项目资助：本书获2011—2013北京市属高等学校人才强教深化计划“中青年骨干人才培养计划”经费资助并为其阶段性成果。

20世纪美国女性文学作品选读

吕静薇　孟静宜　编著

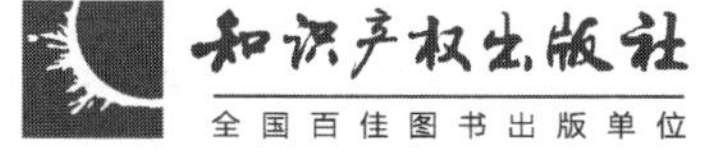

图书在版编目（CIP）数据

20世纪美国女性文学作品选读：英文/吕静薇，孟静宜编著. — 北京：知识产权出版社，2014.4

ISBN 978 - 7 - 5130 - 2668 - 0

Ⅰ.①2… Ⅱ.①吕…②孟… Ⅲ.①英语 — 阅读教学 — 高等学校 — 教材②妇女文学 — 文学评论 — 美国 — 20世纪 Ⅳ.①H319.4：I

中国版本图书馆CIP数据核字（2014）第059410号

内容提要

美国文学在20世纪，尤其是第一次世界大战后才真正走向繁荣，称霸世界文坛。这期间，一大批成绩斐然的作家脱颖而出，而女性作家的表现尤为突出。20世纪后半叶，女性文学研究在美国蓬勃发展，其势头之猛烈，影响之深远，也引起了我国学界和文学爱好者的强烈兴趣。本书以20世纪美国女性文学作品为脉络，按照时间顺序编著，以供有兴趣的教师做选修课程教材，或供英语专业高年级学生作为课外阅读材料，丰富知识，提高其文学鉴赏能力，并了解20世纪美国女性文学在美国文学发展中不可或缺的作用。

责任编辑：唐学贵　　**责任出版：**谷　洋

执行编辑：于晓菲

20世纪美国女性文学作品选读

20SHIJI MEIGUO NÜXING WENXUE ZUOPIN XUANDU

吕静薇　孟静宜　编著

出版发行：	知识产权出版社有限责任公司	**网　　址：**	http：//www.ipph.cn
电　　话：	010 - 82004826		http：//www.laichushu.com
社　　址：	北京市海淀区马甸南村1号	**邮　　编：**	100088
责编电话：	010 - 82000860转8363	**责编邮箱：**	yuxiaofei@cnipr.com
发行电话：	010 - 82000860转8101/8029	**发行传真：**	010 - 82000893/82003279
印　　刷：	北京中献拓方科技发展有限公司	**经　　销：**	各大网上书店、新华书店及相关专业书店
开　　本：	720mm×960mm　1/16	**印　　张：**	19
版　　次：	2014年9月第1版	**印　　次：**	2014年9月第1次印刷
字　　数：	300千字	**定　　价：**	49.00元

ISBN 978-7-5130-2668-0

前 言

20世纪的美国社会，经历了一战后的经济繁荣；三十年代的经济危机；五十年代的冷战；六七十年代的民权运动、妇女运动。社会的大变迁必然带来艺术创作的大爆发。

美国文学虽然只有200多年的历史，但它的发展在世界文学史上已处于不可忽视的地位，是世界文学的一个重要组成部分。在这一发展过程中，20世纪的美国文学尤为耀眼。可以说，美国文学在20世纪才真正走向世界，走向繁荣。一大批优秀的文学家在这一历史时期脱颖而出，创作出大量高质量的精湛之作。美国文学的繁荣，女性文学功不可没。

本书按照时间顺序，选取了15位20世纪美国重要的女性作家及其作品供读者选读。除了美国本土作家，还特别重点选取了非裔和华裔女作家的作品，期望将美国多元化文学的繁荣呈现在读者面前。

本书面向大学英语专业高年级学生及非专业的英语文学爱好者。有兴趣的教师可选作文学选修课程教材，或供学生作为课外辅助阅读材料，丰富知识，提高其文学鉴赏能力。

本书内容分五个部分：作家简介（英文），主要作品列表（中英对照），代表作品选读（英文），作品注释，讨论问题。作家简介包括作家生平、文学创作发展、文学地位简介。作品列表中罗列的是该作家的主要文学作品，即以小说、诗歌、散文等文体为主的代表作，并非全部作品。列表包括中英文的作品名称、创作（或发表）年代。注释与讨论问题的设置均以帮助读者理解作品的创作背景、主题思想、语言风格为目的，期望有助于读者在阅读后的深层思考。

本书在编撰过程中得到孙万军老师以及张光婴、周建焕两位同学的无私帮助和大力支持，特此致以诚挚谢忱。

最后需要说明的是，虽然我们做出了努力，但本书一定不可避免还存在很多欠缺。敬请老师和同学们，以及所有读者批评指正。

编　者

2014 年 3 月于北京

Contents

Willa Cather (1873—1947)

Willa Cather was born in Virginia, the oldest child of Charles and Virginia Cather, who moved with their family to the Nebraska Divide when she was ten years old. After a year of farming, they relocated to the town of Red Cloud, and her father went into the real estate business. At the age of seventeen, Cather moved on her own to Lincoln, the state capital and seat of the University of Nebraska; she attended preparatory school for two years and graduated from the university in 1896. In college she studied the traditional classics and participated in the lively contemporary cultural life of the city by reviewing books, plays, and musical performances. Following graduation, she moved to Pittsburgh, Pennsylvania, to work as an editor of a women's magazine, the *Home Monthly*, which she gave up five years later to teach high-school English and Latin. During this time she also wrote poems and stories, gathering poems into the book *April Twilights*, in 1903, and stories into *The Troll Garden*, in 1905. Also in Pittsburgh, in 1899, she met Isabelle McClung, from a prominent, wealthy family. She lived in the McClung's from 1901 to 1906, when she moved to New York City to write for the journal *McClure's*. Throughout her life, Cather remained devoted to McClung, experiencing her marriage in 1916 as a severe personal loss, and was devastated by her death in 1938.

Having long wished to write novels, Cather took a leave of absence from *McClure's* in 1911, and wrote *Alexander's Bridge* (1912). This novel was successful, but the next three made her reputation. Each focused on a western heroine: Alexander Bergson in O *Pioneers*! (1913), Thea Kronberg in *The Song of the Lark* (1915), and Ántonia Shimerda in *My Ántonia* (1918). While Alexandra is extraordinary as the most successful farmer — the only woman farmer — on the Nebraska Divide, and Thea is extraordinary as a gifted opera singer, Ántonia has no unusual gifts; for Cather and the novel's many readers she stands for the entire experience of European settlement of the Great Plains. These three novels also manifest Cather's qualities of lyrical yet understand prose writing; they contain a wealth of detail about the lives of Nebraska settlers — Bohemian Czech, German, Danish, Swedish, Norwegian, French, Russian, and "Americans" form the East — as they learned to farm on the prairie and built communities in which their various ethnicities met and mingled. Cather's is no melting pot ethos, however; rather she sees the frontier as a shifting kaleidoscope of overlapping social groups and individuals. Recognizing that even by the second decade of the twentieth century this period in the U. S. history had disappeared, Cather approached her characters with deep respect for what they had endured and accomplished.

Whether these novels (or any of Cather's other work) encode a lesbian sensibility has been a matter of much critical debate. In life Cather showed no romantic interest in men; in 1908 she began to share an apartment with Edith Lewis, a Nebraskan whom she had met in 1903, and they lived together until Cather's death. (They lived mostly in New York City, but Cather also traveled a great deal: to Europe, to New England, to the Southwest, and back to Red Cloud to visit her family.)

Estrangement from conventional sexuality and sex roles is typical of many of her main characters, male and female; but heterosexual romance and sexual behavior is equally present in her novels. It seems fair to say that close friendship, much more than romantic or sexual love, is the great ideal in her fiction.

Around 1922, according to Cather, her world broke in two; she suffered from the combined effects of poor health, dissatisfaction with the progress of her career, and alarm at the increasing mechanization and mass-produced quality of American life. She joined the Episcopal Church, and her novels took a new direction. Although her books had always celebrated alternative values to the material and conventional, this theme became much more urgent, while the motif of heroic woman hood — which had led many to call her a feminist, though Cather herself kept aloof from all movements — receded. Important books form her "middle period" include *A Lost Lady* (1923) and *The Professor's House* (1925), which deal with spiritual and cultural crises in the lives of the main characters.

Published in 1927, the novel *Death Comes for the Archbishop* initiated her "third stage". Like many other writers and artists in the 1920s, she had become entranced with the American Southwest — especially New Mexico; her first trip to the region in 1912 figured in her depiction (in *The Song of the Lark*) of Thea Kronberg finding spiritual renewal in this landscape. *Death Comes for the Archbishop*, partly written at Mary Austin's home in Santa Fe, is based on the career of Jean Baptiste Lamy (1814—1888), archbishop of New Mexico, and the priest Joseph Marchebeuf, his close friend and collaborator. Another historical novel, *Shadows on the Rock* (1913) is set even further back in time, in seventeenth-century Quebec. In both books, a composite image of high French culture, ceremonial spirituality, and the American landscape contrasts to the material trivia and empty banality of contemporary life.

The short story *Neighbour Rosicky* recapitulates Cather's earlier interest in the pioneers. Cather's focus is on character rather than plot; a life story unfolds through a steady but loose accumulation of conversation and internal reminiscence with minimal intrusion by a narrator. Often, Cather chose to use narrative vantage points that keep the reader at a distance from the character. She preferred to evoke rather than explain a character and distrusted all psychological theories that purported to account for human behavior. Indeed, to be evocative rather than explanatory was her general literary aim. She once described her work as "unfurnished", meaning that contained only those details necessary to provoke the reader into imagining her fictional world. "Suggestion rather than enumeration" was another way she described her goal. She believed in art as a high calling and strove to create works of beauty. This commitment to culture and aesthetics set her apart from the social movements of the day but won her considerable critical praise.

Politically, culturally, and aesthetically, Cather was in many respects deeply conservative as well as conflicted — a sophisticated populist, an agrarian urbanite. She believed in high art and superior people, but also thought great human gifts were more often found among the obscure and ordinary than those with great advantages. Her vision of the United States had little room for Native American and African Americans; yet she preferred immigrants from Europe to migrants from the East Coast. She appreciated popular legends and folktales, which appear along with classical myth and allusion in her work. She paid little attention to formal structure; her novels often read more like chronicles than plot-driven stories, which makes them seem artless and real while concealing the sentence-by-sentence care that has gone into the work. The sparseness and clarity of her fiction puts in the modernist tradition, even though in her lifetime she had little interest in the modernist movement.

(The text is selected from *The Norton Anthology of American Literature* (Shorter Fifth Edition))

Major Works:

Novels:

- *Alexander's Bridge*, 1912 《亚历山大的桥》
- *O Pioneers!*, 1913 《啊，拓荒者!》
- *The Song of the Lark*, 1915 《百灵鸟之歌》
- *My Ántonia*, 1918 《我的安东尼亚》

- *One of Ours*, 1922 《我们自己人》
- *A Lost Lady*, 1923 《迷途的女人》
- *The Professor's House*, 1925 《教授的房子》
- *Death Comes for the Archbishop*, 1927 《大主教之死》
- *Sapphira and the Slave Girl*, 1940 《莎菲拉和女奴》

Collections:

- *April Twilights*, 1903 《四月的黄昏》
- *The Troll Garden*, 1905 《精灵花园》
- *Youth and the Bright Medusa*, 1920 《青春和美艳的美杜莎》
- *Obscure Destinies*, 1932 《无常人生》
- *The Old Beauty and Others*, 1948 《美女暮年及其他故事》

The Sculptor's Funeral[1]

A group of the townspeople stood on the station siding of a little Kansas town, awaiting the coming of the night train, which was already twenty minutes overdue. The snow had fallen thick over everything; in the pale starlight the line of bluffs across the wide, white meadows south of the town made soft, smoke-colored curves against the clear sky. The men on the siding stood first on one foot and then on the other, their hands thrust deep into their trousers pockets, their overcoats open, their shoulders screwed up with the cold; and they glanced from time to time toward the southeast, where the railroad track wound along the river shore. They conversed in low tones and moved about restlessly, seeming uncertain as to what was expected of them. There was but one of the company who looked as though he knew exactly why he was there; and he kept conspicuously apart; walking to the far end of the platform, returning to the station door, then pacing up the track again, his chin sunk in the high collar of his overcoat, his burly shoulders drooping forward, his gait heavy and dogged. Presently he was approached by a tall, spare, grizzled man clad

[1] "The Sculptor's Funeral" (1905) is an important early Cather's text, first published in *McClure's Magazine* in January, 1905 and later reprinted in both *The Troll Garden* (1905) and *Youth and the Bright Medusa* (1920).

in a faded Grand Army suit, who shuffled out from the group and advanced with a certain deference, craning his neck forward until his back made the angle of a jack-knife three-quarters open.

"I reckon she's agoin'to be pretty late ag'in tonight, Jim," he remarked in a squeaky falsetto. "S'pose it's the snow?"

"I don't know," responded the other man with a shade of annoyance, speaking from out an astonishing cataract of red beard that grew fiercely and thickly in all directions.

The spare man shifted the quill toothpick he was chewing to the other side of his mouth. "It ain't likely that anybody from the East will come with the corpse, I s'pose," he went on reflectively.

"I don't know," responded the other, more curtly than before.

"It's too bad he didn't belong to some lodge or other. I like an order funeral myself. They seem more appropriate for people of some reputation," the spare man continued, with an ingratiating concession in his shrill voice, as he carefully placed his toothpick in his vest pocket. He always carried the flag at the G. A. R[1]. funerals in the town.

The heavy man turned on his heel, without replying, and walked up the siding. The spare man shuffled back to the uneasy group. "Jim's ez full ez a tick, ez ushel," he commented commiseratingly.

Just then a distant whistle sounded, and there was a shuffling of feet on the platform. A number of lanky boys of all ages appeared as suddenly and slimily as eels wakened by the crack of thunder; some came from the waiting room, where they had been warming themselves by the red stove, or half-asleep on the slat benches; others uncoiled themselves from baggage trucks or slid out of express wagons. Two clambered down from the driver's seat of a hearse that stood backed up against the siding. They straightened their stooping shoulders and lifted their heads, and a flash of momentary animation kindled their dull eyes at that cold, vibrant scream, the world-

[1] G. A. R. was a fraternal organization composed of veterans of the Union Army, US Navy, Marines and Revenue Cutter Service who served in the American Civil War.

wide call for men. It stirred them like the note of a trumpet; just as it had often stirred the man who was coming home tonight, in his boyhood.

The night express shot, red as a rocket, from out the eastward marsh lands and wound along the river shore under the long lines of shivering poplars that sentinelled the meadows, the escaping steam hanging in gray masses against the pale sky and blotting out the Milky Way. In a moment the red glare from the headlight streamed up the snow-covered track before the siding and glittered on the wet, black rails. The burly man with the dishevelled red beard walked swiftly up the platform toward the approaching train, uncovering his head as he went. The group of men behind him hesitated, glanced questioningly at one another, and awkwardly followed his example. The train stopped, and the crowd shuffled up to the express car just as the door was thrown open, the spare man in the G. A. B. suit thrusting his head forward with curiosity. The express messenger appeared in the doorway, accompanied by a young man in a long ulster and traveling cap.

"Are Mr. Merrick's friends here?" inquired the young man.

The group on the platform swayed and shuffled uneasily. Philip Phelps, the banker, responded with dignity: "We have come to take charge of the body. Mr. Merrick's father is very feeble and can't be about."

"Send the agent out here," growled the express messenger, "and tell the operator to lend a hand."

The coffin was got out of its rough box and down on the snowy platform. The townspeople drew back enough to make room for it and then formed a close semicircle about it, looking curiously at the palm leaf which lay across the black cover. No one said anything. The baggage man stood by his truck, waiting to get at the trunks. The engine panted heavily, and the fireman dodged in and out among the wheels with his yellow torch and long oilcan, snapping the spindle boxes. The young Bostonian, one of the dead sculptor's pupils who had come with the body, looked about him helplessly. He turned to the banker, the only one of that black, uneasy, stoop-shouldered group who seemed enough of an individual to be addressed.

"None of Mr. Merrick's brothers are here?" he asked uncertainly.

The man with the red heard for the first time stepped up and joined the group. "No, they have not come yet; the family is scattered. The body will be taken directly to the house." He stooped and took hold of one of the handles of the coffin.

"Take the long hill road up, Thompson, it will be easier on the horses," called the liveryman as the undertaker snapped the door of the hearse and prepared to mount to the driver's seat.

Laird, the red-bearded lawyer, turned again to the stranger: "We didn't know whether there would be anyone with him or not," he explained. "It's a long walk, so you'd better go up in the hack." He pointed to a single battered conveyance, but the young man replied stiffly: "Thank you, but I think I will go up with the hearse. If you don't object," turning to the undertaker, "I'll ride with you."

They clambered up over the wheels and drove off in the starlight tip the long, white hill toward the town. The lamps in the still village were shining from under the low, snow-burdened roofs; and beyond, on every side, the plains reached out into emptiness, peaceful and wide as the soft sky itself, and wrapped in a tangible, white silence.

When the hearse backed up to a wooden sidewalk before a naked, weatherbeaten frame house, the same composite, ill-defined group that had stood upon the station siding was huddled about the gate. The front yard was an icy swamp, and a couple of warped planks, extending from the sidewalk to the door, made a sort of rickety footbridge. The gate hung on one hinge and was opened wide with difficulty. Steavens, the young stranger, noticed that something black was tied to the knob of the front door.

The grating sound made by the casket, as it was drawn from the hearse, was answered by a scream from the house; the front door was wrenched open, and a tall, corpulent woman rushed out bareheaded into the snow and flung herself upon the coffin, shrieking: "My boy, my boy! And this is how you've come home to me!"

As Steavens turned away and closed his eyes with a shudder of unutterable repulsion, another woman, also tall, but flat and angular, dressed entirely in black, darted out of the house and caught Mrs. Merrick by the shoulders, crying sharply:

"Come, come, Mother; you mustn't go on like this!" Her tone changed to one of obsequious solemnity as she turned to the banker: "The parlor is ready, Mr. Phelps."

The bearers carried the coffin along the narrow boards, while the undertaker ran ahead with the coffin-rests. They bore it into a large, unheated room that smelled of dampness and disuse and furniture polish, and set it down under a hanging lamp ornamented with jingling glass prisms and before a "Rogers group" of John Alden and Priscilla, wreathed with smilax. Henry Steavens stared about him with the sickening conviction that there had been some horrible mistake, and that he had somehow arrived at the wrong destination. He looked painfully about over the clover-green Brussels, the fat plush upholstery, among the hand-painted china plaques, and panels and vases, for some mark of identification, for something that might once conceivably have belonged to Harvey Merrick. It was not until he recognized his friend in the crayon portrait of a little boy in kilts and curls, hanging above the piano, that he felt willing to let any of these people approach the coffin.

"Take the lid off, Mr. Thompson; let me see my boy's face," wailed the elder woman between her sobs. This time Steavens looked fearfully, almost beseechingly into her face, red and swollen under its masses of strong, black, shiny hair. He flushed, dropped his eyes, and then, almost incredulously, looked again. There was a kind of power about her face — a kind of brutal handsomeness, even; but it was scarred and furrowed by violence, and so colored and coarsened by fiercer passions that grief seemed never to have laid a gentle finger there. The long nose was distended and knobbed at the end, and there were deep lines on either side of it; her heavy, black brows almost met across her forehead; her teeth were large and square and set far apart — teeth that could tear. She filled the room; the men were obliterated, seemed tossed about like twigs in an angry water, and even Steavens felt himself being drawn into the whirlpool.

The daughter — the tall, raw boned woman in crepe, with a mourning comb in her hair which curiously lengthened her long face — sat stiffly upon the sofa, her hands, conspicuous for their large knuckles, folded in her lap, her mouth and eyes drawn down, solemnly awaiting the opening of the coffin. Near the door stood a mulatto[1] woman, evidently a servant in the house, with a timid bearing and an emaciated face pitifully sad and gentle. She was weeping silently, the corner of her calico apron lifted to her eyes, occasionally suppressing a long, quivering sob. Steavens walked over and stood beside her.

Feeble steps were heard on the stairs, and an old man, tall and frail, odorous of pipe smoke, with shaggy, unkept gray hair and a dingy beard, tobacco stained about the mouth, entered uncertainly. He went slowly up to the coffin and stood, rolling a blue cotton handkerchief between his hands, seeming so pained and embarrassed by his wife's orgy of grief that he had no consciousness of anything else.

"There, there, Annie, dear, don't take on so," he quavered timidly, putting out a shaking hand and awkwardly patting her elbow. She turned with a cry and sank upon his shoulder with such violence that he tottered a little. He did not even glance toward the coffin, but continued to look at her with a dull, frightened, appealing expression, as a spaniel looks at the whip. His sunken cheeks slowly reddened and burned with miserable shame. When his wife rushed from the room, her daughter strode after her with set lips. The servant stole up to the coffin, bent over it for a moment, and then slipped away to the kitchen, leaving Steavens, the lawyer, and the father to themselves. The old man stood trembling and looking down at his dead son's face. The sculptor's splendid head seemed even more noble in its rigid stillness than in life. The dark hair had crept down upon the wide forehead; the face seemed strangely long, but in it there was not that beautiful and chaste repose which we expect to find in the faces of the dead. The brows were so drawn that there were two deep lines above the beaked nose, and the chin was thrust forward defiantly. It was as though the strain of life had been so sharp and bitter that death could not at once wholly relax the tension and smooth the countenance into perfect peace — as though he were still guarding something precious and holy, which might even yet be wrested from him.

---

[1] A word for someone with one black parent and one white parent, which is now usually considered offensive.

The old man's lips were working under his stained beard. He turned to the lawyer with timid deference: "Phelps and the rest are comin' back to set up with Harve, ain't they?" he asked. "Thank'ee, Jim, thank'ee." He brushed the hair back gently from his son's forehead. "He was a good boy, Jim; always a good boy. He was ez gentle ez a child and the kindest of, em all — only we didn't none of us ever understand him." The tears trickled slowly down his beard and dropped upon the sculptor's coat.

"Martin, Martin. Oh, Martin! Come here," his wife wailed from the top of the stairs. The old man started timorously: "Yes, Annie, I'm coming." He turned away, hesitated, stood for a moment in miserable indecision; then he reached back and patted the dead man's hair softly, and stumbled from the room.

"Poor old man, I didn't think he had any tears left. Seems as if his eyes would have gone dry long ago. At his age nothing cuts very deep," remarked the lawyer.

Something in his tone made Steavens glance up. While the mother had been in the room, the young man had scarcely seen anyone else; but now, from the moment he first glanced into Jim Laird's florid face and bloodshot eyes, he knew that he had found what he had been heartsick at not finding before — the feeling, the understanding, that must exist in someone, even here.

The man was red as his beard, with features swollen and blurred by dissipation, and a hot, blazing blue eye. His face was strained — that of a man who is controlling himself with difficulty — and he kept plucking at his beard with a sort of fierce resentment. Steavens, sitting by the window, watched him turn down the glaring lamp, still its jangling pendants with an angry gesture, and then stand with his hands locked behind him, staring down into the master's face. He could not help wondering what link there could have been between the porcelain vessel and so sooty a lump of potter's clay.

From the kitchen an uproar was sounding; when the dining-room door opened the import of it was clear. The mother was abusing the maid for having forgotten to make the dressing for the chicken salad which had been prepared for the watchers. Steavens had never heard anything in the least like it; it was injured, emotional, dramatic abuse, unique and masterly in its excruciating cruelty, as violent and unrestrained as had been her grief of twenty minutes before. With a shudder of disgust the lawyer went into the dining-room and closed the door into the kitchen.

"Poor Roxy's getting it now," he remarked when he came back. "The Mericks took her out of the poor-house years ago; and if her loyalty would let her, I guess the poor old thing could tell tales that would curdle your blood. She's the mulatto woman who was standing in here a while ago, with her apron to her eyes. The old woman is a fury; there never was anybody like her for demonstrative piety and ingenious cruelty. She made Harvey's life a hell for him when he lived at home; he was so sick ashamed of it. I never could see how he kept himself so sweet."

"He was wonderful," said Steavens slowly, "wonderful; but until tonight I have never known how wonderful."

"That is the true and eternal wonder of it, anyway; that it can come even from such a dung heap as this," the lawyer cried, with a sweeping gesture which seemed to indicate much more than the four walls within which they stood.

"I think I'll see whether I can get a little air. The room is so close I am beginning to feel rather faint," murmured Steavens, struggling with one of the windows. The sash was stuck, however, and would not yield, so he sat down dejectedly and began pulling at his collar. The lawyer came over, loosened the sash with one blow of his red fist and sent the window up a few inches. Steavens thanked him, but the nausea which had been gradually climbing into his throat for the last half-hour left him with but one desire — a desperate feeling that he must get away from this place with what was left of Harvey Merrick. Oh, he comprehended well enough now the quiet bitterness of the smile that he had seen so often on his master's lips!

He remembered that once, when Merrick returned from a visit home, he brought with him a singularly feeling and suggestive bas-relief of a thin, faded old woman, sitting and sewing something pinned to her knee; while a full-lipped, full-blooded little urchin, his trousers held up by a single gallows, stood beside her, impatiently twitching her gown to call her attention to a butterfly he had caught. Steavens, impressed by the tender and delicate modeling of the thin, tired face, had asked him if it were his mother. He remembered the dull flush that had burned up in the sculptor's face.

The lawyer was sitting in a rocking-chair beside the coffin, his head thrown back and his eyes closed. Steavens looked at him earnestly, puzzled at the line of the chin, and wondering why a man should conceal a feature of such distinction under that disfiguring shock of beard. Suddenly, as though he felt the young sculptor's keen glance, Jim Laird opened his eyes.

"Was he always a good deal of an oyster?" he asked abruptly. "He was terribly shy as a boy."

"Yes, he was an oyster, since you put it so," rejoined Steavens. "Although he could be very fond of people, he always gave one the impression of being detached. He disliked violent emotion; he was reflective, and rather distrustful of himself — except, of course, as regarded his work. He was surefooted enough there. He distrusted men pretty thoroughly and women even more, yet somehow without believing ill of them. He was determined, indeed, to believe the best, but he seemed afraid to investigate."

"A burnt dog dreads the fire," said the lawyer grimly, and closed his eyes.

Steavens went on and on, reconstructing that whole miserable boyhood. All this raw, biting ugliness had been the portion of the man whose tastes were refined beyond the limits of the reasonable — whose mind was an exhaustless gallery of beautiful impressions, and so sensitive that the mere shadow of a poplar leaf flickering against a sunny wall would be etched and held there forever. Surely, if ever a man had the magic word in his fingertips, it was Merrick. Whatever he touched, he revealed its holiest secret; liberated it from enchantment and restored it to its pristine loveliness, like the Arabian prince who fought the enchantress spell for spell. Upon whatever he had come in contact with, he had left a beautiful record of the experience — a sort of ethereal signature; a scent, a sound, a color that was his own.

Steavens understood now the real tragedy of his master's life; neither love nor wine, as many had conjectured; but a blow which had fallen earlier and cut deeper than anything else could have done — a shame not his, and yet so unescapably his, to bide in his heart from his very boyhood. And without — the frontier warfare; the yearning of a boy, cast ashore upon a desert of newness and ugliness and sordidness, for all that is chastened and old, and noble with traditions.

At eleven o'clock the tall, flat woman in black crepe entered, announced that the watchers were arriving, and asked them "to step into the dining room." As Steavens rose the lawyer said dryly: "You go on — it'll be a good experience for you, doubtless; as for me, I'm not equal to that crowd tonight; I've had twenty years of them."

As Steavens closed the door after him be glanced back at the lawyer, sitting by the coffin in the dim light, with his chin resting on his hand.

The same misty group that had stood before the door of the express car shuffled into the dining-room. In the light of the kerosene lamp they separated and became individuals. The minister, a pale, feeble-looking man with white hair and blond chin-whiskers, took his seat beside a small side table and placed his Bible upon it. The Grand Army man sat down behind the stove and tilted his chair back comfortably against the wall, fishing his quill toothpick from his waistcoat pocket. The two bankers, Phelps and Elder, sat off in a corner behind the dinner table, where they could finish their discussion of the new usury law and its effect on chattel security loans. The real estate agent, an old man with a smiling, hypocritical face, soon joined them. The coal-and-lumber dealer and the cattle shipper sat on opposite sides of the hard coal-burner, their feet on the nickelwork. Steavens took a book from his pocket and began to read. The talk around him ranged through various topics of local interest while the house was quieting down. When it was clear that the members of the family were in bed, the Grand Army man hitched his shoulders and, untangling his long legs, caught his heels on the rounds of his chair.

"S'pose there'll be a will, Phelps?" he queried in his weak falsetto.

The banker laughed disagreeably and began trimming his nails with a pearl-handled pocket knife.

"There'll scarcely be any need for one, will there?" he queried in his turn.

The restless Grand Army man shifted his position again, getting his knees still nearer his chin. "Why, the ole man says Harve's done right well lately," he chirped[1].

The other banker spoke up. "I reckon he means by that Harve ain't asked him to mortgage any more farms lately, so as he could go on with his education."

"Seems like my mind don't reach back to a time when Harve wasn't bein' edycated," tittered the Grand Army man.

There was a general chuckle. The minister took out his handkerchief and blew his nose sonorously. Banker Phelps closed his knife with a snap. "It's too bad the old man's sons didn't turn out better," he remarked with reflective authority. "They never hung together. He spent money enough on Harve to stock a dozen cattle farms and he might as well have poured it into Sand Creek. If Harve had stayed at home and helped nurse what little they had, and gone into stock on the old man's bottom farm, they might all have been well fixed. But the old man had to trust everything to tenants and was cheated right and left."

"Harve never could have handled stock none," interposed the cattleman. "He hadn't it in him to be sharp. Do you remember when he bought Sander's mules for eight-year-olds, when everybody in town knew that Sander's father-in-law give'em to his wife for a wedding present eighteen years before, an' they was full-grown mules then."

Everyone chuckled, and the Grand Army man rubbed his knees with a spasm of childish delight.

"Harve never was much account for anything practical, and he shore was never fond of work," began the coal-and-lumber dealer. "I mind the last time he was home; the day he left, when the old man was out to the barn helpin' his hand hitch up to take Harve to the train, and Cal Moots was patchin' up the fence; Harve, he come out on the step and sings out, in his ladylike voice: 'Cal Moots, Cal Moots! please come cord my trunk.'"

"That's Harve for you," approved the Grand Army man gleefully. "I kin hear

---

[1] Speak in a happy, high voice.

him howlin' yet when he was a big feller in long pants and his mother used to whale him with a rawhide in the barn for lettin' the cows git foundered in the cornfield when he was drivin'' em home from pasture. He killed a cow of mine that-a-way onc't — a pure Jersey and the best milker I had, an' the ole man had to put up for her. Harve, he was watchin' the sun set acros't the marshes when the anamile got away; he argued that sunset was oncommon fine."

"Where the old man made his mistake was in sending the boy East to school," said Phelps, stroking his goatee and speaking in a deliberate, judicial tone. "There was where he got his head full of traipsing to Paris and all such folly. What Harve needed, of all people, was a course in some first-class Kansas City business college."

The letters were swimming before Steavens's eyes. Was it possible that these men did not understand, that the palm on the coffin meant nothing to them? The very name of their town would have remained forever buried in the postal guide had it not been now and again mentioned in the world in connection with Harvey Merrick's. He remembered what his master had said to him on the day of his death, after the congestion of both lungs had shut off any probability of recovery, and the sculptor had asked his pupil to send his body home. "It's not a pleasant place to be lying while the world is moving and doing and bettering," he had said with a feeble smile, "but it rather seems as though we ought to go back to the place we came from in the end. The townspeople will come in for a look at me; and after they have had their say I shan't have much to fear from the judgment of God. The wings of the Victory, in there" — with a weak gesture toward his studio — "will not shelter me."

The cattleman took up the comment. "Forty's young for a Merrick to cash in; they usually hang on pretty well. Probably he helped it along with whisky."

"His mother's people were not long-lived, and Harvey never had a robust constitution," said the minister mildly. He would have liked to say more. He had been the boy's Sunday-school teacher, and had been fond of him; but he felt that he was not in a position to speak. His own sons had turned out badly, and it was not a year since one of them had made his last trip home in the express car, shot in a gambling house in the Black Hills.

"Nevertheless, there is no disputin' that Harve frequently looked upon the wine when it was red, also variegated, and it shore made an oncommon fool of him," moralized the cattleman.

Just then the door leading into the parlor rattled loudly, and everyone started involuntarily, looking relieved when only Jim Laird came out. His red face was convulsed with anger, and the Grand Army man ducked his head when he saw the spark in his blue, bloodshot eye. They were all afraid of Jim; he was a drunkard, but he could twist the law to suit his client's needs as no other man in all western Kansas could do; and there were many who tried. The lawyer closed the door gently behind him, leaned back against it and folded his arms, cocking his head a little to one side. When he assumed this attitude in the courtroom, ears were always pricked up, as it usually foretold a flood of withering sarcasm.

"I've been with you gentlemen before," he began in a dry, even tone, "when you've sat by the coffins of boys born and raised in this town; and, if I remember rightly, you were never any too well satisfied when you checked them up. What's the matter, anyhow? Why is it that reputable young men are as scarce as millionaires in Sand City[1]? It might almost seem to a stranger that there was some way something the matter with your progressive town. Why did Ruben Sayer, the brightest young lawyer you ever turned out, after he had come home from the university as straight as a die, take to drinking and forge a check and shoot himself? Why did Bill Merrit's son die of the shakes in a saloon in Omaha? Why was Mr. Thomas's son, here, shot in a gambling house? Why did young Adams burn his mill to beat the insurance companies and go to the pen?"

The lawyer paused and unfolded his arms, laying one clenched fist quietly on the table. "I'll tell you why. Because you drummed nothing but money and knavery into their ears from the time they wore knickerbockers; because you carped away at them as you've been carping here tonight, holding our friends Phelps and Elder up to

---

[1] A seaside city in California.

them for their models, as our grandfathers held up George Washington and John Adams. But the boys, worse luck, were young and raw at the business you put them to; and how could they match coppers with such artists as Phelps and Elder? You wanted them to be successful rascals; they were only unsuccessful ones — that's all the difference. There was only one boy ever raised in this borderland between ruffianism and civilization who didn't come to grief, and you hated Harvey Merrick more for winning out than you hated all the other boys who got under the wheels. Lord, Lord, how you did hate him! Phelps, here, is fond of saying that he could buy and sell us all out any time he's a mind to; but he knew Harve wouldn't have given a tinker's damn for his bank and all his cattle farms put together; and a lack of appreciation, that way, goes hard with Phelps.

"Old Nimrod, here, thinks Harve drank too much; and this from such as Nimrod and me!

"Brother Elder says Harve was too free with the old man's money — fell short in filial consideration, maybe. Well, we can all remember the very tone in which brother Elder swore his own father was a liar, in the county court; and we all know that the old man came out of that partnership with his son as bare as a sheared lamb. But maybe I'm getting personal, and I'd better be driving ahead at what I want to say."

The lawyer paused a moment, squared his heavy shoulders, and went on: "Harvey Merrick and I went to school together, back East. We were dead in earnest, and we wanted you all to be proud of us some day. We meant to be great men. Even I, and I haven't lost my sense of humor, gentlemen, I meant to be a great man. I came back here to practice, and I found you didn't in the least want me to be a great man. You wanted me to be a shrewd lawyer — oh, yes! Our veteran here wanted me to get him an increase of pension, because he had dyspepsia[1]; Phelps wanted a new county survey that would put the widow Wilson's little bottom farm inside his south line; Elder wanted to lend money at 5 per cent a month and get it

---

[1] A problem that your body has in dealing with the food you eat.

collected; old Stark here wanted to wheedle old women up in Vermont into investing their annuities in real estate mortgages that are not worth the paper they are written on. Oh, you needed me hard enough, and you'll go on needing me; and that's why I'm not afraid to plug the truth home to you this once.

"Well, I came back here and became the damned shyster you wanted me to be. You pretend to have some sort of respect for me; and yet you'll stand up and throw mud at Harvey Merrick, whose soul you couldn't dirty and whose hands you couldn't tie. Oh, you're a discriminating lot of Christians! There have been times when the sight of Harvey's name in some Eastern paper has made me hang my head like a whipped dog; and, again, times when I liked to think of him off there in the world, away from all this hog wallow, doing his great work and climbing the big, clean up-grade he'd set for himself.

"And we? Now that we've fought and lied and sweated and stolen, and hated as only the disappointed strugglers in a bitter, dead little Western town know how to do, what have we got to show for it? Harvey Merrick wouldn't have given one sunset over your marshes for all you've got put together, and you know it. It's not for me to say why, in the inscrutable wisdom of God, a genius should ever have been called from this place of hatred and bitter waters; but I want this Boston man to know that the drivel he's been hearing here tonight is the only tribute any truly great man could ever have from such a lot of sick, side-tracked, burnt-dog, land-poor sharks as the here-present financiers of Sand City — upon which town may God have mercy!"

The lawyer thrust out his hand to Steavens as he passed him, caught up his overcoat in the hall, and had left the house before the Grand Army man had had time to lift his ducked head and crane his long neck about at his fellows.

Next day Jim Laird was drunk and unable to attend the funeral services. Steavens called twice at his office, but was compelled to start East without seeing him. He had a presentiment that he would hear from him again, and left his address on the lawyer's table; but if Laird found it, he never acknowledged it. The thing in him that Harvey Merrick had loved must have gone underground with Harvey Merrick's coffin; for it never spoke again, and Jim got the cold he died of driving across the

Colorado mountains to defend one of Phelps's sons who had got into trouble out there by cutting government timber.

(The text is selected from *http*: *//www. classicreader. com*)

Questions for discussion:

1. What is the theme of *The Sculpture's Funeral*?
2. Why does Harvey leave his hometown? What's the influence of his mother on Harvey's character?
3. Why is Jim Liard so bitter? How do you comment on his relationship with Harvey?
4. What are the two different views of success in *The Sculpture's Funeral* (Harvey Merrick *vs* the townspeople)?

Edith Wharton (1862 — 1937)

Edith Wharton began to write as a very young woman, published some fifty varied volumes in her lifetime and left a number of unpublished manuscripts and a voluminous correspondence at her death. *The House of Mirth* (1905), her second novel, was a best-seller; another novel, The *Age of Innocence* (1920), won the Pulitzer Prize; in 1930 she was awarded the gold medal of the National Institute of Arts and Letters, the first woman to be so honored.

Edith Newbold Jones was born in New York City on January 24, 1862, into a patriarchal, monied, cultivated, and rather rigid family that, like others in its small circle, disdained and feared the drastic social, cultural, and economic changes brought on by post-Civil War expansionism. It is small wonder, then, that her work at its best deals with what she described as the tragic psychic and moral effects on its members of a frivolous society under pressure. She was educated by tutors and governesses, much of the time while the family resided in Europe. In 1885 she married the Bostonian Edward Wharton, a social equal thirteen years her senior. Though they lived together (in New York; Newport; Lenox, Massachusetts; and Paris) for twenty-eight years, their marriage was not happy. That Wharton did not seek a divorce until 1913 (on grounds of her husband's adultery) is more a tribute to what her biographer R. W. B. Lewis characterized as her "moral conservatism and her devotion to family ties and the sanctities of tradition" than to personal affection.

The social circle in which Edith Wharton moved was not given to artistic or intellectual pursuits, and any career — especially a career as a writer — was frowned upon. A young woman from Wharton's background received little formal schooling. Her purpose in life — to find a marriage partner from her own social class — required constant attendance at balls and large parties from adolescence on, as well as much attention to fashion and etiquette. After marriage she took her place as a leisure-class wife, displaying her husband's wealth and inculcating class values in her children. Wharton rejected these values even as a young girl; she spent as much time as she could in her father's library at home — and in similar libraries of her friends. By the time she was fifteen she had written — in secret — a thirty-thousand-word novella titled *Fast and Loose*; at this time she also wrote a great deal of lyric poetry — with what she described as "lamentable facility." When she was sixteen, two of her poems were published, one in the prestigious *Atlantic Monthly*. Although her intense interest in literature, ideas, and the arts never abated, she was not to publish again until 1889, when three recently composed poems were sent out to *Scribner's*, *Harper's*, and the *Century* — and all were accepted. The next year, a sketch of hers was published by *Scribner's*.

It was not until the late 1890s, however, that Wharton, now in her late thirties, fully embraced authorship as a career. The decision was motivated partly by her increasing marital discontent and, perhaps, partly by the fact that she was childless. The first significant product of that commitment was a collection of stories titled *The Greater Inclination* (1899). With the publication in 1905 of *The House of Mirth* Wharton confirmed her unconventional choice to be a writer and immediately found an appreciative public. Although she was later to write about other subjects, she discovered in *The House of Mirth* her central settings, plots, and themes: the old aristocracy of New York in conflict with the nouveau riche; and the futile struggle of characters trapped by social forces larger and individuals morally smaller than themselves. Two novels that embody these themes are among those most critically acclaimed. *The House of Mirth* (1905) tells the story of the beautiful but hapless Lily Bart, trained to be a decorative upper-class wife but unable to sell herself like merchandise. In *The Custom of the Country* (1913), which Wharton considered her "masterpiece," the ruthless Undine Spragg from Ohio makes her way up the social ladder, stepping on Americans and Europeans alike in her pursuit of money and the power that goes with it.

In 1911 Wharton separated from her husband and took up residence in France, where she spent the rest of her life. Although she produced more than eighty short stories, twenty-two novellas and novels, including three very different but distinguished books: *Ethan Frome* (1911), *Summer* (1917), and *The Age of Innocence* (1920). Her autobiography, *A Backward Glance*, was published in 1934. During World War I Wharton organized relief efforts for the refugees and orphans displaced by the advance of the German Army and was active in many other committees and organizations dealing with the devastation wrought by this most savage of modern wars. She also wrote extensively about her visits to the front line, and a collection of these dispatches was published as *Fighting France, from Dunkerque to Belfort* (1915). In recognition of her brave and generous effort on behalf of French citizens and soldiers alike, she was awarded the highest honor given by the French government to foreigners — the Chevalier of the Legion of Honor.

R. W. B. Lewis describes *The Other Two* (1904) as "the most nearly perfect short story Edith Wharton ever wrote and a model in the genre of the comedy of manners..." The "comedy" or satire in the story is much mellower than it is in other stories of this period. Wharton, like the thrice-married mistress of ceremonies Mrs. Waythorn, has learned that charm can redeem what would otherwise be a grotesque situation.

Wharton's early social training persisted throughout her life in the form of a constant sociability. She made and kept numerous friends, especially among the leading male intellectuals of her day. Some of them, Egerton Winthrop, Paul Bourget, and Walter Berry to name three, were important to her as she found her way to her profession as a writer. Others, including Henry James and art critics Bernard Berenson and Kenneth Clark, she met as intellectual equals. Still others, including Jean Cocteau and Sinclair Lewis (who dedicated *Babbit* to her), became her admirers late in her life. In this capacity for friendships among the most distinguished people of her time, Wharton is like Gertrude Stein and Willa Cather, also among the most important American writers of the early twentieth century. Her reputation continues to grow; along with Henry James she is considered a major contributor to the practice of psychological realism and a depicter of life among Americans of the leisure class at home and abroad.

(The text is selected from *The Norton Anthology of American Literature* (Shorter Fifth Edition))

Major Works:

- *The Touchstone*, 1900 《试金石》
- *The Valley of Decision*, 1902 《抉择的山谷》
- *The House of Mirth*, 1905 《欢乐之家》
- *Madame de Treymes*, 1907 《特来梅夫人》
- *The Fruit of the Tree*, 1907 《树的果实》
- *Ethan Frome*, 1911 《伊坦·弗洛美》
- *The Reef*, 1912 《暗礁》
- *The Custom of the Country*, 1913 《乡土风俗》
- *Summer*, 1917 《夏》
- *The Marne*, 1918 《马恩河》
- *The Age of Innocence*, 1920 《纯真年代》(普利策奖)
- *A Son at the Front*, 1923《出征的儿子》
- *Old New York*, 1924 《老纽约》
- *Twilight Sleep*, 1927 《朦胧入睡》

- *The Greater Inclination* (Short Story Collection)   1899   《高尚的嗜好》

The Other Two[1]

I

Waythorn, on the drawing-room hearth, waited for his wife to come down to dinner.

It was their first night under his own roof, and he was surprised at his thrill of boyish agitation. He was not so old, to be sure — his glass gave him little more than the five-and-thirty years to which his wife confessed — but he had fancied himself already in the temperate zone; yet here he was listening for her step with a tender sense of all it symbolized, with some old trail of verse about the garlanded nuptial doorposts floating through his enjoyment of the pleasant room and the good dinner just beyond it.

They had been hastily recalled from their honeymoon by the illness of Lily Haskett, the child of Mrs. Waythorn's first marriage. The little girl, at Waythorn's desire, had been transferred to his house on the day of her mother's wedding, and the doctor, on their arrival, broke the news that she was ill with typhoid, but declared that all the symptoms were favorable. Lily could show twelve years of unblemished health, and the case promised to be a light one. The nurse spoke as reassuringly, and after a moment of alarm Mrs. Waythorn had adjusted herself to the situation. She was very fond of Lily — her affection for the child had perhaps been her decisive charm in Waythorn's eyes — but she had the perfectly balanced nerves which her little girl had inherited, and no woman ever wasted less tissue in unproductive worry. Waythorn was therefore quite prepared to see her come in presently, a little late because of a last look at Lily, but as serene and well-appointed as if her good-night kiss had been laid on the brow of health. Her composure was restful to him; it acted as ballast to his somewhat unstable sensibilities. As he pictured her bending over the child's bed he thought how soothing her presence must be in illness: her very step

[1] First published by Scribner's Sons in the 1904 collection entilled *The Descent of Man and Other Stories*.

would prognosticate recovery.

His own life had been a gray one, from temperament rather than circumstance, and he had been drawn to her by the unperturbed gayety which kept her fresh and elastic at an age when most women's activities are growing either slack or febrile. He knew what was said about her; for, popular as she was, there had always been a faint undercurrent of detraction. When she had appeared in New York, nine or ten years earlier, as the pretty Mrs. Haskett whom Gus Varick had unearthed some where — was it in Pittsburgh or Utica? — society, while promptly accepting her, had reserved the right to cast a doubt on its own discrimination. Inquiry, however, established her undoubted connection with a socially reigning family, and explained her recent divorce as the natural result of a runaway match at seventeen; and as nothing was known of Mr. Haskett it was easy to believe the worst of him.

Alice Haskett's remarriage with Gus Varick was a passport to the set whose recognition she coveted, and for a few years the Varicks were the most popular couple in town. Unfortunately the alliance was brief and stormy, and this time the husband had his champions. Still, even Varick's stanchest supporters admitted that he was not meant for matrimony, and Mrs. Varick's grievances were of a nature to bear the inspection of the New York courts[1]. A New York divorce is in itself a diploma of virtue, and in the semi-widowhood of this second separation Mrs. Varick took on an air of sanctity, and was allowed to confide her wrongs to some of the most scrupulous ears in town. But when it was known that she was to marry Waythorn there was a momentary reaction. Her best friends would have preferred to see her remain in the role of the injured wife, which was as becoming to her as crape to a rosy complexion. True, a decent time had elapsed, and it was not even suggested that Waythorn had supplanted his predecessor. Still, people shook their heads over him, and one grudging friend, to whom he affirmed that he took the step with his eyes open, replied oracularly: "Yes — and with your ears shut."

Waythorn could afford to smile at these innuendoes. In the Wall Street phrase,

---

[1] Divorce in New York State could then be granted only on the grounds of adultery.

he had "discounted" them. He knew that society has not yet adapted itself to the consequences of divorce, and that till the adaptation takes place every woman who uses the freedom the law accords her must be her own social justification. Waythorn had an amused confidence in his wife's ability to justify herself. His expectations were fulfilled, and before the wedding took place Alice Varick's group had rallied openly to her support. She took it all imperturbably: she had a way of surmounting obstacles without seeming to be aware of them, and Waythorn looked back with wonder at the trivialities over which he had worn his nerves thin. He had the sense of having found refuge in a richer, warmer nature than his own, and his satisfaction, at the moment, was humorously summed up in the thought that his wife, when she had done all she could for Lily, would not be ashamed to come down and enjoy a good dinner.

The anticipation of such enjoyment was not, however, the sentiment expressed by Mrs. Waythorn's charming face when she presently joined him. Though she had put on her most engaging teagown she had neglected to assume the smile that went with it, and Waythorn thought he had never seen her look so nearly worried.

"What is it?" he asked. "Is anything wrong with Lily?"

"No; I've just been in and she's still sleeping." Mrs. Waythorn hesitated. "But something tiresome has happened."

He had taken her two hands, and now perceived that he was crushing a paper between them.

"This letter?"

"Yes — Mr. Haskett has written — I mean his lawyer has written."

Waythorn felt himself flush uncomfortably. He dropped his wife's hands.

"What about?"

"About seeing Lily. You know the courts —"

"Yes, yes," he interrupted nervously.

Nothing was known about Haskett in New York. He was vaguely supposed to have remained in the outer darkness from which his wife had been rescued, and Waythorn was one of the few who were aware that he had given up his business in

Utica and followed her to New York in order to be near his little girl. In the days of his wooing, Waythorn had often met Lily on the doorstep, rosy and smiling, on her way "to see papa."

"I am so sorry," Mrs. Waythorn murmured.

He roused himself. "What does he want?"

"He wants to see her. You know she goes to him once a week."

"Well — he doesn't expect her to go to him now, does he?"

"No — he has heard of her illness; but he expects to come here."

"Here?"

Mrs. Waythorn reddened under his gaze. They looked away from each other.

"I'm afraid he has the right... You'll see..." She made a proffer of the letter.

Waythorn moved away with a gesture of refusal. He stood staring about the softly lighted room, which a moment before had seemed so full of bridal intimacy.

"I'm so sorry," she repeated. "If Lily could have been moved —"

"That's out of the question," he returned impatiently.

"I suppose so."

Her lip was beginning to tremble, and he felt himself a brute.

"He must come, of course," he said. "When is — his day?"

"I'm afraid — to-morrow."

"Very well. Send a note in the morning."

The butler entered to announce dinner.

Waythorn turned to his wife. "Come — you must be tired. It's beastly, but try to forget about it," he said, drawing her hand through his arm.

"You're so good, dear. I'll try," she whispered back.

Her face cleared at once, and as she looked at him across the flowers, between the rosy candle-shades, he saw her lips waver back into a smile.

"How pretty everything is!" she sighed luxuriously.

He turned to the butler. "The champagne at once, please. Mrs. Waythorn is tired."

In a moment or two their eyes met above the sparkling glasses. Her own were quite clear and untroubled: he saw that she had obeyed his injunction and forgotten.

II

Waythorn, the next morning, went down town earlier than usual. Haskett was not likely to come till the afternoon, but the instinct of flight drove him forth. He meant to stay away all day — he had thoughts of dining at his club. As his door closed behind him he reflected that before he opened it again it would have admitted another man who had as much right to enter it as himself, and the thought filled him with a physical repugnance.

He caught the "elevated❶" at the employees' hour, and found himself crushed between two layers of pendulous humanity. At Eighth Street the man facing him wriggled out and another took his place. Waythorn glanced up and saw that it was Gus Varick. The men were so close together that it was impossible to ignore the smile of recognition on Varick's handsome overblown face. And after all — why not? They had always been on good terms, and Varick had been divorced before Waythorn's attentions to his wife began. The two exchanged a word on the perennial grievance of the congested trains, and when a seat at their side was miraculously left empty the instinct of self-preservation made Waythorn slip into it after Varick.

The latter drew the stout man's breath of relief.

"Lord — I was beginning to feel like a pressed flower." He leaned back, looking unconcernedly at Waythorn. "Sorry to hear that Sellers is knocked out again."

"Sellers?" echoed Waythorn, starting at his partner's name.

Varick looked surprised. "You didn't know he was laid up with the gout?"

"No. I've been away — I only got back last night." Waythorn felt himself reddening in anticipation of the other's smile.

"Ah — yes; to be sure. And Sellers's attack came on two days ago. I'm afraid he's pretty bad. Very awkward for me, as it happens, because he was just putting through a rather important thing for me."

"Ah?" Waythorn wondered vaguely since when Varick had been dealing in

---

❶ Elevated railway.

"important things". Hitherto he had dabbled only in the shallow pools of speculation, with which Waythorn's office did not usually concern itself.

It occurred to him that Varick might be talking at random, to relieve the strain of their propinquity[1]. That strain was becoming momentarily more apparent to Waythorn, and when, at Cortlandt Street, he caught sight of an acquaintance, and had a sudden vision of the picture he and Varick must present to an initiated eye, he jumped up with a muttered excuse.

"I hope you'll find Sellers better," said Varick civilly, and he stammered back: "If I can be of any use to you —" and let the departing crowd sweep him to the platform.

At his office he heard that Sellers was in fact ill with the gout, and would probably not be able to leave the house for some weeks.

"I'm sorry it should have happened so, Mr. Waythorn," the senior clerk said with affable significance. "Mr. Sellers was very much upset at the idea of giving you such a lot of extra work just now."

"Oh, that's no matter," said Waythorn hastily. He secretly welcomed the pressure of additional business, and was glad to think that, when the day's work was over, he would have to call at his partner's on the way home.

He was late for luncheon, and turned in at the nearest restaurant instead of going to his club. The place was full, and the waiter hurried him to the back of the room to capture the only vacant table. In the cloud of cigar-smoke Waythorn did not at once distinguish his neighbors; but presently, looking about him, he saw Varick seated a few feet off. This time, luckily, they were too far apart for conversation, and Varick, who faced another way, had probably not even seen him; but there was an irony in their renewed nearness.

Varick was said to be fond of good living, and as Waythorn sat despatching his hurried luncheon he looked across half enviously at the other's leisurely degustation of his meal. When Waythorn first saw him he had been helping himself with critical

---

[1] The state of being near in space or time.

deliberation to a bit of Camembert at the ideal point of liquefaction, and now, the cheese removed, he was just pouring his cafe double from its little two-storied earthen pot. He poured slowly, his ruddy profile bent above the task, and one beringed white hand steadying the lid of the coffee-pot; then he stretched his other hand to the decanter of cognac at his elbow, filled a liqueur-glass, took a tentative sip, and poured the brandy into his coffee-cup.

Waythorn watched him in a kind of fascination. What was he thinking of — only of the flavor of the coffee and the liqueur? Had the morning's meeting left no more trace in his thoughts than on his face? Had his wife so completely passed out of his life that even this odd encounter with her present husband, within a week after her remarriage, was no more than an incident in his day? And as Waythorn mused, another idea struck him: had Haskett ever met Varick as Varick and he had just met? The recollection of Haskett perturbed him, and he rose and left the restaurant, taking a circuitous way out to escape the placid irony of Varick's nod.

It was after seven when Waythorn reached home. He thought the footman who opened the door looked at him oddly.

"How is Miss Lily?" he asked in haste.

"Doing very well, sir. A gentleman —"

"Tell Barlow to put off dinner for half an hour," Waythorn cut him off, hurrying upstairs.

He went straight to his room and dressed without seeing his wife. When he reached the drawing-room she was there, fresh and radiant. Lily's day had been good; the doctor was not coming back that evening.

At dinner Waythorn told her of Sellers's illness and of the resulting complications. She listened sympathetically, adjuring him not to let himself be overworked, and asking vague feminine questions about the routine of the office. Then she gave him the chronicle of Lily's day; quoted the nurse and doctor, and told him who had called to inquire. He had never seen her more serene and unruffled. It struck him, with a curious pang, that she was very happy in being with him, so happy that she found a childish pleasure in rehearsing the trivial incidents of her day.

After dinner they went to the library, and the servant put the coffee and liqueurs on a low table before her and left the room. She looked singularly soft and girlish in her rosy pale dress, against the dark leather of one of his bachelor armchairs. A day earlier the contrast would have charmed him.

He turned away now, choosing a cigar with affected deliberation.

"Did Haskett come?" he asked, with his back to her.

"Oh, yes — he came."

"You didn't see him, of course?"

She hesitated a moment. "I let the nurse see him."

That was all. There was nothing more to ask. He swung round toward her, applying a match to his cigar. Well, the thing was over for a week, at any rate. He would try not to think of it. She looked up at him, a trifle rosier than usual, with a smile in her eyes.

"Ready for your coffee, dear?"

He leaned against the mantelpiece, watching her as she lifted the coffee-pot. The lamplight struck a gleam from her bracelets and tipped her soft hair with brightness. How light and slender she was, and how each gesture flowed into the next! She seemed a creature all compact of harmonies. As the thought of Haskett receded, Waythorn felt himself yielding again to the joy of possessorship. They were his, those white hands with their flitting motions, his the light haze of hair, the lips and eyes...

She set down the coffee-pot, and reaching for the decanter of cognac, measured off a liqueur-glass and poured it into his cup.

Waythorn uttered a sudden exclamation.

"What is the matter?" she said, startled.

"Nothing; only — I don't take cognac in my coffee."

"Oh, how stupid of me," she cried.

Their eyes met, and she blushed a sudden agonized red.

III

Ten days later, Mr. Sellers, still house-bound, asked Waythorn to call on his way downtown.

The senior partner, with his swaddled foot propped up by the fire, greeted his associate with an air of embarrassment.

"I'm sorry, my dear fellow; I've got to ask you to do an awkward thing for me."

Waythorn waited, and the other went on, after a pause apparently given to the arrangement of his phrases: "The fact is, when I was knocked out I had just gone into a rather complicated piece of business for — Gus Varick."

"Well?" said Waythorn, with an attempt to put him at his ease.

"Well — it's this way: Varick came to me the day before my attack. He had evidently had an inside tip from somebody, and had made about a hundred thousand. He came to me for advice, and I suggested his going in with Vanderlyn."

"Oh, the deuce!" Waythorn exclaimed. He saw in a flash what had happened. The investment was an alluring one, but required negotiation. He listened intently while Sellers put the case before him, and, the statement ended, he said: "You think I ought to see Varick?"

"I'm afraid I can't as yet. The doctor is obdurate. And this thing can't wait. I hate to ask you, but no one else in the office knows the ins and outs of it."

Waythorn stood silent. He did not care a farthing for the success of Varick's venture, but the honor of the office was to be considered, and he could hardly refuse to oblige his partner.

"Very well," he said, "I'll do it."

That afternoon, apprised by telephone, Varick called at the office. Waythorn, waiting in his private room, wondered what the others thought of it. The newspapers, at the time of Mrs. Waythorn's marriage, had acquainted their readers with every detail of her previous matrimonial❶ ventures, and Waythorn could fancy the clerks smiling behind Varick's back as he was ushered in.

Varick bore himself admirably. He was easy without being undignified, and Waythorn was conscious of cutting a much less impressive figure. Varick had no

---

❶ Connected with marriage or with being married.

head for business, and the talk prolonged itself for nearly an hour while Waythorn set forth with scrupulous precision the details of the proposed transaction.

"I'm awfully obliged to you," Varick said as he rose. "The fact is I'm not used to having much money to look after, and I don't want to make an ass of myself —" He smiled, and Waythorn could not help noticing that there was something pleasant about his smile. "It feels uncommonly queer to have enough cash to pay one's bills. I'd have sold my soul for it a few years ago!"

Waythorn winced at the allusion. He had heard it rumored that a lack of funds had been one of the determining causes of the Varick separation, but it did not occur to him that Varick's words were intentional. It seemed more likely that the desire to keep clear of embarrassing topics had fatally drawn him into one. Waythorn did not wish to be outdone in civility.

"We'll do the best we can for you," he said. "I think this is a good thing you're in."

"Oh, I'm sure it's immense. It's awfully good of you —" Varick broke off, embarrassed. "I suppose the thing's settled now — but if —"

"If anything happens before Sellers is about, I'll see you again," said Waythorn quietly. He was glad, in the end, to appear the more self-possessed of the two.

The course of Lily's illness ran smooth, and as the days passed Waythorn grew used to the idea of Haskett's weekly visit. The first time the day came round, he stayed out late, and questioned his wife as to the visit on his return. She replied at once that Haskett had merely seen the nurse downstairs, as the doctor did not wish any one in the child's sick-room till after the crisis.

The following week Waythorn was again conscious of the recurrence of the day, but had forgotten it by the time he came home to dinner. The crisis of the disease came a few days later, with a rapid decline of fever, and the little girl was pronounced out of danger. In the rejoicing which ensued the thought of Haskett passed out of Waythorn's mind and one afternoon, letting himself into the house with a latch-key, he went straight to his library without noticing a shabby hat and umbrella in the hall.

In the library he found a small effaced-looking man with a thinnish gray beard sitting on the edge of a chair. The stranger might have been a piano-tuner, or one of those mysteriously efficient persons who are summoned in emergencies to adjust some detail of the domestic machinery. He blinked at Waythorn through a pair of gold-rimmed spectacles and said mildly: "Mr. Waythorn, I presume? I am Lily's father."

Waythorn flushed. "Oh —" he stammered uncomfortably. He broke off, disliking to appear rude. Inwardly he was trying to adjust the actual Haskett to the image of him projected by his wife's reminiscences. Waythorn had been allowed to infer that Alice's first husband was a brute.

"I am sorry to intrude," said Haskett, with his over-the-counter politeness.

"Don't mention it," returned Waythorn, collecting himself. "I suppose the nurse has been told?"

"I presume so. I can wait," said Haskett. He had a resigned way of speaking, as though life had worn down his natural powers of resistance.

Waythorn stood on the threshold, nervously pulling off his gloves.

"I'm sorry you've been detained. I will send for the nurse," he said; and as he opened the door he added with an effort: "I'm glad we can give you a good report of Lily." He winced as the we slipped out, but Haskett seemed not to notice it.

"Thank you, Mr. Waythorn. It's been an anxious time for me."

"Ah, well, that's past. Soon she'll be able to go to you." Waythorn nodded and passed out.

In his own room, he flung himself down with a groan. He hated the womanish sensibility which made him suffer so acutely from the grotesque chances of life. He had known when he married that his wife's former husbands were both living, and that amid the multiplied contacts of modern existence there were a thousand chances to one that he would run against one or the other, yet he found himself as much disturbed by his brief encounter with Haskett as though the law had not obligingly removed all difficulties in the way of their meeting.

Waythorn sprang up and began to pace the room nervously. He had not suffered half so much from his two meetings with Varick. It was Haskett's presence in his own house that made the situation so intolerable. He stood still, hearing steps in the passage.

"This way, please," he heard the nurse say. Haskett was being taken upstairs, then: not a corner of the house but was open to him. Waythorn dropped into another chair, staring vaguely ahead of him. On his dressing-table stood a photograph of Alice, taken when he had first known her. She was Alice Varick then — how fine and exquisite he had thought her! Those were Varick's pearls about her neck. At Waythorn's instance they had been returned before her marriage. Had Haskett ever given her any trinkets — and what had become of them, Waythorn wondered? He realized suddenly that he knew very little of Haskett's past or present situation; but from the man's appearance and manner of speech he could reconstruct with curious precision the surroundings of Alice's first marriage. And it startled him to think that she had, in the background of her life, a phase of existence so different from anything with which he had connected her. Varick, whatever his faults, was a gentleman, in the conventional, traditional sense of the term: the sense which at that moment seemed, oddly enough, to have most meaning to Waythorn. He and Varick had the same social habits, spoke the same language, understood the same allusions. But this other man... it was grotesquely uppermost in Waythorn's mind that Haskett had worn a made-up tie attached with an elastic. Why should that ridiculous detail symbolize the whole man? Waythorn was exasperated by his own paltriness, but the fact of the tie expanded, forced itself on him, became as it were the key to Alice's past. He could see her, as Mrs. Haskett, sitting in a "front parlor" furnished in plush, with a pianola, and a copy of "Ben Hur"❶ on the centre-table. He could see her going to the theatre with Haskett — or perhaps even to a "Church Sociable" — she in a "picture hat" and Haskett in a black frock-coat, a little creased, with the made-up tie on an elastic. On the way home they

---

❶ *Ben Hur*: *A Tale of the Christ* (1880), an immensely popular, rather melodramatic romance by Lew Wallace (1827-1905).

would stop and look at the illuminated shop-windows, lingering over the photographs of New York actresses. On Sunday afternoons Haskett would take her for a walk, pushing Lily ahead of them in a white enameled perambulator, and Waythorn had a vision of the people they would stop and talk to. He could fancy how pretty Alice must have looked, in a dress adroitly constructed from the hints of a New York fashion-paper; how she must have looked down on the other women, chafing at her life, and secretly feeling that she belonged in a bigger place.

For the moment his foremost thought was one of wonder at the way in which she had shed the phase of existence which her marriage with Haskett implied. It was as if her whole aspect, every gesture, every inflection, every allusion, were a studied negation of that period of her life. If she had denied being married to Haskett she could hardly have stood more convicted of duplicity than in this obliteration of the self which had been his wife.

Waythorn started up, checking himself in the analysis of her motives. What right had he to create a fantastic effigy of her and then pass judgment on it? She had spoken vaguely of her first marriage as unhappy, had hinted, with becoming reticence, that Haskett had wrought havoc among her young illusions... It was a pity for Waythorn's peace of mind that Haskett's very inoffensiveness shed a new light on the nature of those illusions. A man would rather think that his wife has been brutalized by her first husband than that the process has been reversed.

IV

"Mr. Waythorn, I don't like that French governess of Lily's."

Haskett, subdued and apologetic, stood before Waythorn in the library, revolving his shabby hat in his hand.

Waythorn, surprised in his armchair over the evening paper, stared back perplexedly at his visitor.

"You'll excuse my asking to see you," Haskett continued. "But this is my last visit, and I thought if I could have a word with you it would be a better way than writing to Mrs. Waythorn's lawyer."

Waythorn rose uneasily. He did not like the French governess either; but that was irrelevant.

"I am not so sure of that," he returned stiffly; "but since you wish it I will give your message to — my wife." He always hesitated over the possessive pronoun in addressing Haskett.

The latter sighed. "I don't know as that will help much. She didn't like it when I spoke to her."

Waythorn turned red. "When did you see her?" he asked.

"Not since the first day I came to see Lily — right after she was taken sick. I remarked to her then that I didn't like the governess."

Waythorn made no answer. He remembered distinctly that, after that first visit, he had asked his wife if she had seen Haskett. She had lied to him then, but she had respected his wishes since; and the incident cast a curious light on her character. He was sure she would not have seen Haskett that first day if she had divined that Waythorn would object, and the fact that she did not divine it was almost as disagreeable to the latter as the discovery that she had lied to him.

"I don't like the woman," Haskett was repeating with mild persistency. "She ain't straight, Mr. Waythorn — she'll teach the child to be underhand. I've noticed a change in Lily — she's too anxious to please — and she don't always tell the truth. She used to be the straightest child, Mr. Waythorn —" He broke off, his voice a little thick. "Not but what I want her to have a stylish education," he ended.

Waythorn was touched. "I'm sorry, Mr. Haskett; but frankly, I don't quite see what I can do."

Haskett hesitated. Then he laid his hat on the table, and advanced to the hearth-rug, on which Waythorn was standing. There was nothing aggressive in his manner; but he had the solemnity of a timid man resolved on a decisive measure.

"There's just one thing you can do, Mr. Waythorn," he said. "You can remind Mrs. Waythorn that, by the decree of the courts, I am entitled to have a voice in Lily's bringing up." He paused, and went on more deprecatingly: "I'm not the kind to talk about enforcing my rights, Mr. Waythorn. I don't know as I think a man is entitled to rights he hasn't known how to hold on to; but this business of the child is different. I've never let go there — and I never mean to."

The scene left Waythorn deeply shaken. Shamefacedly, in indirect ways, he had been finding out about Haskett; and all that he had learned was favorable. The little man, in order to be near his daughter, had sold out his share in a profitable business in Utica, and accepted a modest clerkship in a New York manufacturing house. He boarded in a shabby street and had few acquaintances. His passion for Lily filled his life. Waythorn felt that this exploration of Haskett was like groping about with a dark-lantern in his wife's past; but he saw now that there were recesses his lantern had not explored. He had never inquired into the exact circumstances of his wife's first matrimonial rupture. On the surface all had been fair. It was she who had obtained the divorce, and the court had given her the child. But Waythorn knew how many ambiguities such a verdict might cover. The mere fact that Haskett retained a right over his daughter implied an unsuspected compromise. Waythorn was an idealist. He always refused to recognize unpleasant contingencies till he found himself confronted with them, and then he saw them followed by a special train of consequences. His next days were thus haunted, and he determined to try to lay the ghosts by conjuring them up in his wife's presence.

When he repeated Haskett's request a flame of anger passed over her face; but she subdued it instantly and spoke with a slight quiver of outraged motherhood.

"It is very ungentlemanly of him," she said.

The word grated on Waythorn. "That is neither here nor there. It's a bare question of rights."

She murmured: "It's not as if he could ever be a help to Lily —"

Waythorn flushed. This was even less to his taste. "The question is," he repeated, "what authority has he over her?"

She looked downward, twisting herself a little in her seat. "I am willing to see him — I thought you objected," she faltered.

In a flash he understood that she knew the extent of Haskett's claims. Perhaps it was not the first time she had resisted them.

"My objecting has nothing to do with it," he said coldly; "if Haskett has a right to be consulted you must consult him."

She burst into tears, and he saw that she expected him to regard her as a victim.

Haskett did not abuse his rights. Waythorn had felt miserably sure that he would not. But the governess was dismissed, and from time to time the little man demanded an interview with Alice. After the first outburst she accepted the situation with her usual adaptability. Haskett had once reminded Waythorn of the piano-tuner, and Mrs. Waythorn, after a month or two, appeared to class him with that domestic familiar. Waythorn could not but respect the father's tenacity. At first he had tried to cultivate the suspicion that Haskett might be "up to" something, that he had an object in securing a foothold in the house. But in his heart Waythorn was sure of Haskett's single-mindedness; he even guessed in the latter a mild contempt for such advantages as his relation with the Waythorns might offer. Haskett's sincerity of purpose made him invulnerable, and his successor had to accept him as a lien on the property.

Mr. Sellers was sent to Europe to recover from his gout, and Varick's affairs hung on Waythorn's hands. The negotiations were prolonged and complicated; they necessitated frequent conferences between the two men, and the interests of the firm forbade Waythorn's suggesting that his client should transfer his business to another office.

Varick appeared well in the transaction. In moments of relaxation his coarse streak appeared, and Waythorn dreaded his geniality; but in the office he was concise and clear-headed, with a flattering deference to Waythorn's judgment. Their business relations being so affably established, it would have been absurd for the two men to ignore each other in society. The first time they met in a drawing-room, Varick took up their intercourse in the same easy key, and his hostess's grateful glance obliged Waythorn to respond to it. After that they ran across each other frequently, and one evening at a ball Waythorn, wandering through the remoter rooms, came upon Varick seated beside his wife. She colored a little, and faltered in what she was saying; but Varick nodded to Waythorn without rising, and the latter strolled on.

In the carriage, on the way home, he broke out nervously: "I didn't know you spoke to Varick."

Her voice trembled a little. "It's the first time — he happened to be standing near me; I didn't know what to do. It's so awkward, meeting everywhere — and he said you had been very kind about some business."

"That's different," said Waythorn.

She paused a moment. "I'll do just as you wish," she returned pliantly. "I thought it would be less awkward to speak to him when we meet."

Her pliancy was beginning to sicken him. Had she really no will of her own — no theory about her relation to these men? She had accepted Haskett — did she mean to accept Varick? It was "less awkward," as she had said, and her instinct was to evade difficulties or to circumvent them. With sudden vividness Waythorn saw how the instinct had developed. She was "as easy as an old shoe" — a shoe that too many feet had worn. Her elasticity was the result of tension in too many different directions. Alice Haskett — Alice Varick — Alice Waythorn — she had been each in turn, and had left hanging to each name a little of her privacy, a little of her personality, a little of the inmost self where the unknown god abides.

"Yes — it's better to speak to Varick," said Waythorn wearily.

V

The winter wore on, and society took advantage of the Waythorns' acceptance of Varick. Harassed hostesses were grateful to them for bridging over a social difficulty, and Mrs. Waythorn was held up as a miracle of good taste. Some experimental spirits could not resist the diversion of throwing Varick and his former wife together, and there were those who thought he found a zest in the propinquity. But Mrs. Waythorn's conduct remained irreproachable. She neither avoided Varick nor sought him out. Even Waythorn could not but admit that she had discovered the solution of the newest social problem.

He had married her without giving much thought to that problem. He had fancied that a woman can shed her past like a man. But now he saw that Alice was bound to hers both by the circumstances which forced her into continued relation with it, and by the traces it had left on her nature. With grim irony Waythorn compared himself to a member of a syndicate. He held so many shares in his wife's personality and his predecessors were his partners in the business. If there had been any element of passion in the transaction he would have felt less deteriorated by it. The fact that Alice took her change of husbands like a change of weather reduced the situation to mediocrity. He could have forgiven her for blunders, for excesses; for resisting Hackett, for yielding to Varick; for anything but her acquiescence and her tact. She reminded him of a juggler tossing knives; but the knives were blunt and she knew they would never cut her.

And then, gradually, habit formed a protecting surface for his sensibilities. If he paid for each day's comfort with the small change of his illusions, he grew daily to value the comfort more and set less store upon the coin. He had drifted into a dulling propinquity with Haskett and Varick and he took refuge in the cheap revenge of satirizing the situation. He even began to reckon up the advantages which accrued from it, to ask himself if it were not better to own a third of a wife who knew how to make a man happy than a whole one who had lacked opportunity to acquire the art. For it was an art, and made up, like all others, of concessions, eliminations and embellishments; of lights judiciously thrown and shadows skillfully softened. His wife knew exactly how to manage the lights, and he knew exactly to what training she owed her skill. He even tried to trace the source of his obligations, to discriminate between the influences which had combined to produce his domestic happiness: he perceived that Haskett's commonness had made Alice worship good breeding, while Varick's liberal construction of the marriage bond had taught her to value the conjugal virtues; so that he was directly indebted to his predecessors for the devotion which made his life easy if not inspiring.

From this phase he passed into that of complete acceptance. He ceased to satirize himself because time dulled the irony of the situation and the joke lost its humor with its sting. Even the sight of Haskett's hat on the hall table had ceased to touch the springs of epigram. The hat was often seen there now, for it had been decided that it was better for Lily's father to visit her than for the little girl to go to his boarding-house. Waythorn, having acquiesced in this arrangement, had been surprised to find how little difference it made. Haskett was never obtrusive, and the few visitors who met him on the stairs were unaware of his identity. Waythorn did not know how often he saw Alice, but with himself Haskett was seldom in contact.

One afternoon, however, he learned on entering that Lily's father was waiting to see him. In the library he found Haskett occupying a chair in his usual provisional way. Waythorn always felt grateful to him for not leaning back.

"I hope you'll excuse me, Mr. Waythorn," he said rising. "I wanted to see Mrs. Waythorn about Lily, and your man asked me to wait here till she came in."

"Of course," said Waythorn, remembering that a sudden leak had that morning given over the drawing-room to the plumbers.

He opened his cigar-case and held it out to his visitor, and Haskett's acceptance seemed to mark a fresh stage in their intercourse. The spring evening was chilly, and Waythorn invited his guest to draw up his chair to the fire. He meant to find an excuse to leave Haskett in a moment; but he was tired and cold, and after all the little man no longer jarred on him.

The two were inclosed in the intimacy of their blended cigar-smoke when the door opened and Varick walked into the room. Waythorn rose abruptly. It was the first time that Varick had come to the house, and the surprise of seeing him, combined with the singular inopportuneness of his arrival, gave a new edge to Waythorn's blunted sensibilities. He stared at his visitor without speaking.

Varick seemed too preoccupied to notice his host's embarrassment.

"My dear fellow," he exclaimed in his most expansive tone, "I must apologize for tumbling in on you in this way, but I was too late to catch you down town, and so I thought —" He stopped short, catching sight of Haskett, and his sanguine color deepened to a flush which spread vividly under his scant blond hair. But in a moment he recovered himself and nodded slightly. Haskett returned the bow in silence, and Waythorn was still groping for speech when the footman came in carrying a tea-table.

The intrusion offered a welcome vent to Waythorn's nerves. "What the deuce are you bringing this here for?" he said sharply.

"I beg your pardon, sir, but the plumbers are still in the drawing-room, and Mrs. Waythorn said she would have tea in the library." The footman's perfectly respectful tone implied a reflection on Waythorn's reasonableness.

"Oh, very well," said the latter resignedly, and the footman proceeded to open the folding tea-table and set out its complicated appointments. While this interminable process continued the three men stood motionless, watching it with a fascinated stare, till Waythorn, to break the silence, said to Varick: "Won't you have a cigar?"

He held out the case he had just tendered to Haskett, and Varick helped himself with a smile. Waythorn looked about for a match, and finding none, proffered a light from his own cigar. Haskett, in the background, held his ground mildly, examining his cigar-tip now and then, and stepping forward at the right moment to knock its ashes into the fire.

The footman at last withdrew, and Varick immediately began: "If I could just say half a word to you about this business —"

"Certainly," stammered Waythorn; "in the dining-room —"

But as he placed his hand on the door it opened from without, and his wife appeared on the threshold.

She came in fresh and smiling, in her street dress and hat, shedding a fragrance from the boa which she loosened in advancing.

"Shall we have tea in here, dear?" she began; and then she caught sight of Varick. Her smile deepened, veiling a slight tremor of surprise. "Why, how do you do?" she said with a distinct note of pleasure.

As she shook hands with Varick she saw Haskett standing behind him. Her smile faded for a moment, but she recalled it quickly, with a scarcely perceptible side-glance at Waythorn.

"How do you do, Mr. Haskett?" she said, and shook hands with him a shade less cordially.

The three men stood awkwardly before her, till Varick, always the most self-possessed, dashed into an explanatory phrase.

"We — I had to see Waythorn a moment on business," he stammered, brick-red from chin to nape.

Haskett stepped forward with his air of mild obstinacy. "I am sorry to intrude; but you appointed five o'clock —" he directed his resigned glance to the time-piece on the mantel.

She swept aside their embarrassment with a charming gesture of hospitality.

"I'm so sorry — I'm always late; but the afternoon was so lovely." She stood drawing her gloves off, propitiatory and graceful, diffusing about her a sense of ease and familiarity in which the situation lost its grotesqueness. "But before talking business," she added brightly, "I'm sure every one wants a cup of tea."

She dropped into her low chair by the tea-table, and the two visitors, as if drawn by her smile, advanced to receive the cups she held out.

She glanced about for Waythorn, and he took the third cup with a laugh.

(The text is selected from *The Norton Anthology of American Literature* (Shorter Fifth Edition))

Questions for discussion:

1. Waythorn seems well aware of his own anxious nature, but he marries without concerning about his wife's past marriages, even when friends advise him to be cautious. Why does he act so seemingly out of character?
2. We never really know what Alice is thinking through all of this, and her husband is pretty bad at communicating his insecurities to her. What do you think this story would be like if it was told from Alice's perspective?
3. How do you comment on the marriage of Waythorn and Alice?
4. How do you feel about Waythorn's attitude towards women? What message do you think Edith Wharton was trying to convey about his expectations of his wife?

Marianne Moore (1887 — 1972)

Marianne Moore was a radically inventive modernist, greatly admired by other poets of her generation, and a powerful influence on such later writers as Robert Lowell, Randall Jarrell, and Richard Wilbur. Like her forerunner Emily Dickinson, she made of the traditional and constraining "woman's place" a protected space to do her own work, but unlike Emily Dickinson, she was a deliberate professional, publishing her poems regularly, in touch with the movements and artists of her time. She was famous for the statement that poetry, though departing from the real world, re-created that world within its forms: poems were "imaginary gardens with real toads in them." Her earlier work is distinguished but great precision of observation and language, ornate diction, and complex stanza and prosodic patterns. Her later work is much less ornate; and in revising her poetry, she tended to simplify and shorten.

She was born in Kirkwood, Missouri, a suburb of St. Louis. In her childhood, the family was abandoned by her father; they moved to Carlisle, Pennsylvania, where — in a pattern common among both men and women writers of this period — her mother supported them by teaching school. She went to Bryn Mawr College, graduating in 1909; traveled with her mother in England and France in 1911; and taught at the U. S. India School in Carlisle, Pennsylvania, between 1911 and 1915. Having begun to write poetry in college, she was first published in 1915 and 1916 in such little magazines as the *Egoist* (an English magazine with which Ezra Pound was associated), *Poetry*, and *Others* (a journal for experimental writing with which William Carlos Williams was associated, founded by Alfred Kreymbourg, a New York poet and playwright). Through these magazines she entered the avant-garde and modernist world. She never married; in 1916 she and her mother merged their household with that of Moore's brother, a Presbyterian minister, and they moved with him to a parish in Brooklyn, New York. There Moore was close to literary circles and Ebbets Field, where the Dodgers, then a Brooklyn baseball team, had their home stadium. Moore was a lifelong fan.

While holding jobs in schools and libraries, Moore worked at her poetry. A volume called simply *Poems* was brought out in London in 1921 without her knowledge through the efforts of two women friends who were writers, H. D. (whom she had met at Bryn Mawr) and Bryher. Another book, *Observations*, appeared in 1924 and won the Dial Award. In 1925 she began to work as editor of the *Dial*, continuing in this influential position until the magazine was disbanded in 1929. Her reviewers and editorial judgments were greatly respected, although her preference for elegance and decorum over sexual frankness was not shared by some of the writers — Hart Crane and James Joyce among them — whose work she rejected or published only after they revised it.

As a critic of poetry Moore wrote numerous essays — her collected prose makes a larger book than her collected poetry. She believed that poets usually undervalued prose; "precision, economy of statement, logic" were features of good prose that could "liberate" the imagination, she wrote. In writing about animals she was able to take advantage of two different prose modes that attracted her — scientific and historical description. Her poems were an amalgam of her own observation and her readings, which she acknowledged by quotation marks and often by footnotes as well. In Moore's writings, the reader almost never finds the conventional poetic allusions that invoke a great tradition and assert the present poet's place in it. Like many other modernists, Moore was trying to break with traditional and attach poetry to the world in a new way; unlike them, however, she acknowledged no large social mission and did not present her poetry as necessarily reflecting or commenting on the state of modern civilization.

Against the exactitude and "unbearable accuracy" (as she put it) of her language, Moore counterpointed a complex texture of stanza form and versification. Pound worked with the clause, Williams with the line, H. D. with the image, Stevens and Stein with the word; Moore, unlike these modernist contemporaries, used the entire stanza as the unit of her poetry. Her stanza is composed of regular lines counted by syllables, instead of by stress, which are connected in an elaborate verse pattern, and in which rhymes often occur at unaccented syllables and even in the middle of a word. The effects she achieves are complex and subtle; she was often called the "poet's poet" of her day because the reader needed expert technical understanding to recognize what she was doing.

Nevertheless, her poetry also had a thematic, declarative edge; the outbreak of World War II led her to expand this aspect of her writing. The sentiments expressed in her later verse are the need for human decency and the desirability of a political and social system in which dignity is accorded to all. Moore received the Bollingen, National Book, and Pulitzer awards for *Collected Poems* in 1951 and thereafter was a more publish figure. Throughout her lifetime she continued to revise, expand, cut, and select, so that from volume to volume a poem with the same name may become a very different work. Her *Collected Poems* of 1967 represented her poetry as she wanted it remembered, but a full understanding of Moore calls for reading all the versions of her changing work.

(The text is selected from *The Norton Anthology of American Literature* (Shorter Fifth Edition))

Major Works:

- *Poems*, 1921 《诗集》
- *Observations*, 1924 《观察》
- *Selected Poems*, 1935 《诗歌选集》
- *The Pangolin and Other Verse*, 1936 《穿山甲》
- *What Are Years*, 1941 《何谓岁月?》
- *Nevertheless*, 1944 《然而》
- *A Face*, 1949 《面孔》
- *Collected Poems*, 1951 《诗选》(普利策奖)
- *Fables of La Fontaine*, 1954 《拉封丹寓言集》(译著)
- *Predilections: Literary Essays*, 1955 《嗜好》
- *O to Be a Dragon*, 1959 《哦,做一条龙》
- *Poetry and Criticism*, 1965 《诗和评论集》
- *The Complete Poems of Marianne Moore*, 1967 《诗全集》

Poetry[1]

I, too, dislike it: there are things that are important beyond all this fiddle.
Reading it, however, with a perfect contempt for it, one discovers in
it. after all, a place for the genuine.
Hands that can grasp, eyes
that can dilate, hair that can rise
if it must, these things are important not because a

high-sounding interpretation can be put upon them but because they are
useful. When they become so derivative as to become unintelligible,
the same thing may be said for all of us, that we
do not admire what

---

[1] The version printed here follows the text and format of *Selected Poems* (1935).

we cannot understand: the bat
holding on upside down or in quest of something to

eat, elephants pushing, a wild horse taking a roll, a tireless wolf under
a tree, the immovable critic twitching his skin like a horse
that feels a flea, the base-
ball fan, the statistician —
nor is it valid
to discriminate against "business documents and

school-books";❶ all these phenomena are important. One must make
a distinction
however: when dragged into prominence by half poets, the
result is not poetry,
nor till the poets among us can be
"literalists of
the imagination"❷— above
insolence and triviality and can present

for inspection, "imaginary gardens with real toads in them,"
shall we have
it. In the meantime, if you demand on the one hand,
the raw material of poetry in

---

❶ "Dairy of Tolstoy (Dutton), p. 84. 'Where the boundary between prose and poetry lies, I shall never be able to understand. The question is raised in manuals of style, yet the answer to it lies beyond me. Poetry is verse; prose is not verse. Or else poetry is everything with the exception of business documents and school books'" [Moore's note].

❷ "Yeats's *Ideas of Good and Evil* (A. H. Bullen), p. 182. 'The limitation of his view was from the very intensity of his vision; he was a too literal realist of imagination, as others are of nature; and because he believed that the figures seen by the mind's eye, when exalted by inspiration, were "eternal existences," symbols of divine essences, he hated every grace of style that might obscure their lineaments'" [Moore's note].

all its rawness and
that which is on the other hand
genuine, you are interested in poetry.

The Paper Nautilus[1]

For authorities whose hopes
are shaped by mercenaries?
Writers entrapped by
teatime fame and by
commuters' comforts? Not for these
the paper nautilus
constructs her thin glass shell.

Giving her perishable
souvenir of hope, a dull
white outside and smooth-
edged inner surface
glossy as the sea, the watchful
maker of it guards it
day and night; she scarcely

eats until the eggs are hatched.
Buried eight-fold in her eight
arms, for she is in
a sense a devil-
fish, her glass ram'shorn-cradled freight
is hid but is not crushed;

---

[1] The text is from *Complete Poems* (1967).

as Hercules[1], bitten

by a crab loyal to the hydra,
was hindered to succeed,
the intensively
watched eggs coming from
the shell free it when they are freed, —
leaving its wasp-nest flaws
of white on white, and close-

laid Ionic chiton-folds
like the lines in the mane of
a Parthenon horse,
round which the arms had
wound themselves as if they knew love
is the only fortress
strong enough to trust to.

O to Be a Dragon[2]

If I, like Solomon,...
could have my wish —
my wish ... O to be a dragon,
a symbol of the power of Heaven — of silkworm
size or immense; at times invisible.
Felicitous phenomenon!

(The above texts are selected from *The Norton Anthology of American Literature* (Shorter Fifth Edition))

---

[1] Hero of Greek myth, who performed numerous exploits including battle with the hydra, a many-headed monster.

[2] The text is selected from *Complete Poems* (1967).

Silence[1]

My father used to say,
"Superior people never make long visits,
have to be shown Longfellow's grave
nor the glass flowers at Harvard.
Self-reliant like the cat —
that takes its prey to privacy,
the mouse's limp tail hanging like a shoelace from its mouth —
they sometimes enjoy solitude,
and can be robbed of speech
by speech which has delighted them.
The deepest feeling always shows itself in silence;
not in silence, but restraint."
Nor was he insincere in saying, "Make my house your inn."
Inns are not residences.

The Fish

wade
through black jade.
Of the crow-blue mussel-shells, one keeps
adjusting the ash-heaps;
opening and shutting itself like
an
injured fan.
The barnacles which encrust the side
of the wave, cannot hide
there for the submerged shafts of the

---

[1] The text is selected from *Observations* (1924).

sun,
split like spun
glass, move themselves with spotlight swiftness
into the crevices —
in and out, illuminating
the
turquoise sea
of bodies. The water drives a wedge
of iron through the iron edge
of the cliff; whereupon the stars,
pink
rice-grains, ink-
bespattered jelly fish, crabs like green
lilies, and submarine
toadstools, slide each on the other.
All
external
marks of abuse are present on this
defiant edifice —
all the physical features of

ac-
cident — lack
of cornice, dynamite grooves, burns, and
hatchet strokes, these things stand
out on it; the chasm-side is
dead.
Repeated
evidence has proved that it can live
on what can not revive

its youth. The sea grows old in it.

(The above texts are selected from *http*: *//www. poets. org*)

Questions for discussion:

1. Examine closely Moore's skillful writing of free verse in the selected poems.
2. "they sometimes enjoy solitude/ and can be robbed of speech/ by speech which has delighted them". How do you understand these 3 lines from the poem "Silence"?
3. Moore's poems always blend quotations, allusions, and ironies. Study the above poems and try to identify all these characteristics in them.
4. Is the poem "The Fish" an animal poem? What's the idea that Moore wants to convey?

Katherine Anne Porter (1890 — 1980)

Over a long writing life Katherine Anne Porter produced only four books of stories and one novel, *Ship of Fools*, which did not appear until she was over seventy. Her reputation as a prose writer did not depend on quantity; each story was technically skilled, emotionally powerful, combining traditional narration with new symbolic techniques and contemporary subject matter.

Callie Russell Porter — she changed the name to Katherine Anne Porter when she became a writer — was born in the small settlement of Indian Creek, Texas; her mother died soon after giving birth to her fourth child, when Porter was not quite two years old. Her father moved them all to his mother's home in Kyle, Texas, where the maternal grandmother raised the family in extreme poverty. The father gave up all attempts to support them either financially or emotionally; the security provided by the strong, loving, but pious and stern grandmother ended with her death when

Porter was eleven. Porter married to leave home immediately after her sixteenth birthday, only to find that rooted domesticity was not for her. Long before her divorce in 1915, she had separated from her first husband and begun a life of travel, activity, and changes of jobs.

She started writing in 1916 as a reporter for a *Dallas Newspaper*. In 1917 she moved to Denver, the next year to New York City's Greenwich Village. Between 1918 and 1924 she lived mainly in Mexico, freelancing, meeting artists and intellectuals, and becoming involved in revolutionary politics. In Mexico she found the resources of journalism inadequate to her ambitions; using an anecdote she had heard from an archaeologist as a kernel, she wrote her first story, *Maria Conception*, which was published in the prestigious *Century Magazine* in 1922. Like all her other stories, it dealt with powerful emotions and had a strong sense of locale. Critics praised her as a major talent.

Although she considered herself as a serious writer from this time on, Porter was distracted from fiction by many crosscurrents. A self-supporting woman with expensive tastes, she hesitated to give up lucrative freelance offers. She enjoyed travel and gladly took on jobs that sent her abroad. She became involved in political causes, including the Sacco-Vanzetti case. She was married four times.

Porter planned each story meticulously — taking extensive notes, devising scenarios, roughing out dialogue, and revising many times, sometimes over a period of years. She did not write confessional or simple autobiographical fiction, but each story originated in an important real experience of her life and drew on deep feelings. Although not a feminist, Porter devoted much of her work to exploring the tensions in women's lives in the modern era. The story that made her famous for life, so that everything else she published thereafter was looked on as a literary event, was *Flowering Judas* (1930), set in Mexico and dealing with revolutionary politics, lust, and betrayal. The reality of mixed motives and the difference between pure idealism and egotistical opportunism as they are encountered in revolutionary politics are among the themes in this deceptively simple narrative. It appeared in the little magazine *Hound and Horn*. The collections *Flowering Judas* and *Noon Wine* came out in 1930 and 1937. In 1930 Porter went back to Mexico and the following year to Europe on a Guggenheim fellowship; she lived in Berlin, Paris, and Basel before returning to the United States in 1936. Two more collections of stories and novellas appeared in 1939 (*Pale Horse, Pale Rider*) and in 1944 (*The Leaning Tower*). In these later collections there are several stories about Miranda Gay, Porter's most autobiographical protagonist.

Soon after arriving in Europe in 1931 porter began working on a novel, but it was not until 1962 that *Ship of Fools*, which runs to almost five hundred printed pages, appeared. Set on an ocean liner crossing the Atlantic to Germany in August 1931, it explores the characters and developing relationships of a large number of passengers; the ship, as Porter wrote in a preface, stands for "this world on its voyage to eternity." As in *Flowering Judas*, the personal and the political intersect in *Ship of Fools*, since the coming of Nazism in Germany frames the interlinked stories of the travelers. In its film version, *Ship of Fools* brought Porter a great deal of money. Capitalizing on the publicity, her publishers brought out the Collected Stories in 1965, from which followed the National Book Award, the Pulitzer Prize, the Gold Medal for fiction of the National Institute of Arts and letters, and election to the American Academy of Letters, all in the next two years. The happiest occasions in her later years — she lived to be ninety — were connected with endowing and establishing the Katherine Anne Porter Room at the University of Maryland, not far from her last home near Washington, D. C.

(The text is selected from *The Collected Stories of Katherine Anne Porter* (1965))

Major Works:

Short Story Collections:

- *Flowering Judas and Other Stories*, 1930 《盛开的犹大花》
- *The Leaning Tower and Other Stories*, 1934 《斜塔》
- *The Old Order: Stories of the South*, 1955 《前此集》
- *The Collected Stories of Katherine Anne Porter*, 1965, 《小说选集》(普利策奖)

Novels:

- *Noon Wine*, 1937 《中午酒》
- *Pale Horse, Pale Rider*, 1939 《灰白马，灰白骑士》
- *Ship of Fools*, 1962 《愚人船》

Flowering Judas[1]

Braggioni sits heaped upon the edge of a straight-backed chair much too small for him, and sings to Laura in a furry, mournful voice. Laura has begun to find reasons for avoiding her own house until the latest possible moment, for Braggioni is there almost every night. No matter how late she is, he will be sitting there with a surly, waiting expression, pulling at his kinky yellow hair, thumbing the strings of his guitar, snarling a tune under his breath. Lupe the Indian maid meets Laura at the door, and says with a flicker of a glance towards the upper room, "He waits."

Laura wishes to lie down, she is tired of her hairpins and the feel of her long tight sleeves, but she says to him, "Have you a new song for me this evening?" If he says yes, she asks him to sing it. If he says no, she remembers his favorite one, and asks him to sing it again. Lupe brings her a cup of chocolate and a plate of rice, and Laura eats at the small table under the lamp, first inviting Braggioni, whose answer is always the same: "I have eaten, and besides, chocolate thickens the voice."

Laura says, "Sing, then," and Braggioni heaves himself into song. He scratches the guitar familiarly as though it were a pet animal, and sings passionately off key, taking the high notes in a prolonged painful squeal. Laura, who haunts the markets listening to the ballad singers, and stops every day to hear the blind boy playing his reed-flute in Sixteenth of September Street[2], listens to Braggioni with pitiless courtesy, because she dares not smile at his miserable performance. Nobody

[1] One of a genus of trees and shrubs with purplish rosy flowers. According to legend, Judas Iscariot, betrayer of Jesus, hanged himself from such a tree.

[2] A street in Morelia, a city in western Mexico where the story is set.

dares to smile at him. Braggioni is cruel to everyone, with a kind of specialized insolence, but he is so vain of his talents, and so sensitive to slights, it would require a cruelty and vanity greater than his own to lay a finger on the vast cureless wound of his self-esteem. It would require courage, too, for it is dangerous to offend him, and nobody has this courage.

Braggioni loves himself with such tenderness and amplitude and eternal charity that his followers — for he is a leader of men, a skilled revolutionist, and his skin has been punctured in horrible warfare — warm themselves in the reflected glow, and say to each other: "He has a real nobility, a love of humanity raised above mere personal affections." The excess of this self-love has flowed out, inconveniently for her, over Laura, who, with so many others, owes her comfortable situation and her salary to him. When he is in a very good humor, he tells her, "I am tempted to forgive you for being a *gringa*. *Gringita*❶!" and Laura, burning, imagines herself leaning forward suddenly, and with a sound back-handed slap wiping the suety smile from his face. If he notices her eyes at these moments he gives no sign.

She knows what Braggioni would offer her, and she must resist tenaciously without appearing to resist, and if she could avoid it she would not admit even to herself the slow drift of his intention. During these long evenings which have spoiled a long month for her, she sits in her deep chair with an open book on her knees, resting her eyes on the consoling rigidity of the printed page when the sight and sound of Braggioni singing threaten to identify themselves with all her remembered afflictions and to add their weight to her uneasy premonitions of the future. The gluttonous bulk of Braggioni has become a symbol of her many disillusions, for a revolutionist should be lean, animated by heroic faith, a vessel of abstract virtues. This is nonsense, she knows it now and is ashamed of it. Revolution must have leaders, and leadership is a career for energetic men. She is, her comrades tell her, full of romantic error, for what she defines as cynicism in them is merely "a developed sense of reality." She is almost too willing to say, "I am wrong, I suppose I don't really under-

❶ "*Gringa*": non-Mexican woman; used pejoratively, especially for an American. "*Gringita*": diminutive of *gringa*; a young foreigner, non-Mexican girl; a patronizing term meaning "cute little foreign girl."

stand the principles," and afterward she makes a secret truce with herself, determined not to surrender her will to such expedient logic. But she cannot help feeling that she has been betrayed irreparably by the disunion between her way of living and her feeling of what life should be, and at times she is almost contented to rest in this sense of grievance as a private source of consolation. Sometimes she wishes to run away, but she stays. Now she longs to fly out of this room, down the narrow stairs, and into the street where the houses lean together like conspirators under a single mottled lamp, and leave Braggioni singing to himself.

Instead she looks at Braggioni, frankly and clearly, like a good child who understands the rules of behavior. Her knees cling together under sound blue serge, and her round white collar is not purposely nun-like. She wears the uniform of an idea, and has renounced vanities. She was born Roman Catholic, and in spite of her fear of being seen by someone who might make a scandal of it, she slips now and again into some crumbling little church, kneels on the chilly stone, and says a Hail Mary on the gold rosary she bought in Tehuantepec. It is no good and she ends by examining the altar with its tinsel flowers and raged brocades, and feel tender about the battered doll-shape of some male saint whose white, lace-trimmed drawers hang limply around his ankles below the hieratic dignity of his velvet robe. She has encased herself in a set of principles derived from her early training, leaving no detail of gesture or of personal taste untouched, and for this reason she will not wear lace made on machines. This is her private heresy, for in her special group the machine is sacred, and will be the salvation of the workers. She loves fine lace, and there is a tiny edge of fluted cobweb on this collar, which is one of twenty precisely alike, folded in blue tissue paper in the upper drawer of her clothes chest.

Braggioni catches her glance solidly as if he had been waiting for it, leans forward, balancing his paunch between his spread knees, and sings with tremendous emphasis, weighing his words. He has, the song relates, no father and no mother, nor even a friend to console him; lonely as a wave of the sea he comes and goes, lonely as a wave. His mouth opens round and yearns sideway, his balloon cheeks grow oily with the labor of song. He bulges marvelously in his expensive garments.

Over his lavender collar, crushed upon a purple necktie, held by a diamond hoop: over his ammunition belt of tooled leather worked in silver, buckled cruelly around his gasping middle: over the tops of his glossy yellow shoes Braggioni swells with ominous ripeness, his mauve silk hose stretched taut, his ankles bound with the stout leather thongs of his shoes.

When he stretches his eyelids at Laura she notes again that his eyes are the true tawny yellow cat's eyes. He is rich, not in money, he tells her, but in power, and this power brings with it the blameless ownership of things, and the right to indulge his love of small luxuries. "I have a taste for the elegant refinements," he said once, flourishing a yellow silk handkerchief before her nose. "Smell that? It is Jockey Club, imported from New York." Nonetheless he is wounded by life. He will say so presently. "It is true everything turns to dust in the hand, to gall on the tongue." He sighs and his leather belt creaks like a saddle girth. "I am disappointed in everything as it comes. Everything." He shakes his head, "You, poor thing, you will be disappointed too. You are born for it. We are more alike than you realize in some things. Wait and see. Some day you will remember what I have told you, you will know that Braggioni was your friend."

Laura feels a slow chill, a purely physical sense of danger, a warning in her blood that violence, mutilation, a shocking death, wait for her with lessening patience. She has translated this fear into something homely, immediate, and sometimes hesitates before crossing the street. "My personal fate is nothing, except as the testimony of a mental attitude," she reminds herself, quoting from some forgotten philosophic primer, and is sensible enough to add, "Anyhow, I shall not be killed by an automobile if I can help it."

"It may be true I am as corrupt, in another way, as Braggioni," she thinks in spite of herself, "as callous, as incomplete," and if this is so, any kind of death seems preferable. Still she sits quietly, she does not run. Where could she go? Uninvited she has promised herself to this place; she can no longer imagine herself as living in another country, and there is pleasure in remembering her life before she came here.

Precisely what is the nature of this devotion, its true motives, and what are its obligations? Laura cannot say. She spends part of her days in Xochimilco, near by, teaching Indian children to say in English, "The cat is on the mat." When she appears in the classroom they crowed about her with smiles on their wise, innocent, clay-colored faces, crying, "Good morning, my ticher!" in immaculate voices, and they make of her desk a fresh garden of flowers every day.

During her leisure she goes to union meetings and listens to busy important voices quarreling over tactics, methods, internal politics. She visits the prisoners of her own political faith in their cells, where they entertain themselves with counting cockroaches, repenting of their indiscretions, composing their memoirs, writing out manifestoes and plans for their comrades who are still walking about free, hands in pockets, sniffing fresh air. Laura brings them food and cigarettes and a little money, and she brings messages disguised in equivocal phrases from the men outside who dare not set foot in the prison for fear of disappearing into the cells kept empty for them. If the prisoners confuse night and day, and complain, "Dear little Laura, time doesn't pass in this infernal hole, and I won't know when it is time to sleep unless I have a reminder," she brings them their favorite narcotics, and says in a tone that does not wound them with pity, "Tonight will really be night for you," and though her Spanish amuses them, they find her comforting, useful. If they lose patience and all faith, and curse the slowness of their friends in coming to their rescue with money and influence, they trust her not to repeat everything, and if she inquiries, "Where do you think we can find money, or influence?" they are certain to answer, "Well, there is Braggioni, why doesn't he do something?"

She smuggles letters from headquarters to men hiding from firing squads in back streets in mildewed houses, where they sit in tumbled beds and talk bitterly as if all Mexico were at their heels, when Laura know positively they might appear at the band concert in the Alameda❶ on Sunday morning, and no one would notice them. But Braggioni says, "Let them sweat a little. The next time they may be careful. It

---

❶ Public promenade bordered with trees.

is very restful to have them out of the way for a while." She is not afraid to knock on any door in any street after midnight, and enter in the darkness, and say to none of these men who is really in danger: "They will be looking for you — seriously — tomorrow morning after six. Here is some money from Vincente. Go to Vera Cruz and wait."

She borrows money from the Roumanian agitator to give to his bitter enemy the Polish agitator. The favor of Braggioni is their disputed territory, and Braggioni holds the balance nicely, for he can use them both. The Polish agitator talks love to her over café tables, hoping to exploit what he believes is her secret sentimental preference for him, and he gives her misinformation which he begs her to repeat as the solemn truth to certain persons. The Roumanian is more adroit. He is generous with his money in all good causes, and lies to her with an air of ingenuous candor, as if he were her good friend and confidant. She never repeats anything they may say. Braggioni never asks questions. He has other ways to discover all that he wishes to know about them.

Nobody touches her, but all praise her gray eyes, and the soft, round under lip which promises gayety, yet is always grave, nearly always firmly closed: and they cannot understand why she is in Mexico. She walks back and forth on her errands, with puzzled eyebrows, carrying her little folder of drawings and music and school papers. No dancer dances more beautifully than Laura walks, and she inspires some amusing, unexpected ardors, which cause little gossip, because nothing comes of them. A young captain who had been a soldier in Zapata's[1] army attempted, during a horseback ride near Cuernavaca, to express his desire for her with the noble simplicity befitting a rude folk-hero: but gently, because he was gentle. This gentleness was his defeat, for when he alighted, and removed her foot from the stirrup, and essayed to draw her down into his arms, her horse, ordinarily a tame one, shied fiercely, reared and plunged away. The young hero's horse careered blindly

[1] Emiliano Zapata (c. 1879-1919), Mexican peasant revolutionary general whose movement, *zapatismo*, combined agrarian and Mexican Indian cultural aspirations; one of the most significant figures in Mexico from 1910 to 1919, when he was murdered.

after his stable-mate, and the hero did not return to the hotel until rather late that evening. At breakfast he came to her tale in full charro[1] dress, gray buckskin jacket and trousers with strings of silver buttons down the leg, and he was in a humorous, careless mood. "May I sit with you?" and "You are a wonderful rider. I was terrified that you might be thrown and dragged. I should never have forgiven myself. But I cannot admire you enough for your riding!"

"I learned to ride in Arizona," said Laura.

"If you will ride with me again this morning, I promise you a horse that will not shy with you," he said. But Laura remembered that she must return to Mexico City at noon.

Next morning the children made a celebration and spent their playtime writing on the blackboard, "We love ar ticher," and with tinted chalks they drew wreaths of flowers around the words. The young hero wrote her a letter: "I am a very foolish, wasteful, impulsive man. I should have first said I love you, and then you would not have run away. But you shall see me again." Laura thought, "I must send him a box of colored crayons." But she was trying to forgive herself for having spurred her horse at the wrong moment.

A brown, shock-haired youth came and stood in her patio one night and sang like a lost soul for two hours, but Laura could think of nothing to do about it. The moonlight spread a wash of gauzy silver over the clear spaces of the garden, and the shadows were cobalt blue. The scarlet blossoms of the Judas tree were dull purple, and the names of the colors repeated themselves automatically in her mind, while she watched not the boy, but his shadow, fallen like a dark garment across the fountain rim, trailing in the water. Lupe came silently and whispered expert counsel in her ear: "If you will throw him one little flower, he will sing another song or two and go away." Laura threw the flower, and he sang a last song and went away with the flower tucked in the band of his hat. Lupe said, "He is one of the organizers of the Typographers Union, and before that he sold corridos[2] in the Merced market, and

---

[1] Costume worn by a peasant horseman of special status.

[2] Popular ballads.

before that, he came from Guanajuato, where I was born. I would not trust any man, but I trust least those from Guanajuato."

She did not tell Laura that he would be back again the next night and the next, or that he would follow her at a certain fixed distance around the Merced market, through the Zócalo, up Francisco I. Madero Avenue, and so along the Paseo de la Reforma to Chapultepec Park, and into the Philosopher's Footpath, still with that flower withering in his hat, and an indivisible attention in his eyes.

Now Laura is accustomed to him, it means nothing except that he is nineteen years old and is observing a convention with all propriety, as though it were founded on a law of nature, which in the end it might well prove to be. He is beginning to write poems which he prints on a wooden press, and he leaves them stuck like handbills in her door. She is pleasantly disturbed by the abstract, unhurried watchfulness of his black eye which will in time turn easily towards another object. She tells herself that throwing the flower was a mistake, for she is twenty-two years old and knows better; but she refuses to regret it, and persuade herself that her negation of all external events as they occur is a sign that she is gradually perfecting herself in the stoicism she strives to cultivate against that disaster she fear, though she cannot name it.

She is not at home in the world. Every day she teaches children who remain strangers to her, though she loves their tender round hands and their charming opportunist savagery. She knocks at unfamiliar doors not knowing whether a friend or a stranger shall answer, and even if a known face emerges from the sour gloom of that unknown interior, still it is the face of a stranger. No matter what this stranger says to her, nor what her message to him, the very cells of her flesh reject knowledge and kinship in one monotonous word. No. No. No. She draws her strength from this one holy talismanic word which does not suffer her to be led into evil. Denying everything, she may walk anywhere in safety, she looks at everything without amazement.

No, repeats this firm unchanging voice of her blood; and she looks at Braggioni without amazement. He is a great man, he wishes to impress this simple girl who covers her great round breasts with thick dark cloth, and who hides long, invaluably beautiful legs under a heavy skirt. She is almost thin except for the incomprehensible fullness of her breasts, like a nursing mother's, and Braggioni, who considers himself a judge of women, speculates again on the puzzle of her notorious virginity, and takes the liberty of speech which she permits without a sign of modesty, indeed, without any sort of sign, which is disconcerting.

"You think you are so cold, *gringita*! Wait and see. You will surprise yourself some day! May I be there to advise you!" He stretches his eyelids at her, and his ill-humored cat's eyes waver in a separate glance for the two points of light marking the opposite ends of a smoothly drawn path between the swollen curve of her breasts. He is not put off by that blue serge, nor by her resolutely fixed gaze. There is all the time in the world. His cheeks are bellying with the wind of song. "O girl with the dark eyes," he sings, and reconsiders. "But yours are not dark. I can change all that. O girl with the green eyes, you have stolen my heart away!" Then his mind wanders to the song, and Laura feels the weight of his attention being shifted elsewhere. Singing thus, he seems harmless, he is quite harmless, there is nothing to do but sit patiently and say "No," when the moment comes. She draws a full breath, and her mind wanders also, but not far. She dares not wander too far.

Not for nothing has Braggioni taken pains to be a good revolutionist and a professional lover of humanity. He will never die of it. He has the malice, the cleverness, the wickedness, the sharpness of wit, the hardness of heart, stipulated for loving the world profitably. He will live to see himself kicked out form his feeding trough by other hungry world-saviors. Traditionally he must sing in spite of his life which drives him to bloodshed, he tells Laura, for his father was a Tuscany❶ peasant who drifted to Yucatan and married a Maya woman: a woman of race, an aristocrat. They gave him the love and knowledge of music: and under the rip of his thumbnail, the strings of the instrument complain like exposed nerves.

Once he was called Delgadito by all the girls and married women who ran after him; he was so scrawny all his bones showed under his thin cotton clothing, and he could squeeze his emptiness to the very backbone with his two hands. He was a poet

---

❶ A region in north-central Italy.

and the revolution was only a dream then; too many women loved him and sapped away his youth, and he could never find enough to eat anywhere, anywhere! Now he is a leader of men, crafty men who whisper in his ear, hungry men who wait for hours outside his office for a word with him, emaciated men with wild faces who waylay him at the street gate with a timid, "Comrade, let me tell you..." and they blow the foul breath from their empty stomachs in his face.

He is always sympathetic. He gives them handfuls of small coins from his own pocket, he promises them work, there will be demonstrations, they must join the unions and attend the meetings, above all they must be on the watch for spies. They are closer to him than his own brothers, without them he can do nothing — until tomorrow, comrade!

Until tomorrow. "They are stupid, they are lazy, they are treacherous, they would cut my throat for nothing," he says to Laura. He has good food and abundant drink, he hires an automobile and drives in the Paseo on Sunday morning, and enjoys plenty of sleep in a soft bed beside a wife who dares not disturb him; and he sits pampering his bones in easy billows of fat, singing to Laura, who knows and thinks these things about him. When he was fifteen, he tried to drown himself because he loved a girl, his first love, and she laughed at him. "A thousand women have paid for that," and his tight little mouth turns down at the corners. Now he perfumes his hair with Jockey Club, and confides to Laura: "One woman is really as good as another for me, in the dark. I prefer them all."

His wife organizes unions among the girls in the cigarette factories, and walks in picket lines, and even speaks at meetings in the evenings. But she cannot be brought to acknowledge the benefits of true liberty. "I tell her I must have my freedom, net. She does not understand my point of view." Laura has heard this many times. Braggioni scratches the guitar and meditates. "She is an instinctively virtuous woman, pure gold, no doubt of that. If she were not, I should lock her up, and she knows it."

His wife, who works so hard for the good of the factory girls, employs part of her leisure lying on the floor weeping because there are so many women in the world, and only one husband for her, and she never knows where nor when to look for him. He told her, "Unless you can learn to cry when I am not here, I must go away for good." That day he went away and took a room at the Hotel Madrid.

It is this month of separation for the sake of higher principles that has been spoiled not only for Mrs. Braggioni, whose sense of reality is beyond criticism, but for Laura, who feels herself bogged in a nightmare. Tonight Laura envies Mrs. Braggioni, who is alone, and free to weep as much she pleases about a concrete wrong. Laura has just come from a visit to the prison, and she is waiting for tomorrow with a bitter anxiety as if tomorrow may not come, but time may be caught immovably in this hour, with herself transfixed, Braggioni singing on forever, and Eugenio's body not yet discovered by the guard.

Braggioni says: "Are you going to sleep?" Almost before she can shake her head, he begins telling her about the May-day disturbances coming on in Morelia, for the Catholics hold a festival in honor of the Blessed Virgin, and the Socialists celebrate their martyrs on that day. "There will be two independent processions, starting from either end of town, and they will march until they meet, and the rest depends..." he asks her to oil and load his pistols. Standing up, he unbuckles his ammunition belt, and spreads it laden across her knees. Laura sits with the shell slipping through the cleaning cloth dipped in oil, and he says again he cannot understand why she works so hard for the revolutionary idea unless she loves some man who is in it. "Are you not in love with someone?" "No," says Laura. "And no one is in love with you?" "No." "Then it is your own fault. No woman need go begging. Why, what is the matter with you? The legless beggar woman in the Alameda has a perfectly faithful lover. Did you know that?"

Laura peers down the pistol barrel and says nothing, but a long, slow faintness rises and subsides in her; Braggioni curves his swollen fingers around the throat of the guitar and softly smothers the music out of it, and when she hears him again he seems to have forgotten her, and is speaking in the hypnotic voice he uses when talking in small rooms to a listening, close-gathered crowd. Some day this world, now seemingly so composed and eternal, to the edges of every sea shall be merely a tangle of gaping trenches, of crashing walls and broken bodies. Everything must be torn from its accustomed place where it has rotted for centuries, hurled skyward and distributed, cast down again clean as rain, without separate identity. Nothing shall survive that the stiffened hands of poverty have created for the rich and no one shall be left alive except the elect spirits destined to procreate a new world cleansed of cruelty and injustice, ruled by benevolent anarchy: "Pistols are good, I love them, cannon are even better, but in the end I pin my faith to good dynamite," he concludes, and strokes the pistol lying in her hands. "Once I dreamed of destroying this city, in case it offered resistance to General Ortíz, but it fell into his hands like an overripe pear."

He is made restless by his own works, rises and stands waiting. Laura holds up the belt to him: "Put that on, and go kill somebody in Morelia, and you will be happier," she says softly. The presence of death in the room makes her bold. "Today, I found Eugenio going into a stupor. He refused to allow me to call the prison doctor. He had taken all the tablets I brought him yesterday. He said he took them because he was bored."

"He is a fool, and his death is his own business," says Braggioni, fastening his belt carefully.

"I told him if he had waited only a little while longer, you would have got him set free," says Laura. "He said he did not want to wait."

"He is a fool and we are rid of him," says Braggioni, reaching for his hat.

He goes away. Laura knows his mod has changed, she will not see him any more for a while. He will send word when he needs her to go on errands into strange streets, to speak to the strange faces that will appear, like clay masks with the power of human speech, to mutter their thanks to Braggioni for his help. Now she is free, and she thinks, I must run while there is time. But she does not go.

Braggioni enters his own house where for a month his wife has spent many hours every night weeping and tangling her hair upon her pillow. She is weeping now, and she weeps more at the sight of him, the cause of all her sorrows. He looks about the room. Nothing is changed, the smells are good and familiar, he is well acquainted with the woman who comes toward him with no reproach except grief on her face. He says to her tenderly: "You are so good, please don't cry any more, you dear good creature." She says, "Are you tired, my angel? Sit here and I will wash your feet." She brings a bowl of water, and kneeling, unlaces his shoes, and when from her knees she raises her sad eyes under her blackened lids, he is sorry for everything, and bursts into tears. "Ah, yes, I am hungry, I am tired, let us eat something together," he says, between sobs. His wife leans her head on his arm and says, "Forgive me!" and this time he is refreshed by solemn, endless rain of her tears.

Laura takes off her serge dress and puts on a white linen nightgown and goes to bed. She turns her head a little to one side, and lying still, reminds herself that it is time to sleep. Numbers tick in her brain like little clocks, soundless doors close of themselves around her. If you would sleep, you must not remember anything, the children will say tomorrow, good morning, my teacher, the poor prisoners who come every day bringing flowers to their jailor. 1-2-3-4-5— it is monstrous to confuse love with revolution, night with day, life with death — ah, Eugenio.

The tolling of the midnight bell is a signal, but what does it mean? Get up, Laura, and follow me: come out of your sleep, out of your bed, out of this strange house. What are you doing in this house? Without a word, without fear she rose and reached for Eugenio's hand, but he eluded her with a sharp, sly smile and drifted away. This is not all, you shall see — Murderer, he said, follow me, I will show you a new country, but it is far away and we must hurry. No, said Laura, not unless you take my hand, no; and she clung first to the stair rail, and then to the topmost branch of the Judas tree that bent down slowly and set her upon the earth, and then to the rocky ledge of a cliff, and then to the jagged wave of a sea that was not water but a desert of crumbling stone. Where are you taking me, she asked in wonder but without fear. To death, and it is along way off, and we must hurry, said Eugenio. No, said Laura, not unless you take my hand. Then eat these flowers, poor prisoner, said Eugenio in a voice of pity, take and eat: and form the Judas tree he stripped the warm bleeding flowers, and held them to her lips. She saw that his hand was fleshless, a cluster of small white petrified branches, and his eye sockets were without light, but she ate the flowers greedily for they satisfied both hunger and thirst. Murderer! Said Eugenio, and Cannibal! This is my body and my blood. Laura cried No! and at the sound of her own voice, she awoke trembling, and was afraid to sleep again.

(The text is selected from *The Norton Anthology of American Literature* (Shorter Fifth Edition))

Questions for discussion:

1. How do you understand the symbolism used in this story? What are the symbolic images presented? Make a summary of them.
2. Why is Braggioni's wife so devoted to her husband?
3. Do you believe Laura suffered from a mental problem that shaped her outlook on life? Explain your answer.
4. Obviously, Laura is very attractive, for men regularly make passes at her. In addition, she appears to have many other appealing qualities besides beauty. For example, her students love and admire her, and the revolutionaries she visits trust her. Summarize the positive and negative qualities of this woman, and try to discover what makes her tick.

Pearl S. Buck (1892 — 1973)

Pearl Sydenstricker was born on June 26, 1892, in Hillsboro, West Virginia. Her parents, Absalom and Caroline Sydenstricker, were Southern Presbyterian missionaries, stationed in China. Pearl was the fourth of seven children (and one of only three who would survive to adulthood). She was born when her parents were near the end of a furlough in the United States; when she was three months old, she was taken back to China, where she spent most of the first forty years of her life.

The Sydenstrickers lived in Chinkiang (Zhenjiang), in Kiangsu (Jiangsu) province, then a small city lying at the junction of the Yangtze River and the Grand Canal. Pearl's father spent months away from home, itinerating in the Chinese countryside in search of Christian converts; Pearl's mother ministered to Chinese women in a small dispensary she established.

From childhood, Pearl spoke both English and Chinese. She was taught principally by her mother and by a Chinese tutor, Mr. Kung. In 1900, during the Boxer Uprising, Caroline and the children evacuated to Shanghai, where they spent several anxious months waiting for word of Absalom's fate. Later that year, the family returned to the U. S. for another home leave.

In 1910, Pearl enrolled in Randolph-Macon Woman's College, in Lynchburg, Virginia, from which she graduated in 1914. Although she had intended to remain in the U. S., she returned to China shortly after graduation when she received word that her mother was gravely ill. In 1915, she met a young Cornell graduate, an agricultural economist named John Lossing Buck. They married in 1917, and immediately moved to Nanhsuchou (Nanxuzhou) in rural Anhwei (Anhui) province. In this impoverished community, Pearl Buck gathered the material that she would later use in *The Good Earth* and other stories of China.

The Bucks' first child, Carol, was born in 1921; a victim of PKU, she proved to be profoundly retarded. Furthermore, because of a uterine tumor discovered during the delivery, Pearl underwent a hysterectomy. In 1925, she and Lossing adopted a baby girl, Janice. The Buck marriage was unhappy almost from the beginning, but would last for eighteen years.

From 1920 to 1933, Pearl and Lossing made their home in Nanking (Nanjing), on the campus of Nanking University, where both had teaching positions. In 1921, Pearl's mother died and shortly afterwards her father moved in with the Bucks. The tragedies and dislocations which Pearl suffered in the 1920s reached a climax in March, 1927, in the violence known as the "Nanking Incident." In a confused battle involving elements of Chiang Kai-shek's Nationalist troops, Communist forces, and assorted warlords, several Westerners were murdered. The Bucks spent a terrified day in hiding, after which they were rescued by American gunboats. After a trip downriver to Shanghai, the Buck family sailed to Unzen, Japan, where they spent the following year. They then moved back to Nanking, though conditions remained dangerously unsettled.

Pearl had begun to publish stories and essays in the 1920s, in magazines such as *Nation*, *The Chinese Recorder*, *Asia*, and *Atlantic Monthly*. Her first novel, *East Wind, West Wind*, was published by the John Day Company in 1930. John Day's publisher, Richard Walsh, would eventually become Pearl's second husband, in 1935, after both received divorces.

In 1931, John Day published Pearl's second novel, *The Good Earth*. This became the best-selling book of both 1931 and 1932, won the Pulitzer Prize and the Howells Medal in 1935, and would be adapted as a major MGM film in 1937. Other novels and books of non-fiction quickly followed. In 1938, less than a decade after her first book had appeared, Pearl won the Nobel Prize in literature, the first American woman to do so. By the time of her death in 1973, Pearl would publish over seventy books: novels, collections of stories, biography and autobiography, poetry, drama, children's literature, and translations from the Chinese.

In 1934, because of the conditions in China, and also to be closer to Richard Walsh and her daughter Carol, whom she had placed in an institution in New Jersey, Pearl moved permanently to the U. S.. She bought an old farmhouse, Green Hills Farm, in Bucks County, PA. She and Richard adopted six more children over the following years. Green Hills Farm is now on the Registry of Historic Buildings; fifteen thousand people visit each year.

From the day of her move to the U. S., Pearl was active in American civil rights and women's rights activities. She published essays in both *Crisis*, the journal of the NAACP, and *Opportunity*, the magazine of the Urban League; she was a trustee of Howard University for twenty years, beginning in the early 1940s. In 1942, Pearl and Richard founded the East and West Association, dedicated to cultural exchange and understanding between Asia and the West. In 1949, outraged that existing adoption services considered Asian and mixed-race children unadoptable, Pearl established Welcome House, the first international, inter-racial adoption agency; in the nearly five decades of its work, Welcome House has assisted in the placement of over five thousand children. In 1964, to provide support for Amerasian children who were not eligible for adoption, Pearl also established the Pearl S. Buck Foundation, which provides sponsorship funding for thousands of children in half-a-dozen Asian countries.

Pearl S. Buck died of lung cancer on March 6, 1973, in Danby, Vermont, just two months before her eighty-first birthday. She is buried at Green Hills Farm. Today, she continues to be regarded as a legendary American writer and humanitarian.

(The text is selected from *https://www.english.upenn.edu/Projects/Buck/biography.html*)

Major Works:

Autobiographies:

- *My Several Worlds: A Personal Record*, 1954 《我的几个世界：一部个人的记录》
- *A Bridge For Passing*, 1962 《为了达到彼岸的桥梁》

Biographies:

- *The Exile*, 1936 《流亡》
- *Fighting Angel*, 1936 《奋斗的天使》

Fictions:

- *East Wind: West Wind*, 1930 《东风·西风》
- *The House of Earth*, 1931 《大地之家》
- *The Good Earth*, 1931《大地》(普利策奖)
- *The First Wife and Other Stories*, 1933 《发妻和其他故事》
- *Sons*, 1933 《儿子们》
- *The Mother*, 1933 《母亲》
- *All Men Are Brothers*, 1933 英译本《四海之内皆兄弟》(即中国古典小说《水浒传》)
- *A House Divided*, 1935 《分家》
- *This Proud Heart*, 1938 《这高傲的心》
- *The Patriot*, 1939 《爱国者》
- *Other Gods*, 1940 《另一种神祇：一个美国的传说》(又译《其他的神》)

- *China Sky*, 1941 《中国天空》
- *Today and Forever: Stories of China*, 1941 《今天和永远：中国短篇小说集》
- *Dragon Seed*, 1942 《龙种》(又译《龙子》、《炎黄子孙》)
- *The Promise*, 1943 《希望》(又译《诺言》)
- *China Flight*, 1943 《中国的航程》
- *Twenty-Seven Stories*, 1943《二十七个故事》
- *The Townsman*, 1945 《市民》(又译《镇民》、《城里人》)
- *Portrait of a Marriage*, 1945 《结婚照》
- *Pavilion of Women*, 1946 《群芳庭》(又译《庭院里的女人》)
- *The Angry Wife*, 1947 《愤怒的妻子》
- *Peony*, 1948 《牡丹》
- *The Big Wave*, 1948 《巨浪》
- *The Long Love*, 1949 《漫长的爱情》
- *Far and near: stories of Japan, China, and America*, 1949 《远与近：日本、中国和美国小说集》
- *Kinfolk*, 1950 《亲友们》
- *The Child Who Never Grew*, 1950 《永远长不大的孩子》
- *God's Men*, 1951 《上帝的子民》(又译《圣徒》)
- *The Hidden Flower*, 1952 《羞涩的花朵》(又译《匿花》)
- *Come, My Beloved*, 1953 《来吧，亲爱的》
- *Voices in the House*, 1953 《家声》
- *The Man Who Changed China: The Story of Sun Yat-sen*, 1953《改变了中国的人：孙逸仙的故事》
- *Imperial Woman*, 1956 《帝国女性》
- *Letter from Peking*, 1957 《北京来信》
- *Command the Morning*, 1959 《命令与清晨》
- *Fourteen Stories*, 1961 《十四个故事》
- *Satan Never Sleeps*, 1962 《撒旦永不眠》
- *Hearts Come Home and Other Stories*, 1962 《归心和其他故事》

- *The Living Reed*, 1963 《生芦苇》
- *Death in the Castle*, 1965 《死在城堡中》
- *The Time Is Noon*, 1966 《时当正午》
- *Matthew, Mark, Luke and John*, 1967 《马克·洛克和约翰》
- *The New Year*, 1968 《新年》
- *The Three Daughters of Madame Liang*, 1969 《梁太太的三个女儿》
- *The Good Deed*, 1969 《丰功伟绩》(又译《善行》)
- *Mandala*, 1970 《佛坛》
- *The Goddess Abides*, 1972 《女神的等待》
- *All Under Heaven*, 1973 《全在天底下》
- *The Rainbow*, 1974 《霓虹》
- *East and West Stories*, 1975 《东方与西方》
- *Secrets of the Heart: Stories*, 1976 《心灵的秘密》
- *The Lovers and Other Stories* (1977) 《情人及其他故事》
- *The Woman Who Was Changed and Other Stories*, 1979 《被改变的妇女及其他故事》
- *The Eternal Wonder*, 2013《永恒的怀疑》

The Good Earth

Chapter 1

It was Wang Lung's marriage day. At first, opening his eyes in the blackness of the curtains about his bed, he could not think why the dawn seemed different from any other. The house was still except for the faint, gasping cough of his old father, whose room was opposite to his own across the middle room. Every morning the old man's cough was the first sound to be heard. Wang Lung usually lay listening to it and moved only when he heard it approaching nearer and when he heard the door of his father's room squeak upon its wooden hinges.

But this morning he did not wait. He sprang up and pushed aside the curtains of his bed. It was a dark, ruddy dawn, and through a small square hole of a window, where the tattered paper fluttered, a glimpse of bronze sky gleamed. He went to the hole and tore the paper away.

"It is spring and I do not need this," he muttered.

He was ashamed to say aloud that he wished the house to look neat on this day. The hole was barely large enough to admit his hand and he thrust it out to feel of the air. A small soft wind blew gently from the east, a wind mild and murmurous and full of rain. It was a good omen. The fields needed rain for fruition. There would be no rain this day, but within a few days, if this wind continued, there would be water. It was good. Yesterday he had said to his father that if this brazen, glittering sunshine continued, the wheat could not fill in the ear. Now it was as if Heaven had chosen this day to wish him well. Earth would bear fruit.

He hurried out into the middle room, drawing on his blue outer trousers as he went, and knotting about the fullness at his waist his girdle of blue cotton cloth. He left his upper body bare until he had heated water to bathe himself. He went into the shed which was the kitchen, leaning against the house, and out of its dusk an ox twisted its head from behind the corner next the door and lowed at him deeply. The kitchen was made of earthen bricks as the house was, great squares of earth dug from their own fields, and thatched with straw from their own wheat. Out of their own earth had his grandfather in his youth fashioned also the oven, baked and black with many years of meal preparing. On top of this earthen structure stood a deep, round, iron cauldron.

This cauldron❶ he filled partly full of water, dipping it with a half gourd from an earthen jar that stood near, but he dipped cautiously, for water was precious. Then, after a hesitation, he suddenly lifted the jar and emptied all the water into the cauldron. This day he would bathe his whole body. Not since he was a child upon his mother's knee had anyone looked upon his body. Today one would, and he would have it clean.

He went around the oven to the rear, and selecting a handful of the dry grass and stalks standing in the corner of the kitchen, he arranged it delicately in the

❶ A large deep pot for boiling liquids or cooking food over a fire.

mouth of the oven, making the most of every leaf. Then from an old flint and iron he caught a flame and thrust it into the straw and there was a blaze.

This was the last morning he would have to light the fire. He had lit it every morning since his mother died six years before. He had lit the fire, boiled water, and poured the water into a bowl and taken it into the room where his father sat upon his bed, coughing and fumbling for his shoes upon the floor. Every morning for these six years the old man had waited for his son to bring in hot water to ease him of his morning coughing. Now father and son could rest. There was a woman coming to the house. Never again would Wang Lung have to rise summer and winter at dawn to light the fire. He could lie in his bed and wait, and he also would have a bowl of water brought to him, and if the earth were fruitful there would be tea leaves in the water. Once in some years it was so.

And if the woman wearied, there would be her children to light the fire, the many children she would bear to Wang Lung. Wang Lung stopped, struck by the thought of children running in and out of their three rooms. Three rooms had always seemed much to them, a house half empty since his mother died. They were always having to resist relatives who were more crowded — his uncle, with his endless brood of children, coaxing.

"Now, how can two lone men need so much room? Cannot father and son sleep together? The warmth of the young one's body will comfort the old one's cough."

But the father always replied, "I am saving my bed for my grandson. He will warm my bones in my age."

Now the grandsons were coming, grandsons upon grandsons! They would have to put beds along the walls and in the middle room. The house would be full of beds. The blaze in the oven died down while Wang Lung thought of all the beds there would be in the half empty house, and the water began to chill in the cauldron. The shadowy figure of the old man appeared in the doorway, holding his unbuttoned garments about him. He was coughing and spitting and he gasped.

"How is it that there is not water yet to heat my lungs?"

Wang Lung stared and recalled himself and was ashamed.

"This fuel is damp," he muttered from behind the stove. "The damp wind —"

The old man continued to cough perseveringly and would not cease until the water boiled. Wang Lung dipped some into a bowl, and then, after a moment, he opened a glazed jar that stood upon a ledge of the stove and took from it a dozen or so of the curled dried leaves and sprinkled them upon the surface of the water. The old man's eyes opened greedily and immediately he began to complain.

"Why are you wasteful? Tea is like eating silver."

"It is the day," replied Wang Lung with a short laugh. "Eat and be comforted."

The old man grasped the bowl in his shriveled, knotty fingers, muttering, uttering little grunts. He watched the leaves uncurl and spread upon the surface of the water, unable to bear drinking the precious stuff.

"It will be cold," said Wang Lung.

"True — true —" said the old man in alarm, and he began to take great gulps of the hot tea. He passed into an animal satisfaction, like a child fixed upon its feeding. But he was not too forgetful to see Wang Lung dipping the water recklessly from the cauldron into a deep wooden tub. He lifted his head and stared at his son.

"Now there is water enough to bring a crop to fruit," he said suddenly.

Wang Lung continued to dip the water to the last drop. He did not answer.

"Now then!" cried his father loudly.

"I have not washed my body all at once since the New Year," said Wang Lung in a low voice.

He was ashamed to say to his father that he wished his body to be clean for a woman to see. He hurried out, carrying the tub to his own room. The door was hung loosely upon a warped wooden frame and it did not shut closely, and the old man tottered into the middle room and put his mouth to the opening and bawled,

"It will be ill if we start the woman like this — tea in the morning water and all this washing!"

"It is only one day," shouted Wang Lung. And then he added, "I will throw the water on the earth when I am finished and it is not all waste."

The old man was silent at this, and Wang Lung unfastened his girdle and stepped out of his clothing. In the light that streamed in a square block from the hole he wrung a small towel from the steaming water and he scrubbed his dark slender body vigorously. Warm though he had thought the air, when his flesh was wet he was cold, and he moved quickly, passing the towel in and out of the water until from his whole body there went up a delicate cloud of steam. Then he went to a box that had been his mother's and drew from it a fresh suit of blue cotton cloth. He might be a little cold this day without the wadding of the winter garments, but he suddenly could not bear to put them on against his clean flesh. The covering of them was torn and filthy and the wadding stuck out of the holes, grey and sodden. He did not want this woman to see him for the first time with the wadding sticking out of his clothes. Later she would have to wash and mend, but not the first day. He drew over the blue cotton coat and trousers a long robe made of the same material — his one long robe, which he wore on feast days only, ten days or so in the year, all told. Then with swift fingers he unplaited the long braid of hair that hung down his back, and taking a wooden comb from the drawer of the small, unsteady table, he began to comb out his hair.

His father drew near again and put his mouth to the crack of the door.

"Am I to have nothing to eat this day?" he complained. "At my age the bones are water in the morning until food is given them."

"I am coming," said Wang Lung, braiding his hair quickly and smoothly and weaving into the strands a tasseled, black silk cord.

Then after a moment he removed his long gown and wound his braid about his head and went out, carrying the tub of water. He had quite forgotten the breakfast. He would stir a little water into corn meal and give it to his father. For himself he could not eat. He staggered with the tub to the threshold and poured the water upon the earth nearest the door, and as he did so he remembered he had used all the water in the cauldron for his bathing and he would have to start the fire again. A wave of anger passed over him at his father.

"That old head thinks of nothing except his eating and his drinking," he muttered into the mouth of the oven; but aloud he said nothing. It was the last morning he would have to prepare food for the old man. He put a very little water into the cauldron, drawing it in a bucket from the well near the door, and it boiled quickly and he stirred meal together and took it to the old man.

"We will have rice this night, my father," he said. "Meanwhile, here is corn."

"There is only a little rice left in the basket," said the old man, seating himself at the table in the middle room and stirring with his chopsticks the thick yellow gruel.

"We will eat a little less then at the spring festival," said Wang Lung. But the old man did not hear. He was supping loudly at his bowl.

Wang Lung went into his own room then, and drew about him again the long blue robe and let down the braid of his hair. He passed his hand over his shaven brow and over his cheeks. Perhaps he had better be newly shaven? It was scarcely sunrise yet. He could pass through the Street of the Barbers and be shaved before he went to the house where the woman waited for him. If he had the money he would do it.

He took from his girdle❶ a small greasy pouch of grey cloth and counted the money in it. There were six silver dollars and a double handful of copper coins. He had not yet told his father he had asked friends to sup that night. He had asked his male cousin, the young son of his uncle, and his uncle for his father's sake, and three neighboring farmers who lived in the village with him. He had planned to bring back from the town that morning pork, a small pond fish, and a handful of chestnuts. He might even buy a few of the bamboo sprouts from the south and a little beef to stew with the cabbage he had raised in his own garden. But this only if there were any money left after the bean oil and the soybean sauce had been bought. If he shaved his head he could not, perhaps, buy the beef. Well, he would shave his head, he decided suddenly.

He left the old man without speech and went out into the early morning. In spite

❶ A piece of underwear that fits closely around the body.

of the dark red dawn the sun was mounting the horizon clouds and sparkled upon the dew on the rising wheat and barley. The farmer in Wang Lung was diverted for an instant and he stooped to examine the budding heads. They were empty as yet and waiting for the rain. He smelled the air and looked anxiously at the sky. Rain was there, dark in the clouds, heavy upon the wind. He would buy a stick of incense and place it in the little temple to the Earth God❶. On a day like this he would do it.

He wound his way in among the fields upon the narrow path. In the near distance the grey city wall arose. Within that gate in the wall through which he would pass stood the great house where the woman had been a slave girl since her childhood, the House of Hwang. There were those who said, "It is better to live alone than to marry a woman who has been slave in a great house." But when he had said to his father, "Am I never to have a woman?" his father replied, "With weddings costing as they do in these evil days and every woman wanting gold rings and silk clothes before she will take a man, there remain only slaves to be had for the poor."

His father had stirred himself, then, and gone to the House of Hwang and asked if there were a slave to spare.

"Not a slave too young, and above all, not a pretty one," he had said.

Wang Lung had suffered that she must not be pretty. It would be something to have a pretty wife that other men would congratulate him upon having. His father, seeing his mutinous face, had cried out at him,

"And what will we do with a pretty woman? We must have a woman who will tend the house and bear children as she works in the fields, and will a pretty woman do these things? She will be forever thinking about clothes to go with her face! No, not a pretty woman in our house. We are farmers. Moreover, who has heard of a pretty slave who was virgin in a wealthy house? All the young lords have had their fill of her. It is better to be first with an ugly woman than the hundredth with a beauty. Do you imagine a pretty woman will think your farmer's hands as pleasing as the soft

---

❶ The god protecting the local place, according to Chinese folklore.

hands of a rich man's son, and your sunblack face as beautiful as the golden skin of the others who have had her for their pleasure?"

Wang Lung knew his father spoke well. Nevertheless, he had to struggle with his flesh before he could answer. And then be said violently, "At least, I will not have a woman who is pock-marked, or who has a split upper lip."

"We will have to see what is to be had," his father replied.

Well, the woman was not pock-marked nor had she a split upper lip. This much he knew, but nothing more. He and his father had bought two silver rings, washed with gold, and silver earrings, and these his father had taken to the woman's owner in acknowledgment of betrothal. Beyond this, he knew nothing of the woman who was to be his, except that on this day he could go and get her.

He walked into the cool darkness of the city gate. Water carriers, just outside, their barrows laden with great tubs of water, passed to and fro all day, the water splashing out of the tubs upon the stones. It was always wet and cool in the tunnel of the gate under the thick wall of earth and brick; cool even upon a summer's day, so that the melon vendors spread their fruits upon the stones, melons split open to drink in the moist coolness. There were none yet, for the season was too early, but baskets of small hard green peaches stood along the walls, and the vendor cried out,

"The first peaches of spring — the first peaches! Buy, eat, purge your bowels of the poisons of winter!"

Wang Lung said to himself,

"If she likes them, I will buy her a handful when we return." He could not realize that when he walked back through the gate there would be a woman walking behind him.

He turned to the right within the gate and after a moment was in the Street of Barbers. There were few before him so early, only some farmers who had carried their produce into the town the night before in order that they might sell their vegetables at the dawn markets and return for the day's work in the fields. They had slept shivering and crouching over their baskets, the baskets now empty at their feet. Wang Lung avoided them lest some recognize him, for he wanted none of their joking on this day. All down the street in a long line the barbers stood behind their small stalls, and Wang Lung went to the furthest one and sat down upon the stool and motioned to the barber who stood chattering to his neighbor. The barber came at once and began quickly to pour hot water, from a kettle on his pot of charcoal, into his brass basin.

"Shave everything?" he said in a professional tone.

"My head and my face," replied Wang Lung.

"Ears and nostrils cleaned?" asked the barber.

"How much will that cost extra?" asked Wang Lung cautiously.

"Four pence," said the barber, beginning to pass a black cloth in and out of the hot water.

"I will give you two," said Wang Lung.

"Then I will clean one ear and one nostril," rejoined the barber promptly. "On which side of the face do you wish it done?" He grimaced at the next barber as he spoke and the other burst into a guffaw. Wang Lung perceived that he had fallen into the hands of a joker, and feeling inferior in some unaccountable way, as he always did, to these town dwellers, even though they were only barbers and the lowest of persons, he said quickly,

"As you will — as you will —"

Then he submitted himself to the barber's soaping and rubbing and shaving, and being after all a generous fellow enough, the barber gave him without extra charge a series of skilful poundings upon his shoulders and back to loosen his muscles. He commented upon Wang Lung as he shaved his upper forehead,

"This would not be a bad-looking farmer if he would cut off his hair. The new fashion is to take off the braid."

His razor hovered so near the circle of hair upon Wang Lung's crown that Wang Lung cried out,

"I cannot cut it off without asking my father!" And the barber laughed and skirted the round spot of hair.

When it was finished and the money counted into the barber's wrinkled, water-soaked hand, Wang Lung had a moment of horror. So much money! But walking down the street again with the wind fresh upon his shaven skin, he said to himself, "It is only once."

He went to the market, then, and bought two pounds of pork and watched the butcher as he wrapped it in a dried lotus leaf, and then, hesitating, he bought also six ounces of beef. When all had been bought, even to fresh squares of beancurd, shivering in a jelly upon its leaf, he went to a candlemaker's shop and there he bought a pair of incense sticks. Then he turned his steps with great shyness toward the House of Hwang.

Once at the gate of the house he was seized with terror. How had he come alone? He should have asked his father — his uncle — even his nearest neighbor, Ching — anyone to come with him. He had never been in a great house before. How could he go in with his wedding feast on his arm, and say, "I have come for a woman?"

He stood at the gate for a long time, looking at it. It was closed fast, two great wooden gates, painted black and bound and studded with iron, closed upon each other. Two lions made of stone stood on guard, one at either side. There was no one else. He turned away. It was impossible.

He felt suddenly faint. He would go first and buy a little food. He had eaten nothing — had forgotten food. He went into a small street restaurant, and putting two pence upon the table, he sat down. A dirty waiting boy with a shiny black apron came near and he called out to him, "Two bowls of noodles!" And when they were come, he ate them down greedily, pushing them into his mouth with his bamboo chopsticks, while the boy stood and spun the coppers between his black thumb and forefinger.

"Will you have more?" asked the boy indifferently.

Wang Lung shook his head. He sat up and looked about. There was no one he knew in the small, dark, crowded room full of tables. Only a few men sat eating or drinking tea. It was a place for poor men, and among them he looked neat and clean and almost well-to-do, so that a beggar, passing, whined at him,

"Have a good heart, teacher, and give me a small cash — I starve!"

Wang Lung had never had a beggar ask of him before, nor had any ever called him teacher. He was pleased and he threw into the beggar's bowl two small cash, which are one fifth of a penny, and the beggar pulled back with swiftness his black claw of a hand, and grasping the cash, fumbled them within his rags.

Wang Lung sat and the sun climbed upwards. The waiting boy lounged about impatiently. "If you are buying nothing more," he said at last with much impudence, "you will have to pay rent for the stool."

Wang Lung was incensed at such impudence and he would have risen except that when he thought of going into the great House of Hwang and of asking there for a woman, sweat broke out over his whole body as though he were working in a field.

"Bring me tea," he said weakly to the boy. Before he could turn it was there and the small boy demanded sharply, "Where is the penny?"

And Wang Lung, to his horror, found there was nothing to do but to produce from his girdle yet another penny.

"It is robbery," he muttered, unwilling. Then he saw entering the shop his neighbor whom he had invited to the feast, and he put the penny hastily upon the table and drank the tea at a gulp and went out quickly by the side door and was once more upon the street.

"It is to be done," he said to himself desperately, and slowly he turned his way to the great gates.

This time, since it was after high noon, the gates were ajar and the keeper of the gate idled upon the threshold, picking his teeth with a bamboo sliver after his meal. He was a tall fellow with a large mole upon his left cheek, and from the mole hung three long black hairs which had never been cut. When Wang Lung appeared he shouted roughly, thinking from the basket that he had come to sell something.

"Now then, what?"

With great difficulty Wang Lung replied, "I am Wang Lung, the farmer."

"Well, and Wang Lung, the farmer, what?" retorted the gateman, who was polite to none except the rich friends of his master and mistress.

"I am come — I am come —" faltered Wang Lung.

"That I see," said the gateman with elaborate patience, twisting the long hairs of his mole.

"There is a woman," said Wang Lung, his voice sinking helplessly to a whisper. In the sunshine his face was wet.

The gateman gave a great laugh.

"So you are he!" he roared. "I was told to expect a bridegroom today. But I did not recognize you with a basket on your arm."

"It is only a few meats," said Wang Lung apologetically, waiting for the gateman to lead him within. But the gateman did not move. At last Wang Lung said with anxiety, "Shall I go alone?"

The gateman affected a start of horror. "The Old Lord would kill you!"

Then seeing that Wang Lung was too innocent he said, "A little silver is a good key."

Wang Lung saw at last that the man wanted money of him.

"I am a poor man," he said pleadingly.

"Let me see what you have in your girdle," said the gateman.

And he grinned when Wang Lung in his simplicity actually put his basket upon the stones and lifting his robe took out the small bag from his girdle and shook into his left hand what money was left after his purchases. There was one silver piece and fourteen copper pence.

"I will take the silver," said the gateman coolly, and before Wang Lung could protest the man had the silver in his sleeve and was striding through the gate, bawling loudly, "The bridegroom, the bridegroom!"

Wang Lung, in spite of anger at what had just happened and horror at this loud announcing of his coming, could do nothing but follow, and this he did, picking up his basket and looking neither to the right nor left.

Afterwards, although it was the first time he had ever been in a great family's house, he could remember nothing. With his face burning and his head bowed, he walked through court after court, hearing that voice roaring ahead of him, hearing tinkles of laughter on every side. Then suddenly when it seemed to him he had gone through a hundred courts, the gateman fell silent and pushed him into a small waiting room. There he stood alone while the gateman went into some inner place, returning in a moment to say, "The Old Mistress says you are to appear before her."

Wang Lung started forward, but the gateman stopped him, crying in disgust, "You cannot appear before a great lady with a basket on your arm — a basket of pork and beancurd! How will you bow?"

"True — true — " said Wang Lung in agitation. But he did not dare to put the basket down because he was afraid something might be stolen from it. It did not occur to him that all the world might not desire such delicacies as two pounds of pork and six ounces of beef and a small pond fish. The gateman saw his fear and cried out in great contempt, "In a house like this we feed these meats to the dogs!" and seizing the basket he thrust it behind the door and pushed Wang Lung ahead of him.

Down a long narrow veranda they went, the roofs supported by delicate carven posts, and into a hall the like of which Wang Lung had never seen. A score of houses such as his whole house could have been put into it and have disappeared, so wide were the spaces, so high the roofs. Lifting his head in wonder to see the great carven and painted beams above him he stumbled upon the high threshold of the door and would have fallen except that the gateman caught his arm and cried out, "Now will you be so polite as to fall on your face like this before the Old Mistress?"

And collecting himself in great shame Wang Lung looked ahead of him, and upon a dais[1] in the center of the room he saw a very old lady, her small fine body clothed in lustrous, pearly grey satin, and upon the low bench beside her a pipe of opium stood, burning over its little lamp. She looked at him out of small, sharp, black eyes, as sunken and sharp as a monkey's eyes in her thin and wrinkled face. The skin of her hand that held the pipe's end was stretched over her little bones as smooth and as yellow as the gilt upon an idol. Wang Lung fell to his knees and knocked his head on the tiled floor.

"Raise him," said the old lady gravely to the gateman, "these obeisances are

---

[1] A stage, especially at one end of a room, on which people stand to make speeches to an audience.

not necessary. Has he come for the woman?"

"Yes, Ancient One," replied the gateman.

"Why does he not speak for himself?" asked the old lady.

"Because he is a fool, Ancient One," said the gateman, twirling the hairs of his mole.

This roused Wang Lung and he looked with indignation at the gateman.

"I am only a coarse person, Great and Ancient Lady," he said. "I do not know what words to use in such a presence."

The old lady looked at him carefully and with perfect gravity and made as though she would have spoken, except that her hand closed upon the pipe which a slave had been tending for her and at once she seemed to forget him. She bent and sucked greedily at the pipe for a moment and the sharpness passed from her eyes and a film of forgetfulness came over them. Wang Lung remained standing before her until in passing her eyes caught his figure.

"What is this man doing here?" she asked with sudden anger. It was as though she had forgotten everything. The gateman's face was immovable. He said nothing.

"I am waiting for the woman, Great Lady," said Wang Lung in much astonishment.

"The woman? What woman?..." the old lady began, but the slave girl at her side stooped and whispered and the lady recovered herself. "Ah, yes, I forgot for the moment — a small affair — you have come for the slave called O-lan. I remember we promised her to some farmer in marriage. You are that farmer?"

"I am he," replied Wang Lung.

"Call O-lan quickly," said the old lady to her slave. It was as though she was suddenly impatient to be done with all this and to be left alone in the stillness of the great room with her opium pipe.

And in an instant the slave appeared leading by the hand a square, rather tall figure, clothed in clean blue cotton coat and trousers. Wang Lung glanced once and then away, his heart beating. This was his woman.

"Come here, slave," said the old lady carelessly. "This man has come for you."

The woman went before the lady and stood with bowed head and hands clasped.

"Are you ready?" asked the lady.

The woman answered slowly as an echo, "Ready."

Wang Lung, hearing her voice for the first time, looked at her back as she stood before him. It was a good enough voice, not loud, not soft, plain, and not ill-tempered. The woman's hair was neat and smooth and her coat clean. He saw with an instant's disappointment that her feet were not bound. But this he could not dwell upon, for the old lady was saying to the gateman,

"Carry her box out to the gate and let them begone[1]." And then she called Wang Lung and said, "Stand beside her while I speak." And when Wang had come forward she said to him, "This woman came into our house when she was a child of ten and here she has lived until now, when she is twenty years old. I bought her in a year of famine when her parents came south because they had nothing to eat. They were from the north in Shantung and there they returned, and I know nothing further of them. You see she has the strong body and the square cheeks of her kind. She will work well for you in the field and drawing water and all else that you wish. She is not beautiful but that you do not need. Only men of leisure have the need for beautiful women to divert them. Neither is she clever. But she does well what she is told to do and she has a good temper. So far as I know she is virgin. She has not beauty enough to tempt my sons and grandsons even if she had not been in the kitchen. If there has been anything it has been only a serving man. But with the innumerable and pretty slaves running freely about the courts, I doubt if there has been anyone. Take her and use her well. She is a good slave, although somewhat slow and stupid, and had I not wished to acquire merit at the temple for my future existence by bringing more life into the world I should have kept her, for she is good enough for the kitchen. But I marry my slaves off if any will have them and the lords do not want them."

---

[1] A way of telling somebody to go away immediately.

And to the woman she said, "Obey him and bear him sons and yet more sons. Bring the first child to me to see."

"Yes, Ancient Mistress," said the woman submissively.

They stood hesitating, and Wang Lung was greatly embarrassed, not knowing whether he should speak or what.

"Well, go, will you!" said the old lady in irritation, and Wang Lung, bowing hastily, turned and went out, the woman after him, and after her the gateman, carrying on his shoulder the box. This box he dropped down in the room where Wang Lung returned to find his basket and would carry it no further, and indeed he disappeared without another word.

Then Wang Lung turned to the woman and looked at her for the first time. She had a square, honest face, a short, broad nose with large black nostrils, and her mouth was wide as a gash in her face. Her eyes were small and of a dull black in color, and were filled with some sadness that was not clearly expressed. It was a face that seemed habitually silent and unspeaking, as though it could not speak if it would. She bore patiently Wang Lung's look, without embarrassment or response, simply waiting until he had seen her. He saw that it was true there was not beauty of any kind in her face — a brown, common, patient face. But there were no pockmarks on her dark skin, nor was her lip split. In her ears he saw his rings hanging, the gold-washed rings he had bought, and on her hands were the rings he had given her. He turned away with secret exultation. Well, he had his woman!

"Here is this box and this basket," he said gruffly.

Without a word she bent over and picking up one end of the box she placed it upon her shoulder and, staggering under its weight, tried to rise. He watched her at this and suddenly he said, "I will take the box. Here is the basket."

And he shifted the box to his own back, regardless of the best robe he wore, and she, still speechless, took the handle of the basket. He thought of the hundred courts he had come through and of his figure, absurd under its burden.

"If there were a side gate —" he muttered, and she nodded after a little thought, as though she did not understand too quickly what he said. Then she led the way through a small unused court that was grown up with weed, its pool choked, and there under a bent pine tree was an old round gate that she pulled loose from its bar, and they went through and into the street.

Once or twice he looked back at her. She plodded along steadily on her big feet as though she had walked there all her life, her wide face expressionless. In the gate of the wall he stopped uncertainly and fumbled in his girdle with one hand for the pennies he had left, holding the box steady on his shoulder with the other hand. He took out two pence and with these he bought six small green peaches.

"Take these and eat them for yourself," he said gruffly.

She clutched them greedily as a child might and held them in her hand without speech. When next he looked at her as they walked along the margin of the wheat fields she was nibbling[1] one cautiously, but when she saw him looking at her she covered it again with her hand and kept her jaws motionless.

And thus they went until they reached the western field where stood the temple to the earth. This temple was a small structure, not higher in all than a man's shoulder and made of grey bricks and roofed with tile. Wang Lung's grandfather, who had farmed the very fields upon which Wang Lung now spent his life, had built it, hauling the bricks from the town upon his wheelbarrow. The walls were covered with plaster on the outside and a village artist had been hired in a good year once to paint upon the white plaster a scene of hills and bamboo. But the rain of generations had poured upon this painting until now there was only a faint feathery shadow of bamboos left, and the hills were almost wholly gone.

Within the temple snugly under the roof sat two small, solemn figures, earthen, for they were formed from the earth of the fields about the temple. These were the god himself and his lady. They wore robes of red and gilt paper, and the god had a scant, drooping moustache of real hair. Each year at the New Year Wang Lung's father bought sheets of red paper and carefully cut and pasted new robes for the pair. And each year rain and snow beat in and the sun of summer shone in and spoiled

---

[1] To take small bites of something, especially food.

their robes.

At this moment, however, the robes were still new, since the year was but well begun, and Wang Lung was proud of their spruce appearance. He took the basket from the woman's arm and carefully he looked about under the pork for the sticks of incense he had bought. He was anxious lest they were broken and thus make an evil omen, but they were whole, and when he had found them he stuck them side by side in the ashes of other sticks of incense that were heaped before the gods, for the whole neighborhood worshipped these two small figures. Then fumbling for his flint and iron he caught, with a dried leaf for tinder, a flame to light the incense.

Together this man and this woman stood before the gods of their fields. The woman watched the ends of the incense redden and turn grey. When the ash grew heavy she leaned over and with her forefinger she pushed the head of ash away. Then as though fearful for what she had done, she looked quickly at Wang Lung, her eyes dumb. But there was something he liked in her movement. It was as though she felt that the incense belonged to them both; it was a moment of marriage. They stood there in complete silence, side by side, while the incense smouldered into ashes; and then because the sun was sinking, Wang Lung shouldered the box and they went home.

At the door of the house the old man stood to catch the last rays of the sun upon him. He made no movement as Wang Lung approached with the woman. It would have been beneath him to notice her. Instead he feigned great interest in the clouds and he cried, "That cloud which hangs upon the left horn of the new moon speaks of rain. It will come not later than tomorrow night." And then as he saw Wang Lung take the basket from the woman he cried again, "And have you spent money?"

Wang Lung set the basket on the table. "There will be guests tonight," he said briefly, and he carried the box into the room where he slept and set it down beside the box where his own clothes were. He looked at it strangely. But the old man came to the door and said volubly, "There is no end to the money spent in this house!"

Secretly he was pleased that his son had invited guests, but he felt it would not do to give out anything but complaints before his new daughter-in-law lest she be set from the first in ways of extravagance. Wang Lung said nothing, but he went out and took the basket into the kitchen and the woman followed him there. He took the food piece by piece from the basket and laid it upon the ledge of the cold stove and he said to her, "Here is pork and here beef and fish. There are seven to eat. Can you prepare food?"

He did not look at the woman as he spoke. It would not have been seemly. The woman answered in her plain voice, "I have been kitchen slave since I went into the House of Hwang. There were meats at every meal."

Wang Lung nodded and left her and did not see her again until the guests came crowding in, his uncle jovial and sly and hungry, his uncle's son an impudent lad of fifteen, and the farmers clumsy and grinning with shyness. Two were men from the village with whom Wang Lung exchanged seed and labor at harvest time, and one was his next door neighbor, Ching, a small, quiet man, ever unwilling to speak unless he were compelled to it. After they had been seated about the middle room with demurring and unwillingness to take seats, for politeness, Wang Lung went into the kitchen to bid the woman serve. Then he was pleased when she said to him, "I will hand you the bowls if you will place them upon the table. I do not like to come out before men."

Wang Lung felt in him a great pride that this woman was his and did not fear to appear before him, but would not before other men. He took the bowls from her hands at the kitchen door and he set them upon the table in the middle room and called loudly, "Eat, my uncle and my brothers." And when the uncle, who was fond of jokes, said, "Are we not to see the moth-browed bride?" Wang Lung replied firmly, "We are not yet one. It is not meet that other men see her until the marriage is consummated."

And he urged them to eat and they ate heartily of the good fare, heartily and in silence, and this one praised the brown sauce on the fish and that one the well-done pork, and Wang Lung said over and over in reply,

"It is poor stuff — it is badly prepared."

But in his heart he was proud of the dishes, for with what meats she had the woman had combined sugar and vinegar and a little wine and soy sauce and she had skillfully brought forth all the force of the meat itself, so that Wang Lung himself had never tasted such dishes upon the tables of his friends.

That night after the guests had tarried long over their tea and had done with their jokes, the woman still lingered behind the stove, and when Wang Lung had seen the last guest away he went in and she cowered there in the straw piles asleep beside the ox. There was straw in her hair when he roused her, and when he called her she put up her arm suddenly in her sleep as though to defend herself from a blow. When she opened her eyes at last, she looked at him with her strange speechless gaze, and he felt as though he faced a child. He took her by the hand and led her into the room where that morning he had bathed himself for her, and he lit a red candle upon the table. In this light he was suddenly shy when he found himself alone with the woman and he was compelled to remind himself, "There is this woman of mine. The thing is to be done."

And he began to undress himself doggedly. As for the woman, she crept around the corner of the curtain and began without a sound to prepare for the bed. Wang Lung said gruffly, "When you lie down, put the light out first."

Then he lay down and drew the thick quilt about his shoulders and pretended to sleep. But he was not sleeping. He lay quivering, every nerve of his flesh awake. And when, after a long time, the room went dark, and there was the slow, silent, creeping movement of the woman beside him, an exultation filled him fit to break his body. He gave a hoarse laugh into the darkness and seized her.

(The text is selected from *The Good Earth* (2004))

Questions for discussion:

1. The novel begins with Wang Lung's expectation of rain, the daily boiling of water for his father, and his bathing for his wedding. What might this water imagery foreshadow?
2. Did you notice the different way they used to address the old lady in the House of Hwang?
3. Is Wang Lung satisfied with his bride? How do you know it? What's the woman's reaction?

Margaret Mitchell (1900 — 1949)

Margaret Munnerlyn Mitchell was born on November 8, 1900, in Atlanta. Her great-great-great-grandfather Thomas Mitchell fought in the American Revolution (1775 — 1783), and his son William Mitchell took part in the War of 1812. Her great-grandfather Isaac Green Mitchell was a circuit-riding Methodist minister who settled in Marthasville, which later was named Atlanta. Mitchell was thus a fourth-generation Atlantan. Her grandfather Russell Mitchell fought in the Civil War and suffered two bullet wounds to the head during the fighting at Antietam. Twice married, he had twelve children, the oldest of whom was Mitchell's father, Eugene.

Mitchell's mother's family was Irish Catholic. Her great-grandfather Phillip Fitzgerald came to America from Ireland and eventually settled on a plantation near Jonesboro in Fayette County. (This portion of the county now lies in Clayton County.) The Fitzgeralds had seven daughters. Annie Fitzgerald, Mitchell's grandmother, married John Stephens, who had emigrated from Ireland and settled in

Atlanta. Stephens amassed large real-estate properties and helped found a trolley-car system in the city. The Stephenses had twelve children; Mary Isobel (May Belle), Mitchell's mother, was the seventh. May Belle married Eugene Muse Mitchell on November 8, 1892. Eugene was a noted Atlanta attorney, and May Belle was a staunch supporter of woman suffrage. They had a son, Stephens, followed four years later by a daughter, Margaret Munnerlyn.

Mitchell began making up stories before she could write, dictating them to her mother. Later she made her own books with cardboard covers and filled them with adventure stories using her friends, relatives, and herself as characters. As she grew older she switched to copybooks, which her mother stored in inexpensive enamel bread boxes. A few of the hundreds of tales that she wrote have survived, including two Civil War tales. When the family moved to Peachtree Street, the young Mitchell attended the Tenth Street School and later Woodberry School, a private school. She branched out to writing, directing, and starring in plays, coercing the neighborhood children to take part.

From 1914 to 1918 Mitchell attended the Washington Seminary, a prestigious Atlanta finishing school, where she was a founding member and officer of the drama club. She was also the literary editor of *Facts and Fancies*, the high school yearbook, in which two of her stories were featured. She was president of the Washington Literary Society.

When America entered World War I (1917 — 1918), the seminary girls were in demand at dances for the young servicemen stationed at Camp Gordon and Fort McPherson. At one such dance in the summer of 1918 Mitchell met twenty-two-year-old Clifford Henry, a wealthy and socially prominent New Yorker who was a bayonet instructor at Camp Gordon. The two fell in love and became engaged shortly before he was shipped overseas. He was killed in October 1918 while fighting in France.

In September 1918 Mitchell entered Smith College in Northampton, Massachusetts, where she began using the nickname "Peggy." Her freshman year at college was disrupted when an influenza epidemic forced the cancellation of classes. In January her mother contracted influenza and died the day before her daughter reached home. Mitchell completed her freshman year at Smith, then returned to Atlanta to take her place as mistress of the household and to enter the upcoming debutante season. During the last charity ball of the season, Mitchell created a scandal by performing a sensuous dance popular in the nightclubs of Paris, France.

Soon Mitchell met Berrien Kinnard Upshaw, who was from a prominent Raleigh, North Carolina, family. They were wed in 1922, but the marriage was brief. After four months Upshaw left Atlanta for the Midwest and never returned. The marriage was annulled two years later.

In the same year that she married, Mitchell landed a job with the *Atlanta Journal Sunday Magazine*. She used "Peggy Mitchell" as her byline. Her interviews, profiles, and sketches of life in Georgia were well received. During her four years with the *Sunday Magazine*, Mitchell wrote 129 articles, worked as a proofreader, substituted for the advice columnist, reviewed books, and occasionally did hard news stories for the paper. Complications from a broken ankle led her to end her career as a journalist.

Mitchell's second marriage was to John Robert Marsh on July 4, 1925, and the couple set up housekeeping in a small apartment affectionately called "the Dump." They entertained the newspaper crowd and other friends on a regular basis. Marsh, originally from Maysville, Kentucky, worked for the Georgia Railway and Power Company (later Georgia Power Company) as director of the publicity department.

In 1926, to relieve the boredom of being cooped up with a broken ankle, Mitchell began to write *Gone With the Wind*. Setting up her Remington typewriter on an old sewing table, she completed the majority of the book in three years. She wrote the last chapter first and the other chapters in no particular order. Stuffing the chapters into manila envelopes, she eventually accumulated almost seventy chapters. When visitors appeared, she covered her work with a towel, keeping her novel a secret. There has been much speculation on whether the characters were based on real people, but Mitchell claimed they were her own creations.

In April 1935 Harold Latham, an editor for the Macmillan publishing company in New York City, toured the South looking for new manuscripts. Latham heard that

Mitchell had been working on a manuscript and asked her if he could see it, but she denied having one. When a friend commented that Mitchell was not serious enough to write a novel, Mitchell gathered up many of the envelopes and took them to Latham at his hotel. He had to purchase a suitcase to carry them. He read part of the manuscript on the train to New Orleans, Louisiana, and sent it straight to New York. By July Macmillan had offered her a contract. She received a $500 advance and 10 percent of the royalties.

As she revised the manuscript, Mitchell cut and rearranged chapters, confirmed details, wrote the first chapter, changed the name of the main character (originally called Pansy), and struggled to think of a title that suited her. Titles considered included *Tomorrow Is Another Day*, *Another Day*, *Tote the Weary Load*, *Milestones*, *Ba! Ba! Blacksheep*, *Not in Our Stars*, and *Bugles Sang True*. Finally she settled on a phrase from a favorite poem by Ernest Dowson: "I have forgot much, Cynara! Gone with the wind, / Flung roses, roses riotously with the throng." Published in 1936, *Gone With the Wind* was 1,037 pages long and sold for three dollars.

Gone With the Wind was a phenomenal success and received rave reviews. Overnight, Mitchell became a celebrity and remained very much in the public spotlight through the production and premiere of the film based on her novel in 1939. She was in constant demand for speaking engagements and interviews. At first she complied, but later, pleading poor health, she usually declined these requests and stopped autographing copies of her book. She said she wanted to remain simply Mrs. John Marsh.

Gone With the Wind was Mitchell's only published novel. At her request, the original manuscript (except for a few pages retained to validate her authorship) and all other writings were destroyed. These included a novella in the Gothic style, a ghost story set in an old plantation home left vacant after the Civil War. According to the recollections of Lois Cole, a friend of Mitchell's and a Macmillan employee, three people had read this tale (written before *Gone With the Wind*) and thought it was worth publishing by one of the bigger publishing houses. Cole suggested that Mitchell enter it in the Little, Brown novelette contest.

Possibly one of the reasons that Mitchell never wrote another novel was that she spent so much time working with her brother and her husband to protect the copyright of her book abroad. Up until the publication of *Gone With the Wind*, international copyright laws were ambiguous and varied from country to country. Correspondence also took much of her time. During the years following publication, she personally answered every letter she received about her book. With the outbreak of World War II (1941 — 1945), she worked tirelessly for the American Red Cross, even outfitting a hospital ship. She also set up scholarships for black medical students.

On August 11, 1949, Mitchell and her husband decided to go to a movie, *A Canterbury Tale*, at the Peachtree Art Theatre. Just as they started to cross Peachtree Street, near 13th Street, a speeding taxi crested the hill. Mitchell stepped back; Marsh stepped forward. The driver applied the brakes, skidded, and hit Mitchell. She was rushed to Grady Hospital but never regained consciousness. During the five days before she died, crowds waited outside for news. U. S. president Harry Truman, Georgia governor Herman Talmadge, and Atlanta mayor William B. Hartsfield all asked to be kept informed of her condition. Special phone lines were installed at Grady Hospital, and friends manned the lines in four-hour shifts. Mitchell died on August 16, 1949, and was buried in Oakland Cemetery in Atlanta.

Mitchell was inducted into Georgia Women of Achievement in 1994 and into the Georgia Writers Hall of Fame in 2000.

(The text is selected from *The New Georgia Encyclopedia*, 09/27/2004)

Major Works:

Gone with the Wind, 1936 《飘》

Gone with the Wind

CHAPTER XXIII

After Prissy had gone, Scarlett went wearily into the downstairs hall and lit a lamp. The house felt steamingly hot, as though it held in its walls all the heat of the noontide. Some of her dullness was passing now and her stomach was clamoring for food. She remembered she had had nothing to eat since the night before except a spoonful of hominy, and picking up the lamp she went into the kitchen. The fire in the oven had died but the room was stifling hot. She found half a pone of hard corn bread in the skillet and gnawed hungrily on it while she looked about for other food. There was some hominy left in the pot and she ate it with a big cooking spoon, not waiting to put it on a plate. It needed salt badly but she was too hungry to hunt for it. After four spoonfuls of it, the heat of the room was too much and, taking the lamp in one hand and a fragment of pone in the other, she went out into the hall.

She knew she should go upstairs and sit beside Melanie. If anything went wrong, Melanie would be too weak to call. But the idea of returning to that room where she had spent so many nightmare hours was repulsive to her. Even if Melanie were dying, she couldn't go back up there. She never wanted to see that room again. She set the lamp on the candle stand by the window and returned to the front porch. It was so much cooler here, and even the night was drowned in soft warmth. She sat down on the steps in the circle of faint light thrown by the lamp and continued gnawing on the corn bread.

When she had finished it, a measure of strength came back to her and with the strength came again the pricking of fear. She could hear a humming of noise far down the street, but what it portended she did not know. She could distinguish nothing but a volume of sound that rose and fell. She strained forward trying to hear and soon she found her muscles aching from the tension. More than anything in the world she yearned to hear the sound of hooves and to see Rhett's careless, self-confident eyes laughing at her fears. Rhett would take them away, somewhere. She didn't know where. She didn't care.

As she sat straining her ears toward town, a faint glow appeared above the trees. It puzzled her. She watched it and saw it grow brighter. The dark sky became pink and then dull red, and suddenly above the trees, she saw a huge tongue of flame leap high to the heavens. She jumped to her feet, her heart beginning again its sickening thudding and bumping.

The Yankees[1] had come! She knew they had come and they were burning the town. The flames seemed to be off to the east of the center of town. They shot higher and higher and widened rapidly into a broad expanse of red before her terrified eyes. A whole block must be burning. A faint hot breeze that had sprung up bore the smell of smoke to her.

She fled up the stairs to her own room and hung out the window for a better view. The sky was a hideous lurid color and great swirls of black smoke went twisting up to hand in billowy clouds above the flames. The smell of smoke was stronger now. Her mind rushed incoherently here and there, thinking how soon the flames would spread up Peachtree Street and burn this house, how soon the Yankees would be rushing in upon her, where she would run, what she would do. All the fiends of hell seemed screaming in her ears and her brain swirled with confusion and panic so overpowering she clung to the window sill for support.

"I must think," she told herself over and over. "I must think."

But thoughts eluded her, darting in and out of her mind like frightened humming birds. As she stood hanging to the sill, a deafening explosion burst on her ears, louder than any cannon she had ever heard. The sky was rent with gigantic flame. Then other explosions. The earth shook and the glass in the panes above her head shivered and came down around her.

The world became an inferno of noise and flame and trembling earth as one explosion followed another in ear-splitting succession. Torrents of sparks shot to the sky and descended slowly, lazily, through blood-colored clouds of smoke. She thought she heard a feeble call from the next room but she paid it no heed. She had no time for Melanie now. No time for anything except a fear that licked through her veins as swiftly as the flames she saw. She was a child and mad with fright and she wanted to bury her head in her mother's lap and shut out this sight. If she were only home! Home with Mother.

Through the nerve-shivering sounds, she heard another sound, that of fear-sped

---

[1] Yankees refer to people who come from or live in any of the northern states of the US, especially New England. Here it refers to soldiers who fought for the Union (= the northern states) in the American Civil War.

feet coming up the stairs three at a time, heard a voice yelping like a lost hound. Prissy broke into the room and, flying to Scarlett, clutched her arm in a grip that seemed to pinch out pieces of flesh.

"The Yankees —" cried Scarlett.

"No'm, its our gempmums!" yelled Prissy between breaths, digging her nails deeper into Scarlett's arm. "Dey's buhnin' de foun'ry an' de ahmy supply depots an' de wa'houses an', fo' Gawd, Miss Scarlett, dey done set off dem seventy freight cahs of cannon balls an' gunpowder an', Jesus, we's all gwine ter buhn up!"

She began yelping again shrilly and pinched Scarlett so hard she cried out in pain and fury and shook off her hand.

The Yankees hadn't come yet! There was still time to get away! She rallied her frightened forces together.

"If I don't get a hold on myself," she thought, "I'll be squalling like a scalded cat!" and the sight of Prissy's abject terror helped steady her. She took her by the shoulders and shook her.

"Shut up that racket and talk sense. The Yankees haven't come, you fool! Did you see Captain Butler? What did he say? Is he coming?"

Prissy ceased her yelling but her teeth chattered.

"Yas'm, Ah finely foun' him. In a bahroom, lak you told me. He —"

"Never mind where you found him. Is he coming? Did you tell him to bring his horse?"

"Lawd, Miss Scarlett, he say our gempmums done tuck his hawse an' cah' ige fer a amberlance."

"Dear God in Heaven!"

"But he comin' —"

"What did he say?"

Prissy had recovered her breath and a small measure of control but her eyes still rolled.

"Well'm, lak you tole me, Ah foun' him in a bahroom. Ah stood outside an' yell fer him an' he come out. An' ter-reckly he see me an' Ah starts tell him, de sojers tech off a sto' house down Decatur Street an' it flame up an' he say Come on an' he grab me an' we runs ter Fibe Points an' he say den: What now? Talk fas'. An' Ah say you say, Cap' n Butler, come quick an' bring yo' hawse an' cah' ige. Miss Melly done had a chile an' you is bustin' ter get outer town. An' he say: Where all she studyin' 'bout goin'? An' Ah say: Ah doan know, suh, but you is boun' ter go fo' de Yankees gits hyah an' wants him ter go wid you. An' he laugh an' say dey done tuck his hawse."

Scarlett' s heart went leaden as the last hope left her. Fool that she was, why hadn' t she thought that the re-treating army would naturally take every vehicle and animal left in the city? For a moment she was too stunned to hear what Prissy was saying but she pulled herself together to hear the rest of the story.

"An' den he say, Tell Miss Scarlett ter res' easy. Ah'll steal her a hawse outer de ahmy crall effen dey's ary one lef. An' he say, Ah done stole hawses befo' dis night. Tell her Ah git her a hawse effen Ah gits shot fer it. Den' he laugh agin an' say, Cut an' run home. An' befo' Ah gits started Ker-bloom! Off goes a noise an' Ah lak ter drap in mah tracks an' he tell me twarnt nuthin' but de ammernition our gempmums blowin' up so's de Yankees don't git it an' — "

"He is coming? He's going to bring a horse?"

"So he say."

She drew a long breath of relief. If there was any way of getting a horse, Rhett Butler would get one. A smart man, Rhett. She would forgive him anything if he got them out of this mess. Escape! And with Rhett she would have no fear. Rhett would protect them. Thank God for Rhett! With safety in view she turned practical.

"Wake Wade up and dress him and pack some clothes for all of us. Put them in the small trunk. And don't tell Miss Mellie we're going. Not yet. But wrap the baby in a couple of thick towels and be sure and pack his clothes."

Prissy still dang to her skirts and hardly anything showed in her eyes except the whites. Scarlett gave her a shove and loosened her grip.

"Hurry," she cried, and Prissy went off like a rabbit.

Scarlett knew she should go in and quiet Melanie's fear, knew Melanie must be frightened out of her senses by the thunderous noises that continued unabated and the glare that lighted the sky. It looked and sounded like the end of the world.

But she could not bring herself to go back into that room just yet. She ran down the stairs with some idea of packing up Miss Pittypat's china and the little silver she had left when she refugeed to Macon. But when she reached the dining room, her hands were shaking so badly she dropped three plates and shattered them. She ran out onto the porch to listen and back again to the dining room and dropped the silver clattering to the floor. Everything she touched she dropped. In her hurry she slipped on the rag rug and fell to the floor with a jolt but leaped up so quickly she was not even aware of the pain. Upstairs she could hear Prissy galloping about like a wild animal and the sound maddened her, for she was galloping just as aimlessly.

For the dozenth time, she ran out onto the porch but this time she did not go back to her futile packing. She sat down. It was just impossible to pack anything. Impossible to do anything but sit with hammering heart and wait for Rhett. It seemed hours before he came. At last, far up the road, she heard the protesting screech of unoiled axles and the slow uncertain plodding of hooves. Why didn't he hurry? Why didn't he make the horse trot?

The sounds came nearer and she leaped to her feet and called Rhett's name. Then, she saw him dimly as he climbed down from the seat of a small wagon, heard the clicking of the gate as he came toward her. He came into view and the light of the lamp showed him plainly. His dress was as debonair as if he were going to a ball, well-tailored white linen coat and trousers, embroidered gray watered-silk waistcoat and a hint of ruffle on his shirt bosom. His wide Panama hat was set dashingly on one side of his head and in the belt of his trousers were thrust two ivory-handled, long-barreled dueling pistols. The pockets of his coat sagged heavily with ammunition.

He came up the walk with the springy stride of a savage and his fine head was carried like a pagan prince. The dangers of the night which had driven Scarlett into panic had affected him like an intoxicant. There was a carefully restrained ferocity in his dark face, a ruthlessness which would have frightened her had she the wits to see it.

His black eyes danced as though amused by the whole affair, as though the earth-splitting sounds and the horrid glare were merely things to frighten children. She swayed toward him as he came up the steps, her face white, her green eyes burning.

"Good evening," he said, in his drawling voice, as he removed his hat with a sweeping gesture. "Fine weather we're having. I hear you're going to take a trip."

"If you make any jokes, I shall never speak to you again," she said with quivering voice.

"Don't tell me you are frightened!" He pretended to be surprised and smiled in a way that made her long to push him backwards down the steep steps.

"Yes, I am! I'm frightened to death and if you had the sense God gave a goat, you'd be frightened too. But we haven't got time to talk. We must get out of here."

"At your service, Madam. But just where were you figuring on going? I made the trip out here for curiosity, just to see where you were intending to go. You can't go north or east or south or west. The Yankees are all around. There's just one road out of town which the Yankees haven't got yet and the army is retreating by that road. And that road won't be open long. General Steve Lee's cavalry is fighting a rear-guard action at Rough and Ready to hold it open long enough for the army to get away. If you follow the army down the McDonough road, they'll take the horse away from you and, while it's not much of a horse, I did go to a lot of trouble stealing it. Just where are you going?"

She stood shaking, listening to his words, hardly hearing them. But at his question she suddenly knew where she was going, knew that all this miserable day she had known where she was going. The only place.

"I'm going home," she said.

"Home? You mean to Tara?"

"Yes, yes! To Tara! Oh, Rhett, we must hurry!"

He looked at her as if she had lost her mind.

"Tara? God Almighty, Scarlett! Don't you know they fought all day at Jonesboro?

Fought for ten miles up and down the road from Rough and Ready even into the streets of Jonesboro? The Yankees may be all over Tara by now, all over the County. Nobody knows where they are but they're in that neighborhood. You can't go home! You can't go right through the Yankee army!"

"I will go home!" she cried. "I will! I will!"

"You little fool," and his voice was swift and rough. "You can't go that way. Even if you didn't run into the Yankees, the woods are full of stragglers and deserters from both armies. And lots of our troops are still retreating from Jonesboro. They'd take the horse away from you as quickly as the Yankees would. Your only chance is to follow the troops down the McDonough road and pray that they won't see you in the dark. "You can't go to Tara. Even if you got there, you'd probably find it burned down. I won't let you go home. It's insanity."

"I will go home!" she cried and her voice broke and rose to a scream. "I will go home! You can't stop me! I will go home! I want my mother! I'll kill you if you try to stop me! I will go home!"

Tears of fright and hysteria streamed down her face as she finally gave way under the long strain. She beat on his chest with her fists and screamed again: "I will! I will! If I have to walk every step of the way!"

Suddenly she was in his arms, her wet cheek against the starched ruffle of his shirt, her beating hands stilled against him. His hands caressed her tumbled hair gently, soothingly, and his voice was gentle too. So gentle, so quiet, so devoid of mockery, it did not seem Rhett Butler's voice at all but the voice of some kind strong stranger who smelled of brandy and tobacco and horses, comforting smells because they reminded her of Gerald.

"There, there, darling," he said softly. "Don't cry. You shall go home, my brave little girl. You shall go home. Don't cry."

She felt something brush her hair and wondered vaguely through her tumult if it were his lips. He was so tender, so infinitely soothing, she longed to stay in his arms forever. With such strong arms about her, surely nothing could harm her.

He fumbled in his pocket and produced a handkerchief and wiped her eyes.

"Now, blow your nose like a good child," he ordered, a glint of a smile in his eyes, "and tell me what to do. We must work fast."

She blew her nose obediently, still trembling, but she could not think what to tell him to do. Seeing how her lip quivered and her eyes looked up at him helplessly, he took command.

"Mrs. Wilkes has had her child? It will be dangerous to move her — dangerous to drive her twenty-five miles in that rickety wagon. We'd better leave her with Mrs. Meade."

"The Meades aren't home. I can't leave her."

"Very well. Into the wagon she goes. Where is that simple-minded little wench?"

"Upstairs packing the trunk."

"Trunk? You can't take any trunk in that wagon. It's almost too small to hold all of you and the wheels are ready to come off with no encouragement. Call her and tell her to get the smallest feather bed in the house and put it in the wagon."

Still Scarlett could not move. He took her arm in a strong grasp and some of the vitality which animated him seemed to flow into her body. If only she could be as cool and casual as he was! He propelled her into the hall but she still stood helplessly looking at him. His lip went down mockingly: "Can this be the heroic young woman who assured me she feared neither God nor man?"

He suddenly burst into laughter and dropped her arm. Stung, she glared at him, hating him.

"I'm not afraid," she said.

"Yes, you are. In another moment you'll be in a swoon and I have no smelling salts about me."

She stamped her foot impotently because she could not think of anything else to do — and without a word picked up the lamp and started up the stairs. He was close behind her and she could hear him laughing softly to himself. That sound stiffened her spine. She went into Wade's nursery and found him sitting clutched in Prissy's arms, half dressed, hiccoughing quietly. Prissy was whimpering. The feather tick on Wade's bed was small and she ordered Prissy to drag it down the stairs and into the wagon. Prissy put down the child and obeyed. Wade followed her down the stairs, his hiccoughs stilled by his interest in the proceedings.

"Come," said Scarlett, turning to Melanie's door and Rhett followed her, hat in hand.

Melanie lay quietly with the sheet up to her chin. Her face was deathly white but her eyes, sunken and black circled, were serene. She showed no surprise at the sight of Rhett in her bedroom but seemed to take it as a matter of course. She tried to smile weakly but the smile died before it reached the corners of her mouth.

"We are going home, to Tara," Scarlett explained rapidly. "The Yankees are coming. Rhett is going to take us. It's the only way, Melly."

Melanie tried to nod her head feebly and gestured toward the baby. Scarlett picked up the small baby and wrapped him hastily in a thick towel. Rhett stepped to the bed.

"I'll try not to hurt you," he said quietly, tucking the sheet about her. "See if you can put your arms around my neck."

Melanie tried but they fell back weakly. He bent, slipped an arm under her shoulders and another across her knees and lifted her gently. She did not cry out but Scarlett saw her bite her lip and go even whiter. Scarlett held the lamp high for Rhett to see and started toward the door when Melanie made a feeble gesture toward the wall.

"What is it?" Rhett asked softly.

"Please," Melanie whispered, trying to point. "Charles."

Rhett looked down at her as if he thought her delirious but Scarlett understood and was irritated. She knew Melanie wanted the daguerreotype❶ of Charles which hung on the wall below his sword and pistol.

"Please," Melanie whispered again, "the sword."

"Oh, all right," said Scarlett and, after she had lighted Rhett's careful way

---

❶ Daguerreotype is a photograph made by an early process that used a silver plate and mercury gas.

down the steps, she went back and unhooked the sword and pistol belts. It would be awkward, carrying them as well as the baby and the lamp. That was just like Melanie, not to be at all bothered over nearly dying and having the Yankees at her heels but to worry about Charles' things.

As she took down the daguerreotype, she caught a glimpse of Charles' face. His large brown eyes met hers and she stopped for a moment to look at the picture curiously. This man had been her husband, had lain beside her for a few nights, had given her a child with eyes as soft and brown as his. And she could hardly remember him.

The child in her arms waved small fists and mewed softly and she looked down at him. For the first time, she realized that this was Ashley's baby and suddenly wished with all the strength left in her that he were her baby, hers and Ashley's.

Prissy came bounding up the stairs and Scarlett handed the child to her. They went hastily down, the lamp throwing uncertain shadows on the wall. In the hall, Scarlett saw a bonnet and put it on hurriedly, tying the ribbons under her chin. It was Melanie's black mourning bonnet and it did not fit Scarlett's head but she could not recall where she had put her own bonnet.

She went out of the house and down the front steps, carrying the lamp and trying to keep the saber from banging against her legs. Melanie lay full length in the back of the wagon, and, beside her, were Wade and the towel-swathed baby. Prissy climbed in and took the baby in her arms.

The wagon was very small and the boards about the sides very low. The wheels leaned inward as if their first revolution would make them come off. She took one look at the horse and her heart sank. He was a small emaciated animal and he stood with his head dispiritedly low, almost between his forelegs. His back was raw with sores and harness galls and he breathed as no sound horse should.

"Not much of an animal, is it?" grinned Rhett. "Looks like he'll die in the shafts. But he's the best I could do. Some day I'll tell you with embellishments just where and how I stole him and how narrowly I missed getting shot. Nothing but my devotion to you would make me, at this stage of my career, turn horse thief — and thief of such a horse. Let me help you in."

He took the lamp from her and set it on the ground. The front seat was only a narrow plank across the sides of the wagon. Rhett picked Scarlett up bodily and swung her to it. How wonderful to be a man and as strong as Rhett, she thought, tucking her wide skirts about her. With Rhett beside her, she did not fear anything, neither the fire nor the noise nor the Yankees.

He climbed onto the seat beside her and picked up the reins.

"Oh, wait!" she cried. "I forgot to lock the front door."

He burst into a roar of laughter and slapped the reins upon the horse's back.

"What are you laughing at?"

"At you — locking the Yankees out," he said and the horse started off, slowly, reluctantly. The lamp on the sidewalk burned on, making a tiny yellow circle of light which grew smaller and smaller as they moved away.

Rhett turned the horse's slow feet westward from Peachtree and the wobbling wagon jounced into the rutty lane with a violence that wrenched an abruptly stilled moan from Melanie. Dark trees interlaced above their heads, dark silent houses loomed up on either side and the white palings of fences gleamed faintly like a row of tombstones. The narrow street was a dim tunnel, but faintly through the thick leafy ceiling the hideous red glow of the sky penetrated and shadows chased one another down the dark way like mad ghosts. The smell of smoke came stronger and stronger, and on the wings of the hot breeze came a pandemonium of sound from the center of town, yells, the dull rumbling of heavy army wagons and the steady tramp of marching feet. As Rhett jerked the horse's head and turned him into another street, another deafening explosion tore the air and a monstrous skyrocket of flame and smoke shot up in the west.

That must be the last of the ammunition trains," Rhett said calmly. "Why didn't they get them out this morning, the fools! There was plenty of time. Well, too bad for us. I thought by circling around the center of town, we might avoid the fire and that drunken mob on Decatur Street and get through to the southwest part of town without any danger. But we've got to cross Marietta Street somewhere and that explosion was near Marietta Street or I miss my guess."

"Must — must we go through the fire?" Scarlett quavered.

"Not if we hurry," said Rhett and, springing from the wagon, he disappeared into the darkness of a yard. When he returned he had a small limb of a tree in his hand and he laid it mercilessly across the horse's galled back. The animal broke into a shambling trot, his breath panting and labored, and the wagon swayed forward with a jolt that threw them about like popcorn in a popper. The baby wailed, and Prissy and Wade cried out as they bruised themselves against the sides of the wagon. But from Melanie there was no sound.

As they neared Marietta Street, the trees thinned out and the tall flames roaring up above the buildings threw street and houses into a glare of light brighter than day, casting monstrous shadows that twisted as wildly as torn sails flapping in a gale on a sinking ship.

Scarlett's teeth chattered but so great was her terror she was not even aware of it. She was cold and she shivered, even though the heat of the flames was already hot against their faces. This was hell and she was in it and, if she could only have conquered her shaking knees, she would have leaped from the wagon and run screaming back the dark road they had come, back to the refuge of Miss Pittypat's house. She shrank closer to Rhett, took his arm in fingers that trembled and looked up at him for words, for comfort, for something reassuring. In the unholy crimson[1] glow that bathed them, his dark profile stood out as clearly as the head on an ancient coin, beautiful, cruel and decadent. At her touch he turned to her, his eyes gleaming with a light as frightening as the fire. To Scarlett, he seemed as exhilarated and contemptuous as if he got strong pleasure from the situation, as if he welcomed the inferno they were approaching.

"Here," he said, laying a hand on one of the long-barreled pistols in his belt. "If anyone, black or white, comes up on your side of the wagon and tries to lay hand on the horse, shoot him and we'll ask questions later. But for God's sake,

---

[1] Dark red in color.

don't shoot the nag in your excitement."

"I — I have a pistol," she whispered, clutching the weapon in her lap, perfectly certain that if death stared her in the face, she would be too frightened to pull the trigger.

"You have? Where did you get it?"

"It's Charles."

"Charles?"

"Yes, Charles — my husband."

"Did you ever really have a husband, my dear?" he whispered and laughed softly.

If he would only be serious! If he would only hurry!

"How do you suppose I got my boy?" she cried fiercely.

"Oh, there are other ways than husbands —"

"Will you hush and hurry?"

But he drew rein abruptly, almost at Marietta Street, in the shadow of a warehouse not yet touched by the flames.

"Hurry!" It was the only word in her mind. Hurry! Hurry!

"Soldiers," he said.

The detachment came down Marietta Street, between the burning buildings, walking at route step, tiredly, rifles held any way, heads down, too weary to hurry, too weary to care if timbers were crashing to right and left and smoke billowing about them. They were all ragged, so ragged that between officers and men there were no distinguishing insignia except here and there a torn hat brim pinned up with a wreathed "C. S. A." Many were barefooted and here and there a dirty bandage wrapped a head or arm. They went past, looking neither to left nor right, so silent that had it not been for the steady tramp of feet they might all have been ghosts.

"Take a good look at them," came Rhett's gibing voice, "so you can tell your grandchildren you saw the rear guard of the Glorious Cause in retreat."

Suddenly she hated him, hated him with a strength that momentarily overpowered her fear, made it seem petty and small. She knew her safety and that of the others in the back of the wagon depended on him and him alone, but she hated him for his sneering at those ragged ranks. She thought of Charles who was dead and Ashley who might be dead and all the gay and gallant young men who were rotting in shallow graves and she forgot that she, too, had once thought them fools. She could not speak, but hatred and disgust burned in her eyes as she stared at him fiercely.

As the last of the soldiers were passing, a small figure in the rear rank, his rifle butt dragging the ground, wavered, stopped and stared after the others with a dirty face so dulled by fatigue he looked like a sleepwalker. He was as small as Scarlett, so small his rifle was almost as tall as he was, and his grime-smeared face was unbearded. Sixteen at the most, thought Scarlett irrelevantly, must be one of the Home Guard or a runaway schoolboy.

As she watched, the boy's knees buckled slowly and he went down in the dust. Without a word, two men fell out of the last rank and walked back to him. One, a tall spare man with a black beard that hung to his belt, silently handed his own rifle and that of the boy to the other. Then, stooping, he jerked the boy to his shoulders with an ease that looked like sleight of hand. He started off slowly after the retreating column, his shoulders bowed under the weight, while the boy, weak, infuriated like a child teased by its elders, screamed out: Put me down, damn you! Put me down! I can walk!"

The bearded man said nothing and plodded on out of sight around the bend of the road.

Rhett sat still, the reins lax in his hands, looking after them, a curious moody look on his swarthy face. Then, there was a crash of falling timbers near by and Scarlett saw a thin tongue of flame lick up over the roof of the warehouse in whose sheltering shadow they sat. Then pennons and battle flags of flame flared triumphantly to the sky above them. Smoke burnt her nostrils and Wade and Prissy began coughing. The baby made soft sneezing sounds.

"Oh, name of God, Rhett! Are you crazy? Hurry! Hurry!"

Rhett made no reply but brought the tree limb down on the horse's back with a cruel force that made the animal leap forward. With all the speed the horse could summon, they jolted and bounced across Marietta Street. Ahead of them was a tunnel of fire where buildings were blaring on either side of the short, narrow street that led down to the railroad tracks. They plunged into it. A glare brighter than a dozen suns dazzled their eyes, scorching heat seared their skins and the roaring, crackling and crashing beat upon their ears in painful waves. For an eternity, it seemed, they were in the midst of flaming torment and then abruptly they were in semidarkness again.

As they dashed down the street and bumped over the railroad tracks, Rhett applied the whip automatically. His face looked set and absent, as though he had forgotten where he was. His broad shoulders were hunched forward and his chin jutted out as though the thoughts in his mind were not pleasant. The heat of the fire made sweat stream down his forehead and cheeks but he did not wipe it off.

They pulled into a side street, then another, then turned and twisted from one narrow street to another until Scarlett completely lost her bearings and the roaring of the flames died behind them. Still Rhett did not speak. He only laid on the whip with regularity. The red glow in the sky was fading now and the road became so dark, so frightening, Scarlett would have welcomed words, any words from him, even jeering, insulting words, words that cut. But he did not speak.

Silent or not, she thanked Heaven for the comfort of his presence. It was so good to have a man beside her, to lean close to him and feel the hard swell of his arm and know that he stood between her and unnamable terrors, even though he merely sat there and stared.

"Oh, Rhett," she whispered clasping his arm, "What would we ever have done without you? I'm so glad you aren't in the army!"

He turned his head and gave her one look, a look that made her drop his arm and shrink back. There was no mockery in his eyes now. They were naked and there was anger and something like bewilderment in them. His lip curled down and he turned his head away. For a long time they jounced along in a silence unbroken except for the faint wails of the baby and sniffles from Prissy. When she was able to bear the sniffling noise no longer, Scarlett turned and pinched her viciously, causing

Prissy to scream in good earnest before she relapsed into frightened silence.

Finally Rhett turned the horse at right angles and after a while they were on a wider, smoother road. The dim shapes of houses grew farther and farther apart and unbroken woods loomed wall-like on either side.

"We're out of town now," said Rhett briefly, drawing rein, "and on the main road to Rough and Ready."

"Hurry. Don't stop!"

"Let the animal breathe a bit." Then turning to her, he asked slowly: "Scarlett, are you still determined to do this crazy thing?"

"Do what?'

"Do you still want to try to get through to Tara? It's suicidal. Steve Lee's cavalry and the Yankee Army are between you and Tara."

Oh, Dear God! Was he going to refuse to take her home, after all she'd gone through this terrible day?

"Oh, yes! Yes! Please, Rhett, let's hurry. The horse isn't tired."

"Just a minute. You can't go down to Jonesboro[1] on this road. You can't follow the train tracks. They've been fighting up and down mere all day from Rough and Ready on south. Do you know any other roads, small wagon roads or lanes that don't go through Rough and Ready or Jonesboro?"

"Oh, yes," cried Scarlett in relief. "If we can just get near to Rough and Ready, I know a wagon trace that winds off from the main Jonesboro road and wanders around for miles. Pa and I used to ride it. It comes out right near the Macintosh place and that's only a mile from Tara."

"Good. Maybe you can get past Rough and Ready all right. General Steve Lee was there during the afternoon covering the retreat. Maybe the Yankees aren't there yet. Maybe you can get through there, if Steve Lee's men don't pick up your horse."

"I can get through?"

---

[1] A city in Arkansas.

"Yes, you." His voice was rough.

"But Rhett — You — Aren't going to take us?"

"No. I'm leaving you here."

She looked around wildly, at the livid sky behind them, at the dark trees on either hand hemming them in like a prison wall, at the frightened figures in the back of the wagon — and finally at him. Had she gone crazy? Was she not hearing right?

He was grinning now. She could just see his white teeth in the faint light and the old mockery was back in his eyes.

"Leaving us? Where — where are you going?"

"I am going, dear girl, with the army."

She sighed with relief and irritation. Why did he joke at this time of all times? Rhett in the army! After all he'd said about stupid fools who were enticed into losing their lives by a roll of drums and brave words from orators — fools who killed themselves that wise men might make money!

"Oh, I could choke you for scaring me so! Let's get on."

"I'm not joking, my dear. And I am hurt, Scarlett that you do not take my gallant sacrifice with better spirit. Where is your patriotism, your love for Our Glorious Cause? Now is your chance to tell me to return with my shield or on it. But, talk fast, for I want time to make a brave speech before departing for the wars."

His drawling voice gibed[1] in her ears. He was jeering at her and, somehow, she knew he was jeering at himself too. What was he talking about? Patriotism, shields, brave speeches? It wasn't possible that he meant what he was saying. It just wasn't believable that he could talk so blithely of leaving her here on this dark road with a woman who might be dying, a new-born infant, a foolish black wench and a frightened child, leaving her to pilot them through miles of battle fields and stragglers and Yankees and fire and God knows what.

Once, when she was six years old, she had fallen from a tree, flat on her stomach. She could still recall that sickening interval before breath came back into

---

[1] Gibe = jibe. To say something that is intended to embarrass somebody or make them look silly.

her body. Now, as she looked at Rhett, she felt the same way she had felt then, breathless, stunned, nauseated.

"Rhett, you are joking!"

She grabbed his arm and felt her tears of fright splash down her wrist. He raised her hand and kissed it angrily.

"Selfish to the end, aren't you, my dear? Thinking only of your own precious hide and not of the gallant Confederacy. Think how our troops will be heartened by my eleventh-hour appearance." There was a malicious tenderness in his voice.

"Oh, Rhett," she wailed, "how can you do this to me? Why are you leaving me?"

"Why?" he laughed jauntily. "Because, perhaps, of the betraying sentimentality that lurks in all of us Southerners. Perhaps — perhaps because I am ashamed. Who knows?"

"Ashamed? You should die of shame. To desert us here, alone, helpless —"

"Dear Scarlett! You aren't helpless. Anyone as selfish and determined as you are is never helpless. God help the Yankees if they should get you."

He stepped abruptly down from the wagon and, as she watched him, stunned with bewilderment, he came around to her side of the wagon.

"Get out," he ordered.

She stared at him. He reached up roughly, caught her under the arms and swung her to the ground beside him. With a tight grip on her he dragged her several paces away from the wagon. She felt the dust and gravel in her slippers hurting her feet. The still hot darkness wrapped her like a dream.

"I'm not asking you to understand or forgive. I don't give a damn whether you do either, for I shall never understand or forgive myself for this idiocy. I am annoyed at myself to find that so much quixoticism still lingers in me. But our fair Southland needs every man. Didn't our brave Governor Brown say just that? Not matter. I'm off to the wars." He laughed suddenly, a ringing, free laugh that startled the echoes in the dark woods.

" 'I could not love thee, Dear, so much, loved I not Honor more.' That's a pat speech, isn't it? Certainly better than anything I can think up myself, at the present moment. For I do love you, Scarlett, in spite of what I said that night on the porch last month."

His drawl was caressing and his hands slid tip her bare arms, warm strong hands. "I love you, Scarlett, because we are so much alike, renegades, both of us, dear, and selfish rascals. Neither of us cares a rap if the whole world goes to pot so long as we are safe and comfortable."

His voice went on in the darkness and she heard words, but they made no sense to her. Her mind was tiredly trying to take in the harsh truth that he was leaving her here to face the Yankees alone. Her mind said: "He's leaving me. He's leaving me." But no emotion stirred.

Then his arms went around her waist and shoulders and she felt the hard muscles of his thighs against her body and the buttons of his coat pressing into her breast. A warm tide of feeling, bewildering, frightening, swept over her, carrying out of her mind the time and place and circumstances. She felt as limp as a rag doll, warm, weak and helpless, and his supporting arms were so pleasant.

"You don't want to change your mind about what I said last month? There's nothing like danger and death to give an added fillip. Be patriotic, Scarlett. Think how you would be sending a soldier to his death with beautiful memories."

He was kissing her now and his mustache tickled her mouth, kissing her with slow, hot lips that were so leisurely as though he had the whole night before him. Charles had never kissed her like this. Never had the kisses of the Tarleton and Calvert boys made her go hot and cold and shaky like this. He bent her body backward and his lips traveled down her throat to where the cameo fastened her basque.

"Sweet," he whispered. "Sweet."

She saw the wagon dimly in the dark and heard the treble piping of Wade's voice.

"Muvver! Wade fwightened!"

Into her swaying, darkened mind, cold sanity came back with a rush and she remembered what she had forgotten for the moment — that she was frightened too, and Rhett was leaving her, leaving her, the damned cad. And on top of it all, he had the consummate gall to stand here in the road and insult her with his infamous proposals. Rage and hate flowed into her and stiffened her spine and with one wrench she tore herself loose from his arms.

"Oh, you cad!" she cried and her mind leaped about, trying to think of worse things to call him, things she had heard Gerald call Mr. Lincoln, the Macintoshes and balky mules, but the words would not come. "You low-down, cowardly, nasty, stinking thing!" And because she could not think of anything crushing enough, she drew back her arm and slapped him across the mouth with all the force she had left. He took a step backward, his hand going to his face.

"Ah," he said quietly and for a moment they stood facing each other in the darkness. Scarlett could hear his heavy breathing, and her own breath came in gasps as if she had been running hard.

"They were right! Everybody was right! You aren't a gentleman!"

"My dear girl," he said, "how inadequate."

She knew he was laughing and the thought goaded[1] her.

"Go on! Go on now! I want you to hurry. I don't want to ever see you again. I hope a cannon ball lands right on you. I hope it blows you to a million pieces. I —"

"Never mind the rest. I follow your general idea. When I'm dead on the altar of my country, I hope your conscience hurts you."

She heard him laugh as he turned away and walked back toward the wagon. She saw him stand beside it, heard him speak and his voice was changed, courteous and respectful as it always was when he spoke to Melanie.

"Mrs. Wilkes?"

Prissy's frightened voice made answer from the wagon.

"Gawdlmighty. Cap'n Butler! Miss Melly done fainted away back yonder."

"She's not dead? Is she breathing?"

"Yassuh, she breathin'."

---

[1] "To goad somebody" means to keep irritating or annoying somebody or something until they react.

"Then she's probably better off as she is. If she were conscious, I doubt if she could live through all the pain. Take good care of her, Prissy. Here's a shinplaster for you. Try not to be a bigger fool than you are."

"Yassuh. Thankee suh."

"Goodbye, Scarlett."

She knew he had turned and was facing her but she did not speak. Hate choked all utterance. His feet ground on the pebbles of the road and for a moment she saw his big shoulders looming up in the dark. Then he was gone. She could hear the sound of his feet for a while and then they died away. She came slowly back to the wagon, her knees shaking.

Why had he gone, stepping off into the dark, into the war, into a Cause that was lost, into a world that was mad? Why had he gone, Rhett who loved the pleasures of women and liquor, the comfort of good food and soft beds, the feel of fine linen and good leather, who hated the South and jeered at the fools who fought for it? Now he had set his varnished boots upon a bitter road where hunger tramped with tireless stride and wounds and weariness and heartbreak ran like yelping wolves. And the end of the road was death. He need not have gone. He was safe, rich, comfortable. But he had gone, leaving her alone in a night as black as blindness, with the Yankee Army between her and home.

Now she remembered all the bad names she had wanted to call him but it was too late. She leaned her head against the bowed neck of the horse and cried.

(The text is selected from *Gone with the Wind* (1974))

Questions for discussion:

1. Why do you think Rhett is drawn to Scarlett? Can you explain Scarlett's psychological changes in her talking with Rhett?
2. How do you understand the relationship between Scarlett and Melanie?
3. What is Scarlett's attitude towards her first husband, Charles?
4. What does the "Glorious Course" stand for?

Eudora Welty (1909 — 2001)

In her essay titled "Place in Fiction", Eudora Welty spoke of her work as filled with the spirit of place: "Location is the ground conductor of all the currents of emotion and belief and moral conviction that charge out from the story in its course." Both her outwardly uneventful life and her writing are most intimately connected to the topography and atmosphere, the season and the soil of the native Mississippi that has been her lifelong home.

Born in Jackson on 1909, to parents who came from the North, and raised in comfortable circumstances (her father headed an insurance company), she attended Mississippi State College for Women, then graduated from the University of Wisconsin in 1929. After a course in advertising at the Columbia University School of Business, she returned to Mississippi, first working as a radio writer and newspaper society editor, then for the Works Progress Administration, taking photographs of and interviewing local residents. Those travels would be reflected in her fiction and also in a book of her photographs, *One Time and Place*, published in 1971.

She began writing fiction after her return to Mississippi in 1931 and five years later published her first story, *Death of a Traveling Salesman*, in a small magazine. Over the next two years, six of her stories were published in the *Southern Review*, a serious literary magazine, one of whose editors was the poet and novelist Robert Penn Warren. She also received strong support from Katherine Anne Porter, who contributed an introduction to Welty's first book of stories, *A Curtain of Green* (1941). That introduction hailed the arrival of another gifted southern fiction writer, and in fact the volume contained some of the best stories she was ever to write, such as *Petrified Man*. Her profusion of metaphor and the difficult surface of her narrative-often oblique and indirect in its effect-were in part of her admiration for modern writers like Virginia Woolf and (as with any young southern writer) William Faulkner. Although Welty's stories were as sharp as her mentor, Porter, they were more richly idiomatic and comic in their inclination. A second collection, *The Wide Net*, appeared two years later; and her first novel, *The Robber Bridegroom*, was published in 1942.

In that year and the next she was awarded the O. Henry Memorial Prize for the best piece of short fiction, and from then on she received a steady of awards and prizes, including the Pulitzer Prize for novel *The Optimist's Daughter* (1972). Her most ambitious and longest piece of fiction is *Losing Battles* (1970), in which she aimed to compose a narrative made up almost wholly out of her characters' voices in mainly humorous interplay. Like Robert Frost, Welty loves gossip in all its actuality intimacy, and if that love failed in the novels to produce compelling, extended sequences, it did result in many lively and entertaining pages. Perhaps her finest single book after *A Curtain of Green* was *The Golden Apples* (1949), a sequence of tales about a fabulous, invented, small Mississippi community named Morgana. Her characters appear and reappear in these related stories and come together most memorably in the brilliant *June Recital*, perhaps her masterpiece.

As an entertainer, her wonderfully sharp sense of humor is strongly evident. Although the characters and themes that fill the pages of her fiction consist, in part, of involuted southern families, physically handicapped, mentally retarded, or generally unstable kinfolk — and although this fiction is shot through with undercurrents of death, violence, and degradation — everything Welty touches is transformed by the incorrigibly humorous twist of her narrative idiom. No matter how desperate a situation may be, she makes us listen to the way a character talks about it, it is style rather than information we find ourselves paying attention to. And although her attitude toward human folly is satiric, it is satiric devoid of the wish to undermine and make mockery of her characters. Instead, they are given irresistible life and a memorable expressiveness in the vivid realizations of her prose. Her narrative unfolds on the principle of varied repetitions or reiteration that have (she has claimed) the function of a deliberate double exposure in photography. She once remarked in an essay that "fine story writers seem to be in a sense obstructionists." By marking us pay attention to who is speaking and what the implications are of that speech, by asking us to imagine the way in which a silent character is responding to that speech, and by asking us read behind the deceptively simple response she gives to that character, we are made active readers, playfully engaged in the complicated scene of a typical Welty story. *Why I Live at the P. O.*, *Keela, the Outcast Indian Maiden*, the unforgettable "Powerhouse" with its Fats Waller-like hero, *Petrified Man*, *June Recital*, and many others are solid proof of both the strength and the joy of her art. And although she has been called a "regional" writer, she herself has noted the condescending nature of that term, which she says is an "outsider's term; it has no meaning for the insider who is doing the writing, because as far as he knows he is simply writing about life." (*On Writing*) So it is with Eudora Welty's fiction.

(The text is that published in *A Curtain of Green* (1941))

Major Works:

Novels:

A Curtain of Green, and Other Stories, 1994《绿色帷幔和其他故事》

Delta Wedding, 1946 《三角洲婚礼》

The Robber Bridegroom, 1942 《强盗新郎》

The Wide Net and Other Stories, 1943 《宽网和其他故事》

The Golden Apples, 1949 《金苹果》

The Ponder Heart, 1954 《沉思的心》(又译《庞德的心》)

The Bride of the Innisfallen and Other Stories, 1955 《英尼斯法伦号船上的新娘和其他故事》

Losing Battles, 1970 《败局》

The Optimist's Daughter, 1972 《乐观者的女儿》(普利策奖)

Other works:

The Eye of the Story: Selected Essays and Reviews, 1978 《短篇小说的眼睛》

One Writer's Beggings, 1984 《一位作家的起步》

A Worn Path

It was December — a bright frozen day in the early morning. Far out in the country there was an old Negro woman with her head tied red rag, coming along a path through the pinewoods. Her name was Phoenix Jackson. She was very old and small and she walked slowly in the dark pine shadows, moving a little from side to side in her steps, with the balanced heaviness and lightness of a pendulum in a grandfather clock. She carried a thin, small cane made from an umbrella, and with this she kept tapping the frozen earth in front of her. This made a grave and persistent noise in the still air that seemed meditative like the chirping of a solitary little bird.

She wore a dark striped dress reaching down to her shoe tops, and an equally long apron of bleached sugar sacks, with a full pocket: all neat and tidy, but every time she took a step she might have fallen over her shoelaces, which dragged from her unlaced shoes. She looked straight ahead. Her eyes were blue with age. Her skin had a pattern all its own of numberless branching wrinkles and as though a whole little tree stood in the middle of her forehead, but a golden color ran underneath, and the two knobs of her cheeks were illumined by a yellow burning under the dark. Under the red rag her hair came down on her neck in the frailest of ringlets, still black, and with an odor like copper.

Now and then there was a quivering in the thicket. Old Phoenix said, "Out of my way, all you foxes, owls, beetles, jack rabbits, coons and wild animals!... Keep out from under these feet, little bob-whites... Keep the big wild hogs out of my path. Don't let none of those come running my direction. I got a long way." Under her small black-freckled hand her cane, limber as a buggy whip, would switch at the brush as if to rouse up any hiding things.

On she went. The woods were deep and still. The sun made the pine needles almost too bright to look at, up where the wind rocked. The cones dropped as light as feathers. Down in the hollow was the mourning dove — it was not too late for him.

The path ran up a hill. "Seem like there is chains about my feet, time I get this far," she said, in the voice of argument old people keep to use with themselves. "Something always take a hold of me on this hill — pleads I should stay."

After she got to the top, she turned and gave a full, severe look behind her where she had come. "Up through pines," she said at length. "Now down through oaks."

Her eyes opened their widest, and she started down gently. But before she got to the bottom of the hill a bush caught her dress.

Her fingers were busy and intent, but her skirts were full and long, so that before she could pull them free in one place they were caught in another. It was not possible to allow the dress to tear. "I in the thorny bush," she said. "Thorns, you doing your appointed work. Never want to let folks pass, no sir. Old eyes thought you was a pretty little *green* bush."

Finally, trembling all over, she stood free, and after a moment dared to stoop for her cane.

"Sun so high!" she cried, leaning back and looking, while the thick tears went over her eyes. "The time getting all gone here."

At the foot of this hill was a place where a log was laid across the creek.

"Now comes the trial," said Phoenix. Putting her right foot out, she mounted the log and shut her eyes. Lifting her skirt, leveling her cane fiercely before her, like a festival figure in some parade, she began to march across. Then she opened her eyes and she was safe on the other side.

"I wasn't as old as I thought," she said.

But she sat down to rest. She spread her skirts on the bank around her and folded her hands over her knees. Up above her was a tree in a pearly cloud of mistletoe. She did not dare to close her eyes, and when a little boy brought her a plate with a slice of marble-cake on it she spoke to him. "That would be acceptable," she said. But when she went to take it there was just her own hand in the air.

So she left that tree, and had to go through a barbed-wire fence. There she had to creep and crawl, spreading her knees and stretching her fingers like a baby trying to climb the steps. But she talked loudly to herself: she could not let her dress be torn now, so late in the day, and she could not pay for having her arm or her leg sawed off if she got caught fast where she was.

At last she was safe through the fence and risen up out in the clearing. Big dead trees, like black men with one arm, were standing in the purple stalks of the withered cotton field. There sat a buzzard❶.

"Who you watching?"

In the furrow she made her way along.

"Glad this not the season for bulls," she said, looking sideways, "and the good Lord made his snakes to curl up and sleep in the winter. A pleasure I don't see no two-headed snake coming around that tree, where it come once. It took a while to get by him, back in the summer."

She passed through the old cotton and went into a field of dead corn. It whispered and shook, and was taller than her head. "Through the maze now," she said, for there was no path.

---

❶ A type of large bird that eats dead animals.

Then there was something tall, black, and skinny there, moving before her.

At first she took it for a man. It could have been a man dancing in the field. But she stood still and listened, and it did not make a sound. It was as silent as a ghost.

"Ghost," she said sharply, "who be you the ghost of? For I have heard of nary death close by."

But there was no answer — only the ragged dancing in the wind.

She shut her eyes, reached out her hand, and touched a sleeve. She found a coat and inside that an emptiness, cold as ice.

"You scarecrow[1]," she said. Her face lighted. "I ought to be shut up for good," she said with laughter. "My senses is gone. I too old. I the oldest people I ever know. Dance, old scarecrow," she said, "while I dancing with you."

She kicked her foot over the furrow, and with mouth drawn down, shook her head once or twice in a little strutting way. Some husks blew down and whirled in streamers about her skirts.

Then she went on, parting her way from side to side with the cane, through the whispering field. At last she came to the end, to a wagon track where the silver grass blew between the red ruts. The quail were walking around like pullets, seeming all dainty and unseen.

"Walk pretty," she said. "This the easy place. This the easy going." She followed the track, swaying through the quiet bare fields, through the little strings of trees silver in their dead leaves, past cabins silver from weather, with the doors and windows boarded shut, all like old women under a spell sitting there. "I walking in their sleep," she said, nodding her head vigorously.

In a ravine she went where a spring was silently flowing through a hollow log. Old Phoenix bent and drank. "Sweet gum makes the water sweet," she said, and drank more. "Nobody know who made this well, for it was here when I was born."

The track crossed a swampy part where the moss hung as white as lace from

---

[1] An object in the shape of a person that a farmer puts in a field to frighten birds away from seeds.

every limb. "Sleep on, alligators, and blow your bubbles." Then the track went into the road.

Deep, deep the road went down between the high green-colored banks. Overhead the live-oaks met, and it was as dark as a cave.

A black dog with a lolling tongue came up out of the weeds by the ditch. She was meditating, and not ready, and when he came at her she only hit him a little with her cane. Over she went in the ditch, like a little puff of milkweed.

Down there, her senses drifted away. A dream visited her, and she reached her hand up, but nothing reached down and gave her a pull. So she lay there and presently went to talking. "Old woman," she said to herself, "that black dog come up out of the weeds to stall you off, and now there he sitting on his fine tail, smiling at you."

A white man finally came along and found her — a hunter, a young man, with his dog on a chain.

"Well, Granny!" he laughed. "What are you doing there?"

"Lying on my back like a June-bug waiting to be fumed over, mister," she said, reaching up her hand.

He lifted her up, gave her a swing in the air, and set her down. "Anything broken, Granny?"

"No sir, them old dead weeds is springy enough," said Phoenix, when she had got her breath. "I thank you for your trouble."

"Where do you live, Granny?" he asked, while the two dogs were growling at each other.

"Away back yonder, sir, behind the ridge. You can't even see it from here."

"On your way home?"

"No sir, I going to town."

"Why, that's too far! That's as far as I walk when I come out myself, and I get something for my trouble." He patted the stuffed bag he carried, and there hung down a little closed claw. It was one of the bob-whites, with its beak hooked bitterly to show it was dead. "Now you go on home, Granny!"

"I bound to go to town, mister," said Phoenix. "The time come around."

He gave another laugh, filling the whole landscape. "I know you old colored people! Wouldn't miss going to town to see Santa Claus!"

But something held old Phoenix very still. The deep lines in her face went into a fierce and different radiation. Without warning, she had seen with her own eyes a flashing nickel fall out of the man's pocket onto the ground.

"How old are you, Granny?" he was saying.

"There is no telling, mister," she said, "no telling."

Then she gave a little cry and clapped her hands and said, "Git on away from here, dog! Look! Look at that dog!" She laughed as if in admiration. "He ain't scared of nobody. He a big black dog." She whispered, "Sic him!"

"Watch me get rid of that cur," said the man. "Sic him, Pete! Sic him!"

Phoenix heard the dogs fighting, and heard the man running and throwing sticks. She even heard a gunshot. But she was slowly bending forward by that time, further and further forward, the lids stretched down over her eyes, as if she were doing this in her sleep. Her chin was lowered almost to her knees. The yellow palm of her hand came out from the fold of her apron. Her fingers slid down and along the ground under the piece of money with the grace and care they would have in lifting an egg from under a setting hen. Then she slowly straightened up; she stood erect, and the nickel was in her apron pocket. A bird flew by. Her lips moved, "God watching me the whole time. I come to stealing."

The man came back, and his own dog panted about them. "Well, I scared him off that time," he said, and then he laughed and lifted his gun and pointed it at Phoenix.

She stood straight and faced him.

"Doesn't the gun scare you?" he said, still pointing it.

"No, sir, I seen plenty go off closer by, in my day, and for less than what I done," she said, holding utterly still.

He smiled, and shouldered the gun. "Well, Granny," he said, "you must be a hundred years old, and scared of nothing. I'd give you a dime if I had any money with me. But you take my advice and stay home, and nothing will happen to you."

"I bound to go on my way, mister," said Phoenix. She inclined her head in the red rag. Then they went in different directions, but she could hear the gun shooting again and again over the hill.

She walked on. The shadows hung from the oak trees to the road like curtains. Then she smelled wood-smoke, and smelled the river, and she saw a steeple and the cabins on their steep steps. Dozens of little black children whirled around her. There ahead was Natchez[1] shining. Bells were ringing. She walked on.

In the paved city it was Christmas time. There were red and green electric lights strung and crisscrossed everywhere, and all turned on in the daytime. Old Phoenix would have been lost if she had not distrusted her eyesight and depended on her feet to know where to take her.

She paused quietly on the sidewalk where people were passing by. A lady came along in the crowd, carrying an armful of red, green and silver-wrapped presents; she gave off perfume like the red roses in hot summer, and Phoenix stopped her.

"Please, missy, will you lace up my shoe?" She held up her foot.

"What do you want, Grandma?"

"See my shoe," said Phoenix. "Do all right for out in the country, but wouldn't look right to go in a big building."

"Stand still then, Grandma," said the lady. She put her packages down on the sidewalk beside her and laced and tied both shoes tightly.

"Can't lace 'em with a cane," said Phoenix. "Thank you, missy. I don't mind asking a nice lady to tie up my shoe, when I get out on the street."

Moving slowly and from side to side, she went into the big building, and into a tower of steps, where she walked up and around and around until her feet knew to stop.

She entered a door, and there she saw nailed up on the wall the document that

---

[1] A city in Mississippi, U. S.

had been stamped with the gold seal and framed in the gold frame, which matched the dream that was hung up in her head.

"Here I be," she said. There was a fixed and ceremonial stiffness over her body.

"A charity case, I suppose," said an attendant who sat at the desk before her.

But Phoenix only looked above her head. There was sweat on her face, the wrinkles in her skin shone like a bright net.

"Speak up, Grandma," the woman said. "What's your name? We must have your history, you know. Have you been here before? What seems to be the trouble with you?"

Old Phoenix only gave a twitch to her face as if a fly were bothering her.

"Are you deaf?" cried the attendant.

But then the nurse came in.

"Oh, that's just old Aunt Phoenix," she said. "She doesn't come for herself — she has a little grandson. She makes these trips just as regular as clockwork. She lives away back off the Old Natchez Trace." She bent down. "Well, Aunt Phoenix, why don't you just take a seat? We won't keep you standing after your long trip." She pointed.

The old woman sat down, bolt upright in the chair.

"Now, how is the boy?" asked the nurse.

Old Phoenix did not speak.

"I said, how is the boy?"

But Phoenix only waited and stared straight ahead, her face very solemn and withdrawn into rigidity.

"Is his throat any better?" asked the nurse. "Aunt Phoenix, don't you hear me? Is your grandson's throat any better since the last time you came for the medicine?"

With her hands on her knees, the old woman waited, silent, erect and motionless, just as if she were in armor.

"You mustn't take up our time this way, Aunt Phoenix," the nurse said.

"Tell us quickly about your grandson, and get it over. He isn't dead, is he?"

At last there came a flicker and then a flame of comprehension across her face, and she spoke.

"My grandson. It was my memory had left me. There I sat and forgot why I made my long trip."

"Forgot?" The nurse frowned. "After you came so far?"

Then Phoenix was like an old woman begging a dignified forgiveness for waking up frightened in the night. "I never did go to school, I was too old at the Surrender❶," she said in a soft voice. "I'm an old woman without an education. It was my memory fail me. My little grandson, he is just the same, and I forgot it in the coming."

"Throat never heals, does it?" said the nurse, speaking in a loud, sure voice to old Phoenix. By now she had a card with something written on it, a little list. "Yes. Swallowed lye. When was it? — January — two, three years ago?"

Phoenix spoke unasked now. "No, missy, he not dead, he just the same. Every little while his throat begin to close up again, and he not able to swallow. He not get his breath. He not able to help himself. So the time come around, and I go on another trip for the soothing medicine."

"All right. The doctor said as long as you came to get it, you could have it," said the nurse. "But it's an obstinate case."

"My little grandson, he sit up there in the house all wrapped up, waiting by himself," Phoenix went on. "We is the only two left in the world. He suffer and it don't seem to put him back at all. He got a sweet look. He going to last. He wear a little patch quilt and peep out, holding his mouth open like a little bird. I remembers so plain now. I not going to forget him again, no, the whole enduring time. I could tell him from all the others in creation."

"All right." The nurse was trying to hush her now. She brought her a bottle of medicine. "Charity," she said, making a check mark in a book.

---

❶ The Confederate Army's surrender to the Union Army at Appomattox on April 9, 1865.

Old Phoenix held the bottle close to her eyes, and then carefully put it into her pocket.

"I thank you," she said.

"It's Christmas time, Grandma," said the attendant. "Could I give you a few pennies out of my purse?"

"Five pennies is a nickel," said Phoenix stiffly.

"Here's a nickel," said the attendant.

Phoenix rose carefully and held out her hand. She received the nickel and then fished the other nickel out of her pocket and laid it beside the new one. She stared at her palm closely, with her head on one side.

Then she gave a tap with her cane on the floor.

"This is what come to me to do," she said. "I going to the store and buy my child a little windmill they sells, made out of paper. He going to find it hard to believe there such a thing in the world. I'll march myself back where he waiting, holding it straight up in this hand."

She lifted her free hand, gave a little nod, turned around, and walked out of the doctor's office. Then her slow step began on the stairs, going down.

(The text is selected from *http: //wenku. baidu. com*)

Questions for discussion:

1. What are the obstacles old Phoenix has to overcome before she reaches the doctor's office in town? How does she deal with each one?
2. What does "the worn path" symbolize?
3. Why does Phoenix take such a difficult trip to town? What does she plan to do with the money she gets?
4. What do you think is the main idea Welty wants to convey to us?

Elizabeth Bishop (1911 — 1979)

"The enormous power of reticence," the poet Octavio Paz said in a tribute, "that is the great lesson of Elizabeth Bishop." Bishop's reticence originates in a temperament indistinguishable from her style; her remarkable formal gifts allowed her to create ordered and lucid structures that hold strong feelings in place. Chief among these feelings was a powerful sense of loss. The crucial events of Bishop's life occurred within her first eight years. Born in Worcester, Massachusetts, in 1911, she was eight months old when her father died. Her mother suffered a series of breakdowns and was permanently institutionalized when her daughter was five. "I've never concealed this," Bishop once wrote, "although I don't like to make too much of it. But of course it is an important face, to me. I didn't see her again." The understatement in this remark is characteristic. When Bishop wrote about her early life — as she first did in several poems and stories in the 1950s and last did in her extraordinary final book, *Geography III* (1976) — she resisted sentimentality and self-pity. It was as if she could look at the events of her own life with the same unflinching gaze she turned on the landscapes that so consistently compelled her. The deep feeling in her pomes rises up out of direct and particular description, but Bishop does more than simply observe. Whether writing about her childhood landscape of Nova Scotia or her adopted Brazil, she often opens a poem with long perspectives on time, with landscapes that dwarf the merely human, emphasizing the dignified frailty of a human observer and the pervasive mysteries that surround her.

Examining her own case, she traces the observer's instinct to early childhood. *In the Waiting Room*, a poem written in early 1970s, probes the sources and motives behind her interest in detail. Using an incident from 1918 when she was seven — a little girl waits for her aunt in the dentist's anteroom — Bishop shows how in the course of the episode she became aware, as if wounded, of the utter strangeness and engulfing power of the world. The spectator in that poem hangs on to details as a kind of lifejacket; she observes because she has to.

After her father's death, Bishop and her mother went to live with Bishop's maternal grandparents in Great Village, Nova Scotia. She remained there for several years after her mother was institutionalized, until she was removed ("kidnapped," she describes herself feeling in one of her stories) by her paternal grandparents and taken to live in Worcester, Massachusetts. This experience was followed by a series of illnesses (eczema, bronchitis, and asthma), which plagued her for many years. Bishop later lived with an aunt and attended Walnut Hill School, a private high school. She graduated from Vassar College in 1934, where while a student she had been introduced to Marianne Moore. Moore's meticulous taste for fact was to influence Bishop's poetry, but more immediately, Moore's independent life as a poet made that life seem an alternative to Bishop's vaguer intentions to attend medical school. Bishop lived in New York City and in Key West, Florida; a traveling fellowship took her to Brazil, which so appealed to her that she stayed there for more than sixteen years.

Exile and travel were at the heart of Bishop's poems from the very start. The title of her very first book, *North & South* (1946), looks forward to the tropical worlds she was to choose so long as home and backward to the northern seas of Nova Scotia. Her poems are set among these landscapes, where she can stress the sweep and violence of encircling and eroding geological powers or, in the case of Brazil, a bewildering botanical plenty. *Questions of Travel* (1965), her third volume, constitutes a sequence of poems initiating her, with her botanist-geologist-anthropologist's curiosity, into the life of Brazil and the mysteries of what questions a traveler-exile should ask. In this series with its increasing penetration of a new country, a process is at work similar to one Bishop identifies in the great English naturalist Charles Darwin, of whom Bishop once said: "One admires the beautiful solid case being built up out of his endless, heroic observations, almost unconscious or automatic — and then comes a sudden relaxation, a forgetful phrase, and one feels the strangeness of his undertaking, sees the lonely young man, his eyes fixed on facts and minute details, sinking or sliding giddily off into the unknown."

In 1969 Bishop's *Complete Poems* appeared, an ironic title in light of the fact that she continued to write and publish new poetry. *Geography III* contains some of her very best work, poems that, form the settled perspective of her return to the United States, look back and evaluate the appetite for exploration apparent in her earlier verse. The influence of her long friendship with the poet Robert Lowell, and their mutual regard for one another's work, may be felt in the way *Geography III* explores the terrain of memory and autobiography more powerfully and directly than her earlier work. Having left Brazil, Bishop lived in Boston from 1970 and taught at Harvard University until 1977. She received the Pulitzer Prize for the combined volume *North & South and A Cold Spring* (1955), the National Book Award for *The Complete Poems*, and in 1976 was the first woman and the first American to receive the Books Abroad Neustadt International Prize for Literature. Since Bishop's death in 1979, most of her published work has been gathered in two volumes: *The Complete Poems* 1929-1979 and *The Collected Prose*.

(The text is selected from *The Norton Anthology of American Literature* (Shorter Fifth Edition))

Major Works:

Poetry collections:

- *North & South*, 1946 《北方·南方》
- *A Cold Spring*, 1955 《一个寒冷的春天》
- *Questions of Travel*, 1965 《旅行的问题》
- *The Complete Poems*, 1969 《诗集》
- *Geography* Ⅲ, 1976 《地理学Ⅲ》

At the Fishhouses

Although it is a cold evening,
down by one of the fishhouses
an old man sits netting,
his net, in the gloaming almost invisible,
a dark purple-brown,
and his shuttle worn and polished.
The air smells so strong of codfish
it makes one's nose run and one's eyes water.
The five fishhouses have steeply peaked roofs
and narrow, cleated gangplanks slant up
to storerooms in the gables
for the wheelbarrows to be pushed up and down on.
All is silver: the heavy surface of the sea,
swelling slowly as if considering spilling over,
is opaque, but the silver of the benches,
the lobster pots, and masts, scattered
among the wild jagged rocks,
is of an apparent translucence
like the small old buildings with an emerald moss
growing on their shoreward walls.

The big fish tubs are completely lined
with layers of beautiful herring scales
and the wheelbarrows are similarly plastered
with creamy iridescent coats of mail,
with small iridescent flies crawling on them.
Up on the little slope behind the houses,
set in the sparse bright sprinkle of grass,
is an ancient wooden capstan❶,
cracked, with two long bleached handles
and some melancholy stains, like dried blood,
where the ironwork has rusted.
The old man accepts a Lucky Strike❷.
He was a friend of my grandfather.
We talk of the decline in the population
and of codfish and herring
while he waits for a herring boat to come in.
There are sequins on his vest and on his thumb.
He has scraped the scales, the principal beauty,
from unnumbered fish with that black old knife,
the blade of which is almost worn away.

Down at the water's edge, at the place
where they haul up the boats, up the long ramp
descending into the water, thin silver
tree trunks are laid horizontally
across the gray stones, down and down
at intervals of four or five feet.
Cold dark deep and absolutely clear,

---

❶ A rotating vertical cylinder used to life weights by winding in a cable.

❷ Brand of cigarettes.

element bearable to no mortal,
to fish and to seals... One seal particularly
I have seen here evening after evening.
He was curious about me. He was interested in music;
like me a believer in total immersion[1],
so I used to sing him Baptist hymns.
I also sang "A Mighty Fortress Is Our God."
He stood up in the water and regarded me
steadily, moving his head a little.
Then he would disappear, then suddenly emerge
almost in the same spot, with a sort of shrug
as if it were against his better judgment.
Cold dark deep and absolutely clear,
the clear gray icy water... Back, behind us,
the dignified tall firs begin.
Bluish, associating with their shadows,
a million Christmas trees stand
waiting for Christmas. The water seems suspended
above the rounded gray and blue-gray stones.
I have seen it over and over, the same sea, the same,
slightly, indifferently swinging above the stones,
icily free above the stones,
above the stones and then the world.
If you should dip your hand in,
your wrist would ache immediately,
your bones would begin to ache and your hand would burn
as if the water were a transmutation of fire
that feeds on stones and burns with a dark gray flame.

---

[1] Form of baptism used by Baptists, which holds that people must be immersed in water to be baptized.

If you tasted it, it would first taste bitter,
then briny, then surely burn your tongue.
It is like what we imagine knowledge to be:
dark, salt, clear, moving, utterly free,
drawn from the cold hard mouth
of the world, derived from the rocky breasts
forever, flowing and drawn, and since
our knowledge is historical, flowing, and flown.

The Fish

I caught a tremendous fish
and held him beside the boat
half out of water, with my hook
fast in a corner of his mouth.
He didn't fight.
He hadn't fought at all.
He hung a grunting weight,
battered and venerable
and homely. Here and there
his brown skin hung in strips
like ancient wallpaper,
and its pattern of darker brown
was like wallpaper:
shapes like full-blown roses
stained and lost through age.
He was speckled with barnacles,
fine rosettes of lime,
and infested
with tiny white sea-lice,
and underneath two or three

rags of green weed hung down.
While his gills were breathing in
the terrible oxygen
— the frightening gills,
fresh and crisp with blood,
that can cut so badly —
I thought of the coarse white flesh
packed in like feathers,
the big bones and the little bones,
the dramatic reds and blacks
of his shiny entrails,
and the pink swim-bladder
like a big peony.
I looked into his eyes
which were far larger than mine
but shallower, and yellowed,
the irises backed and packed
with tarnished tinfoil
seen through the lenses
of old scratched isinglass[1].
They shifted a little, but not
to return my stare.
— It was more like the tipping
of an object toward the light.
I admired his sullen face,
the mechanism of his jaw,
and then I saw
that from his lower lip

---

[1] A whitish, semitransparent substance, originally obtained from the swim bladders of some freshwater fish and occasionally used for windows.

— if you could call it a lip
grim, wet, and weaponlike,
hung five old pieces of fish-line,
or four and a wire leader
with the swivel still attached,
with all their five big hooks
grown firmly in his mouth.
A green line, frayed at the end
where he broke it, two heavier lines,
and a fine black thread
still crimped from the strain and snap
when it broke and he got away.
Like medals with their ribbons
frayed and wavering,
a five-haired beard of wisdom
trailing from his aching jaw.
I stared and stared
and victory filled up
the little rented boat,
from the pool of bilge
where oil had spread a rainbow
around the rusted engine
to the bailer rusted orange,
the sun-cracked thwarts,
the oarlocks on their strings,
the gunnels — until everything
was rainbow, rainbow, rainbow!
And I let the fish go.

One Art

The art of losing isn't hard to master;

so many things seem filled with the intent
to be lost that their loss is no disaster.

Lose something every day. Accept the fluster
of lost door keys, the hour badly spent.
The art of losing isn't hard to master.

Then practice losing farther, losing faster:
places, and names, and where it was you meant
to travel. None of these will bring disaster.

I lost my mother's watch. And look! my last, or
next-to-last, of three loved houses went.
The art of losing isn't hard to master.

I lost two cities, lovely ones. And, vaster,
some realms I owned, two rivers, a continent.
I miss them, but it wasn't a disaster.

— Even losing you (the joking voice, a gesture
I love) I shan't have lied. It's evident
the art of losing's not too hard to master
though it may look like (*Write* it!) like disaster.

In the Waiting Room

In Worcester, Massachusetts,
I went with Aunt Consuelo
to keep her dentist's appointment
and sat and waited for her
in the dentist's waiting room.

It was winter. It got dark
early. The waiting room
was full of grown-up people,
arctics and overcoats,
lamps and magazines.
My aunt was inside
what seemed like a long time
and while I waited I read
the *National Geographic*
(I could read) and carefully
studied the photographs:
the inside of a volcano,
black, and full of ashes;
then it was spilling over
in rivulets of fire.
Osa and Martin Johnson❶
dressed in riding breeches,
laced boots, and pith helmets.
A dead man slung on a pole
— "Long Pig❷," the caption said.
Babies with pointed heads
wound round and round with string;
black, naked women with necks
wound round and round with wire
like the necks of light bulbs.
Their breasts were horrifying.
I read it right straight through.
I was too shy to stop.

---

❶ Famous explorers and travel writers.

❷ Polynesian cannibals' name for the human carcass.

And then I looked at the cover:
the yellow margins, the date.
Suddenly, from inside,
came an *oh*! of pain
— Aunt Consuelo's voice —
not very loud or long.
I wasn't at all surprised;
even then I knew she was
a foolish, timid woman.
I might have been embarrassed,
but wasn't. What took me
completely by surprise
was that it was *me*:
my voice, in my mouth.
Without thinking at all
I was my foolish aunt,
I — we — were falling, falling,
our eyes glued to the cover
of the *National Geographic*,
February, 1918.

I said to myself: three days
and you'll be seven years old.
I was saying it to stop
the sensation of falling off
the round, turning world.
into cold, blue-black space.
But I felt: you are an *I*,
you are an *Elizabeth*,
you are one of *them*.

Why should you be one, too?
I scarcely dared to look
to see what it was I was.
I gave a sidelong glance
— I couldn't look any higher —
at shadowy gray knees,
trousers and skirts and boots
and different pairs of hands
lying under the lamps.
I knew that nothing stranger
had ever happened, that nothing
stranger could ever happen.

Why should I be my aunt,
or me, or anyone?
What similarities —
boots, hands, the family voice
I felt in my throat, or even
the *National Geographic*
and those awful hanging breasts —
held us all together
or made us all just one?
How — I didn't know any
word for it — how "unlikely"...
How had I come to be here,
like them, and overhear
a cry of pain that could have
got loud and worse but hadn't?

The waiting room was bright
and too hot. It was sliding
beneath a big black wave,
another, and another.

Then I was back in it.
The War was on. Outside,
in Worcester, Massachusetts,
were night and slush and cold,
and it was still the fifth
of February, 1918.
(The texts above are selected from *http://www.poets.org*)

Sestina[1]

September rain falls on the house,
In the failing light, the old grandmother
sits in the kitchen with the child
beside the Little Marvel Stove,
reading the jokes from the almanac,
laughing and talking to hide her tears.

She thinks that her equinoctial tears
and the rain that beats on the roof of the house
were both foretold by the almanac,
But only known to a grandmother,
The iron kettle sings on the stove,
She cuts some bread and says to the child.

---

[1] A fixed verse form in which the end words of the first six-line stanza must be used at the ends of the lines in the next stanza in a rotating order; the final three lines must contain all six words.

It's time for tea now; but the child
is watching the teakettle's small hard tears
dance like mad on the hot black stove,
the way the rain must dance on the house,
Tidying up, the old grandmother
hangs up the clever almanac

on its string. Birdlike, the almanac
hovers half open above the child,
and her teacup full of dark brown tears.
She shivers and says she thinks the house
feels chilly, and puts more wood in the stove.

It was to be, says the Marvel Stove.
I know what I know, says the almanac.
With crayons the child draws a rigid house
and a winding pathway. Then the child
puts in a man with buttons like tears
and shows it proudly to the grandmother.

But secretly, while the grandmother
busies herself about the stove,
the little moons fall down like tears
from between the pages of the almanac
into the flower bet the child
has carefully placed in the front of the house.

Time to plant tears, says the almanac.
The grandmother sings to the marvelous stove
and the child draws another inscrutable house.

(The text above is selected from *The Norton Anthology of American Literature* (Shorter Fifth Edition))

Questions for discussion:

1. How does the poet portray the fish as an object of veneration? Why does she let him go?
2. Each of Bishop's poems seems to build up to a climax, a sudden awareness of something or a "sweet sensation of joy". Would you please point out what it is in each of the selected poems?
3. How would you describe the poetic style of Bishop's poetry?

Flannery O'Connor (1925 — 1964)

Flannery O'Connor, one of this century's finest writers of short stories, was born in Savannah; lived with her mother in Milledgeville, Georgia, for much of her life; and died before her fortieth birthday — victim like her father of disseminated lupus, a rare and incurable disease. She was stricken with the disease in 1950 while at work on her first novel, but injections of a cortisone derivative managed to arrest it, though the cortisone weakened her bones to the extent that from 1955 on she could get around only on crutches. She was able to write, travel, and lecture until 1964 when the lupus reactivated itself and killed her. A Roman Catholic throughout her life, she is quoted as having remarked, apropos of a trip to Lourdes, "I had the best-looking crutches in Europe." This remark suggests the kind of hair-raising jokes that centrally inform her writing as well as a refusal to indulge in self-pity over her fate.

She published two novels, *Wise Blood* (1952) and *The Violent Bear It Away* (1960), both weighty with symbolic and religious concerns and ingeniously contrived in the black-humored manner of Nathanael West, her American predecessor in this mode. But her really memorable creations of characters and actions take place in the stories, which are extremely funny, sometimes unbearably so, and finally we may wonder just what it is we are laughing at. Upon consideration the jokes are seen to be dreadful ones, as with Manley Pointer's treatment of Joy Hopewell's artificial leg in *Good Country People* or Mr. Shiftlet's of his bride in *The Life You Save May Be Your Own.*

Another American "regionalist," the poet Robert Frost, whose own work contains its share of dreadful jokes, once confessed to being more interested in people's speech than in the people themselves. A typical Flannery O'Connor story consists at its most vital level in people talking, clucking their endless reiterations of clichés about life, death, and the universe. These clichés are captured with beautiful accuracy by an artist who had spent her life listening to them, loving and maliciously keeping track until she could put them to use. Early in her life she hoped to be a cartoonist, and there is cartoonlike mastery in her vivid renderings of character through speech and other gesture. Critics have called her a maker of grotesques, a label that like other ones — regionalist, southern lady, or Roman Catholic novelist — might have annoyed if it didn't obviously amuse her too. She once remarked tartly that "anything that comes out of the South is going to be called grotesque by the Northern reader, unless it is grotesque, in which case it is going to be called realistic."

Of course, this capacity for mockery, along with a facility in portraying perverse behavior, may work against other demands we make of the fiction writer, and it is true that O'Connor seldom suggests that her characters have inner lives that are imaginable, let alone worth respect. Instead, the emphasis is on the sharp eye and the ability to tell a tale and keep it moving inevitably toward completion. These completions are usually violent, occurring when the character — in many cases a woman — must confront an experience that she cannot handle by the old trustworthy language and habit-hardened responses. O'Connor's art lies partly in making it impossible for us merely to scorn the banalities of expression and behavior by which these people get through their lives. However dark the comedy, it keeps in touch with the things of this world, even when some force from another world threatens to annihilate the embattled protagonist. And although the stories are filled with religious allusion and parodies, they do not try to inculcate a doctrine. One of her best ones is titled *Revelation*, but a reader often finishes a story with no simple, unambiguous sense of what has been revealed. Instead, we must trust the internal fun and richness of each tale to reveal what it has to reveal. We can agree also, in sadness, with the critic Irving Howe's conclusion to his review of her posthumous collection of stories that it is intolerable for such a writer to have died at the age of thirty-nine.

(The text is selected from *The Norton Anthology of American Literature* (Shorter Fifth Edition))

Major Works:

Novels:

Wise Blood, 1952 《慧血》

A Good Man Is Hard to Find and Other Stories, 1955 《好人难寻》

The Violent Bear It Away, 1960 《暴力得逞》

Everything That Rises Must Converge, 1965 《一切上升皆融合》（又译《殊途同归》）

The Complete Stories of Flannery O'Connor, 1971《奥康纳短篇小说全集》

Other Works:

Mystery and Manners, 1969 《神秘与习俗：散文拾零》

Letters of Flannery O'Conner: The Habit of Being, 1979 《奥康纳书信集：生存习惯》

Good Country People[1]

Besides the neutral expression that she wore when she was alone, Mrs. Freeman had two others, forward and reverse, that she used for all her human dealings. Her

[1] The story is selected from O'Connor's short story collection *A Good Man Is Hard to Find and Other Stories*, which was published in 1955.

forward expression was steady and driving like the advance of a heavy truck. Her eyes never swerved to left or right but turned as the story turned as if they followed a yellow line down the center of it. She seldom used the other expression because it was not often necessary for her to retract a statement, but when she did, her face came to a complete stop, there was an almost imperceptible movement of her black eyes, during which they seemed to be receding, and then the observer would see that Mrs. Freeman, though she might stand there as real as several grain sacks thrown on top of each other, was no longer there in spirit. As for getting anything across to her when this was the case, Mrs. Hopewell had given it up. She might talk her head off. Mrs. Freeman could never be brought to admit herself wrong to any point. She would stand there and if she could be brought to say anything, it was something like, "Well, I wouldn't of said it was and I wouldn't of said it wasn't" or letting her gaze range over the top kitchen shelf where there was an assortment of dusty bottles, she might remark, "I see you ain't ate many of them figs you put up last summer."

They carried on their most important business in the kitchen at breakfast. Every morning Mrs. Hopewell got up at seven o'clock and lit her gas heater and Joy's. Joy was her daughter, a large blonde girl who had an artificial leg. Mrs. Hopewell thought of her as a child though she was thirty-two years old and highly educated. Joy would get up while her mother was eating and lumber into the bathroom and slam the door, and before long, Mrs. Freeman would arrive at the back door. Joy would hear her mother call, "Come on in," and then they would talk for a while in low voices that were indistinguishable in the bathroom. By the time Joy came in, they had usually finished the weather report and were on one or the other of Mrs. Freeman's daughters, Glynese or Carramae. Joy called them Glycerin and Caramel. Glynese, a redhead, was eighteen and had many admirers; Carramae, a blonde, was only fifteen but already married and pregnant. She could not keep anything on her stomach. Every morning Mrs. Freeman told Mrs. Hopewell how many times she had vomited since the last report.

Mrs. Hopewell liked to tell people that Glynese and Carramae were two of the finest girls she knew and that Mrs. Freeman was a lady and that she was never ashamed to take her anywhere or introduce her to anybody they might meet. Then she would tell how she had happened to hire the Freemans in the first place and how they were a godsend to her and how she had had them four years. The reason for her keeping them so long was that they were not trash. They were good country people. She had telephoned the man whose name they had given as reference and he had told her that Mr. Freeman was a good farmer but that his wife was the nosiest woman ever to walk the earth. "She's got to be into everything," the man said. "If she don't get there before the dust settles, you can bet she's dead, that's all. She'll want to know all your business. I can stand him real good," he had said, "but me nor my wife neither could have stood that woman one more minute on this place." That had put Mrs. Hopewell off for a few days.

She had hired them in the end because there were no other applicants but she had made up her mind beforehand exactly how she would handle the woman. Since she was the type who had to be into everything, then, Mrs. Hopewell had decided, she would not only let her be into everything, she would *see to it* that she was into everything — she would give her the responsibility of everything, she would put her in charge. Mrs. Hopewell had no bad qualities of her own but she was able to use other people's in such a constructive way that she had kept them four years.

Nothing is perfect. This was one of Mrs. Hopewell's favorite sayings. Another was: that is life! And still another, the most important, was: well, other people have their opinions too. She would make these statements, usually at the table, in a tone of gentle insistence as if no one held them but her, and the large hulking Joy, whose constant outrage had obliterated every expression from her face, would stare just a little to the side of her, her eyes icy blue, with the look of someone who had achieved blindness by an act of will and means to keep it.

When Mrs. Hopewell said to Mrs. Freeman that life was like that, Mrs. Freeman would say, "I always said so myself." Nothing had been arrived at by anyone that had not first been arrived at by her. She was quicker than Mr. Freeman. When Mrs. Hopewell said to her after they had been on the place for a while, "You know, you're the wheel behind the wheel," and winked, Mrs. Freeman had said, "I know it. I've always been quick. It's some that are quicker than others."

"Everybody is different," Mrs. Hopewell said.

"Yes, most people is," Mrs. Freeman said.

"It takes all kinds to make the world."

"I always said it did myself."

The girl was used to this kind of dialogue for breakfast and more of it for dinner; sometimes they had it for supper too. When they had no guest they ate in the kitchen because that was easier. Mrs. Freeman always managed to arrive at some point during the meal and to watch them finish it. She would stand in the doorway if it were summer but in the winter she would stand with one elbow on top of the refrigerator and look down at them, or she would stand by the gas heater, lifting the back of her skirt slightly. Occasionally she would stand against the wall and roll her head from side to side. At no time was she in any hurry to leave. All this was very trying on Mrs. Hopewell but she was a woman of great patience. She realized that nothing is perfect and that in the Freemans she had good country people and that if, in this day and age, you get good country people, you had better hang onto them.

She had had plenty of experience with trash. Before the Freemans she had averaged one tenant family a year. The wives of these farmers were not the kind you would want to be around you for very long. Mrs. Hopewell, who had divorced her husband long ago, needed someone to walk over the fields with her; and when Joy had to be impressed for these services, her remarks were usually so ugly and her face so glum that Mrs. Hopewell would say, "If you can't come pleasantly, I don't want you at all," to which the girl, standing square and rigid-shouldered with her neck thrust slightly forward, would reply, "If you want me, here I am — LIKE I AM."

Mrs. Hopewell excused this attitude because of the leg (which had been shot off in a hunting accident when Joy was ten). It was hard for Mrs. Hopewell to realize that her child was thirty-two now and that for more than twenty years she had had only one leg. She thought of her still as a child because it tore her heart to think instead of the poor stout girl in her thirties who had never danced a step or had any normal good times. Her name was really Joy but as soon as she was twenty-one and away from home, she had had it legally changed. Mrs. Hopewell was certain that she had thought and thought until she had hit upon the ugliest name in any language. Then she had gone and had the beautiful name, Joy, changed without telling her mother until after she had done it. Her legal name was Hulga.

When Mrs. Hopewell thought the name, Hulga, she thought of the broad blank hull of a battleship. She would not use it. She continued to call her Joy to which the girl responded but in a purely mechanical way.

Hulga had learned to tolerate Mrs. Freeman who saved her from taking walks with her mother. Even Glynese and Carramae were useful when they occupied attention that might otherwise have been directed at her. At first she had thought she could not stand Mrs. Freeman for she had found it was not possible to be rude to her. Mrs. Freeman would take on strange resentments and for days together she would be sullen but the source of her displeasure was always obscure; a direct attack, a positive leer, blatant ugliness to her face — these never touched her. And without warning one day, she began calling her Hulga.

She did not call her that in front of Mrs. Hopewell who would have been incensed but when she and the girl happened to be out of the house together, she would say something and add the name Hulga to the end of it, and the big spectacled Joy-Hulga would scowl and redden as if her privacy had been intruded upon. She considered the name her personal affair. She had arrived at it first purely on the basis of its ugly sound and then the full genius of its fitness had struck her. She had a vision of the name working like the ugly sweating Vulcan[1] who stayed in the furnace and to whom, presumably, the goddess had to come when called. She saw it as the name of her highest creative act. One of her major triumphs was that her mother had not been able to turn her dust into Joy, but the greater one was that she had been able to turn it herself into Hulga. However, Mrs. Freeman's relish for using the name only irritated her. It was as if Mrs. Freeman's beady steel-pointed eyes had penetrated far enough behind her face to reach some secret fact. Something about her seemed to fascinate

---

[1] Vulcan was the Greek god of fire whom Venus, goddess of love, "presumably" obeyed as her consort.

Mrs. Freeman and then one day Hulga realized that it was the artificial leg. Mrs. Freeman had a special fondness for the details of secret infections, hidden deformities, assaults upon children. Of diseases, she preferred the lingering or incurable. Hulga had heard Mrs. Hopewell give her the details of the hunting accident, how the leg had been literally blasted off, how she had never lost consciousness. Mrs. Freeman could listen to it any time as if it had happened an hour ago.

When Hulga stumped into the kitchen in the morning (she could walk without making the awful noise but she made it — Mrs. Hopewell was certain — because it was ugly-sounding), she glanced at them and did not speak. Mrs. Hopewell would be in her red kimono with her hair tied around her head in rags. She would be sitting at the table, finishing her breakfast and Mrs. Freeman would be hanging by her elbow outward from the refrigerator, looking down at the table. Hulga always put her eggs on the stove to boil and then stood over them with her arms folded, and Mrs. Hopewell would look at her — a kind of indirect gaze divided between her and Mrs. Freeman — and would think that if she would only keep herself up a little, she wouldn't be so bad looking. There was nothing wrong with her face that a pleasant expression wouldn't help. Mrs. Hopewell said that people who looked on the bright side of things would be beautiful even if they were not.

Whenever she looked at Joy this way, she could not help but feel that it would have been better if the child had not taken the Ph. D. It had certainly not brought her out any and now that she had it, there was no more excuse for her to go to school again. Mrs. Hopewell thought it was nice for girls to go to school to have a good time but Joy had "gone through." Anyhow, she would not have been strong enough to go again. The doctors had told Mrs. Hopewell that with the best of care, Joy might see forty-five. She had a weak heart. Joy had made it plain that if it had not been for this condition, she would be far from these red hills and good country people. She would be in a university lecturing to people who knew what she was talking about. And Mrs. Hopewell could very well picture here there, looking like a scarecrow and lecturing to more of the same. Here she went about all day in a six-year-old skirt and a yellow sweat shirt with a faded cowboy on a horse embossed on it. She thought this was funny; Mrs. Hopewell thought it was idiotic and showed simply that she was still a child. She was brilliant but she didn't have a grain of sense. It seemed to Mrs. Hopewell that every year she grew less like other people and more like herself — bloated, rude, and squint-eyed. And she said such strange things! To her own mother she had said — without warning, without excuse, standing up in the middle of a meal with her face purple and her mouth half full — "Woman! Do you ever look inside? Do you ever look inside and see what you are *not*? God!" she had cried sinking down again and staring at her plate, "Malebranche[1] was right: we are not our own light. We are not our own light!" Mrs. Hopewell had no idea to this day what brought that on. She had only made the remark, hoping Joy would take it in, that a smile never hurt anyone.

The girl had taken the Ph. D. in philosophy and this left Mrs. Hopewell at a complete loss. You could say, "My daughter is a nurse," or "My daughter is a school teacher," or even, "My daughter is a chemical engineer." You could not say, "My daughter is a philosopher." That was something that had ended with the Greeks and Romans. All day Joy sat on her neck in a deep chair, reading. Sometimes she went for walks but she didn't like dogs or cats or birds or flowers or nature or nice young men. She looked at nice young men as if she could smell their stupidity.

One day Mrs. Hopewell had picked up one of the books the girl had just put down and opening it at random, she read, "Science, on the other hand, has to assert its soberness and seriousness afresh and declare that it is concerned solely with what-is. Nothing — how can it be for science anything but a horror and a phantasm? If science is right, then one thing stands firm: science wishes to know nothing of nothing. Such is after all the strictly scientific approach to Nothing. We know it by wishing to know nothing of Nothing." These words had been underlined with a blue pencil and they worked on Mrs. Hopewell like some evil incantation in gibberish. She shut the book quickly and went out of the room as if she were having a chill.

This morning when the girl came in, Mrs. Freeman was on Carramae. "She

[1] Nicolas Malebranche (1638 — 1715), French philosopher and religious thinker who believed that the mind could not have any knowledge external to itself except through God.

thrown up four times after supper," she said, "and was up twice in the night after three o'clock. Yesterday she didn't do nothing but ramble in the bureau drawer. All she did. Stand up there and see what she could run up on."

"She's got to eat," Mrs. Hopewell muttered, sipping her coffee, while she watched Joy's back at the stove. She was wondering what the child had said to the Bible salesman. She could not imagine what kind of a conversation she could possibly have had with him.

He was a tall gaunt hatless youth who had called yesterday to sell them a Bible. He had appeared at the door, carrying a large black suitcase that weighted him so heavily on one side that he had to brace himself against the door facing. He seemed on the point of collapse but he said in a cheerful voice, "Good morning, Mrs. Cedars!" and set the suitcase down on the mat. He was not a bad-looking young man though he had on a bright blue suit and yellow socks that were not pulled up far enough. He had prominent face bones and a streak of sticky-looking brown hair falling across his forehead.

"I'm Mrs. Hopewell," she said.

"Oh!" he said, pretending to look puzzled but with his eyes sparkling, "I saw it said 'The Cedars' on the mailbox so I thought you was Mrs. Cedars!" and he burst out in a pleasant laugh. He picked up the satchel and under cover of a pant, he fell forward into her hall. It was rather as if the suitcase had moved first, jerking him after it. "Mrs. Hopewell!" he said and grabbed her hand. "I hope you are well!" and he laughed again and then all at once his face sobered completely. He paused and gave her a straight earnest look and said, "Lady, I've come to speak of serious things."

"Well, come in," she muttered, none too pleased because her dinner was almost ready. He came into the parlor and sat down on the edge of a straight chair and put the suitcase between his feet and glanced around the room as if he were sizing her up by it. Her silver gleamed on the two sideboards; she decided he had never been in a room as elegant as this.

"Mrs. Hopewell," he began, using her name in a way that sounded almost intimate, "I know you believe in Chrustian service."

"Well, yes," she murmured.

"I know," he said and paused, looking very wise with his head cocked on one side, "that you're a good woman. Friends have told me."

Mrs. Hopewell never liked to be taken for a fool. "What are you selling?" she asked.

"Bibles," the young man said and his eye raced around the room before he added, "I see you have no family Bible in your parlor, I see that is the one lack you got!"

Mrs. Hopewell could not say, "My daughter is an atheist and won't let me keep the Bible in the parlor." She said, stiffening slightly, "I keep my Bible by my bedside." This was not the truth. It was in the attic somewhere.

"Lady," he said, "the word of God ought to be in the parlor."

"Well, I think that's a matter of taste," she began, "I think..."

"Lady," he said, "for a Chrustian, the word of God ought to be in every room in the house besides in his heart. I know you're a Chrustian because I can see it in every line of your face."

She stood up and said, "Well, young man, I don't want to buy a Bible and I smell my dinner burning."

He didn't get up. He began to twist his hands and looking down at them, he said softly, "Well lady, I'll tell you the truth — not many people want to buy one nowadays and besides, I know I'm real simple. I don't know how to say a thing but to say it. I'm just a country boy." He glanced up into her unfriendly face. "People like you don't like to fool with country people like me!"

"Why!" she cried, "good country people are the salt of the earth! Besides, we all have different ways of doing, it takes all kinds to make the world go 'round. That's life!"

"You said a mouthful," he said.

"Why, I think there aren't enough good country people in the world!" she said, stirred. "I think that's what's wrong with it!"

His face had brightened. "I didn't intraduce myself," he said. "I'm Manley Pointer from out in the country around Willohobie, not even from a place, just from near a place."

"You wait a minute," she said. "I have to see about my dinner." She went out to the kitchen and found Joy standing near the door where she had been listening.

"Get rid of the salt of the earth," she said, "and let's eat."

Mrs. Hopewell gave her a pained look and turned the heat down under the vegetables. "I can't be rude to anybody," she murmured and went back into the parlor.

He had opened the suitcase and was sitting with a Bible on each knee.

"I appreciate your honesty," he said. "You don't see any more real honest people unless you go way out in the country."

"I know," she said, "real genuine folks!" Through the crack in the door she heard a groan.

"I guess a lot of boys come telling you they're working their way through college," he said, "but I'm not going to tell you that. Somehow," he said, "I don't want to go to college. I want to devote my life to Chrustian service. See," he said, lowering his voice, "I got this heart condition. I may not live long. When you know it's something wrong with you and you may not live long, well then, lady..." He paused, with his mouth open, and stared at her.

He and Joy had the same condition! She knew that her eyes were filling with tears but she collected herself quickly and murmured, "Won't you stay for dinner? We'd love to have you!" and was sorry the instant she heard herself say it.

"Yes mam," he said in an abashed voice. "I would sher love to do that!"

Joy had given him one look on being introduced to him and then throughout the meal had not glanced at him again. He had addressed several remarks to her, which she had pretended not to hear. Mrs. Hopewell could not understand deliberate rudeness, although she lived with it, and she felt she had always to overflow with hospitality to make up for Joy's lack of courtesy. She urged him to talk about himself and he did. He said he was the seventh child of twelve and that his father had been crushed under a tree when he himself was eight years old. He had been crushed very badly, in fact, almost cut in two and was practically not recognizable. His mother had got along the best she could by hard working and she had always seen that her children went to Sunday School and that they read the Bible every evening. He was now nineteen years old and he had been selling Bibles for four months. In that time he had sold seventy-seven Bibles and had the promise of two more sales. He wanted to become a missionary because he thought that was the way you could do most for people. "He who losest his life shall find it," he said simply and he was so sincere, so genuine and earnest that Mrs. Hopewell would not for the world have smiled. He prevented his peas from sliding onto the table by blocking them with a piece of bread which he later cleaned his plate with. She could see Joy observing sidewise how he handled his knife and fork and she saw too that every few minutes, the boy would dart a keen appraising glance at the girl as if he were trying to attract her attention.

After dinner Joy cleared the dishes off the table and disappeared and Mrs. Hopewell was left to talk with him. He told her again about his childhood and his father's accident and about various things that had happened to him. Every five minutes or so she would stifle a yawn. He sat for two hours until finally she told him she must go because she had an appointment in town. He packed his Bibles and thanked her and prepared to leave, but in the doorway he stopped and wring her hand and said that not on any of his trips had he met a lady as nice as her and he asked if he could come again. She had said she would always be happy to see him.

Joy had been standing in the road, apparently looking at something in the distance, when he came down the steps toward her, bent to the side with his heavy valise. He stopped where she was standing and confronted her directly. Mrs. Hopewell could not hear what he said but she trembled to think what Joy would say to him. She could see that after a minute Joy said something and that then the boy began to speak again, making an excited gesture with his free hand. After a minute Joy said something else at which the boy began to speak once more. Then to her amazement, Mrs. Hopewell saw the two of them walk off together, toward the gate. Joy had walked all the way to the gate with him and Mrs. Hopewell could not imagine what they had said to each other, and she had not yet dared to ask.

Mrs. Freeman was insisting upon her attention. She had moved from the refrigerator to the heater so that Mrs. Hopewell had to turn and face her in order to seem to be listening. "Glynese gone out with Harvey Hill again last night," she said. "She had this sty."

"Hill," Mrs. Hopewell said absently, "is that the one who works in the garage?"

"Nome, he's the one that goes to chiropractor school," Mrs. Freeman said. "She had this sty. Been had it two days. So she says when he brought her in the other night he says, 'Lemme get rid of that sty for you,' and she says, 'How?' and he says, 'You just lay yourself down acrost the seat of that car and I'll show you.' So she done it and he popped her neck. Kept on a-popping it several times until he made him quit. This morning," Mrs. Freeman said, "she ain't got no sty. She ain't got no traces of a sty."

"I never heard of that before," Mrs. Hopewell said.

"He ast her to marry him before the Ordinary[1]," Mrs. Freeman went on, "and she told him she wasn't going to be married in no office."

"Well, Glynese is a fine girl," Mrs. Hopewell said. "Glynese and Carramae are both fine girls."

"Carramae said when her and Lyman was married Lyman said it sure felt sacred to him. She said he said he wouldn't take five hundred dollars for being married by a preacher."

"How much would he take?" the girl asked from the stove.

"He said he wouldn't take five hundred dollars," Mrs. Freeman repeated.

"Well we all have work to do," Mrs. Hopewell said.

"Lyman said it just felt more sacred to him," Mrs. Freeman said. "The doctor wants Carramae to eat prunes. Says instead of medicine. Says them cramps is coming from pressure. You know where I think it is?"

"She'll be better in a few weeks," Mrs. Hopewell said.

---

[1] Justice of the peace who performs the marriage ceremony in chambers rather than in public.

"In the tube," Mrs. Freeman said. "Else she wouldn't be as sick as she is."

Hulga had cracked her two eggs into a saucer and was bringing them to the table along with a cup of coffee that she had filled too full. She sat down carefully and began to eat, meaning to keep Mrs. Freeman there by questions if for any reason she showed an inclination to leave. She could perceive her mother's eye on her. The first round-about question would be about the Bible salesman and she did not wish to bring it on. "How did he pop her neck?" she asked.

Mrs. Freeman went into a description of how he had popped her neck. She said he owned a'55 Mercury but that Glynese said she would rather marry a man with only a'36 Plymouth who would be married by a preacher. The girl asked what if he had a'32 Plymouth and Mrs. Freeman said what Glynese had said was a'36 Plymouth.

Mrs. Hopewell said there were not many girls with Glynese's common sense. She said what she admired in those girls was their common sense. She said that reminded her that they had had a nice visitor yesterday, a young man selling Bibles. "Lord," she said, "he bored me to death but he was so sincere and genuine I couldn't be rude to him. He was just good country people, you know," she said, "— just the salt of the earth❶."

"I seen him walk up," Mrs. Freeman said, "and then later — I seen him walk off," and Hulga could feel the slight shift in her voice, the slight insinuation, that he had not walked off alone, had he? Her face remained expressionless but the color rose into her neck and she seemed to swallow it down with the next spoonful of egg. Mrs. Freeman was looking at her as if they had a secret together.

"Well, it takes all kinds of people to make the world go 'round'," Mrs. Hopewell said. "It's very good we aren't all alike."

"Some people are more alike than others," Mrs. Freeman said.

Hulga got up and stumped, with about twice the noise that was necessary, into her room and locked the door. She was to meet the Bible salesman at ten o'clock at the gate. She had thought about it half the night. She had started thinking of it as a

---

❶ The salt of the earth: someone who is ordinary but good and honest.

great joke and then she had begun to see profound implications in it. She had lain in bed imagining dialogues for them that were insane on the surface but that reached below the depths that no Bible salesman would be aware of. Their conversation yesterday had been of this kind.

He had stopped in front of her and had simply stood there. His face was bony and sweaty and bright, with a little pointed nose in the center of it, and his look was different from what it had been at the dinner table. He was gazing at her with open curiosity, with fascination, like a child watching a new fantastic animal at the zoo, and he was breathing as if he had run a great distance to reach her. His gaze seemed somehow familiar but she could not think where she had been regarded with it before. For almost a minute he didn't say anything. Then on what seemed an insuck of breath, he whispered, "You ever ate a chicken that was two days old?"

The girl looked at him stonily. He might have just put this question up for consideration at the meeting of a philosophical association. "Yes," she presently replied as if she had considered it from all angles.

"It must have been mighty small!" he said triumphantly and shook all over with little nervous giggles, getting very red in the face, and subsiding finally into his gaze of complete admiration, while the girl's expression remained exactly the same.

"How old are you?" he asked softly.

She waited some time before she answered. Then in a flat voice she said, "Seventeen."

His smiles came in succession like waves breaking on the surface of a little lake. "I see you got a wooden leg," he said. "I think you're real brave. I think you're real sweet."

The girl stood blank and solid and silent.

"Walk to the gate with me," he said. "You're a brave sweet little thing and I liked you the minute I seen you walk in the door."

Hulga began to move forward.

"What's your name?" he asked, smiling down on the top of her head.

"Hulga," she said.

"Hulga," he murmured, "Hulga. Hulga. I never heard of anybody name Hulga before. You're shy, aren't you, Hulga?" he asked.

She nodded, watching his large red hand on the handle of the giant valise.

"I like girls that wear glasses," he said. "I think a lot. I'm not like these people that a serious thought don't ever enter their heads. It's because I may die."

"I may die too," she said suddenly and looked up at him. His eyes were very small and brown, glittering feverishly.

"Listen," he said, "don't you think some people was meant to meet on account of what all they got in common and all? Like they both think serious thoughts and all?" He shifted the valise to his other hand so that the hand nearest her was free. He caught hold of her elbow and shook it a little. "I don't work on Saturday," he said. "I like to walk in the woods and see what Mother Nature is wearing. O'er the hills and far away. Picnics and things. Couldn't we go on a picnic tomorrow? Say yes, Hulga," he said and gave her a dying look as if he felt his insides about to drop out of him. He had even seemed to sway slightly toward her.

During the night she had imagined that she seduced him. She imagined that the two of them walked on the place until they came to the storage barn beyond the two back fields and there, she imagined, that things came to such a pass that she very easily seduced him and that then, of course, she had to reckon with his remorse. True genius can get an idea across even to an inferior mind. She imagined that she took his remorse in hand and changed it into a deeper understanding of life. She took all his shame away and turned it into something useful.

She set off for the gate at exactly ten o'clock, escaping without drawing Mrs. Hopewell's attention. She didn't take anything to eat, forgetting that food is usually taken on a picnic. She wore a pair of slacks and a dirty white shirt, and as an afterthought, she had put some Vapex on the collar of it since she did not own any perfume. When she reached the gate no one was there.

She looked up and down the empty highway and had the furious feeling that she had been tricked, that he only meant to make her walk to the gate after the idea of him. Then suddenly he stood up, very tall, from behind a bush on the opposite embankment. Smiling, he lifted his hat which was new and wide-brimmed. He had not worn it yesterday and she wondered if he had bought it for the occasion. It was toast-colored with a red and white band around it and was slightly too large for him. He stepped from behind the bush still carrying the black valise. He had on the same suit and the same yellow socks sucked down in his shoes from walking. He crossed the highway and said, "I knew you'd come!"

The girl wondered acidly how he had known this. She pointed to the valise and asked, "Why did you bring your Bibles?"

He took her elbow, smiling down on her as if he could not stop. "You can never tell when you'll need the word of God, Hulga," he said. She had a moment in which she doubted that this was actually happening and then they began to climb the embankment. They went down into the pasture toward the woods. The boy walked lightly by her side, bouncing on his toes. The valise did not seem to be heavy today; he even swung it. They crossed half the pasture without saying anything and then, putting his hand easily on the small of her back, he asked softly, "Where does your wooden leg join on?"

She turned an ugly red and glared at him and for an instant the boy looked abashed. "I didn't mean you no harm," he said. "I only meant you're so brave and all. I guess God takes care of you."

"No," she said, looking forward and walking fast, "I don't even believe in God."

At this he stopped and whistled. "No!" he exclaimed as if he were too astonished to say anything else.

She walked on and in a second he was bouncing at her side, fanning with his hat. "That's very unusual for a girl," he remarked, watching her out of the corner of his eye. When they reached the edge of the wood, he put his hand on her back again and drew her against him without a word and kissed her heavily.

The kiss, which had more pressure than feeling behind it, produced that extra surge of adrenalin in the girl that enables one to carry a packed trunk out of a burning house, but in her, the power went at once to the brain. Even before he released her, her mind, clear and detached and ironic anyway, was regarding him from a great distance, with amusement but with pity. She had never been kissed before and she was pleased to discover that it was an unexceptional experience and all a matter of the mind's control. Some people might enjoy drain water if they were told it was vodka. When the boy, looking expectant but uncertain, pushed her gently away, she turned and walked on, saying nothing as if such business, for her, were common enough.

He came along panting at her side, trying to help her when he saw a root that she might trip over. He caught and held back the long swaying blades of thorn vine until she had passed beyond them. She led the way and he came breathing heavily behind her. Then they came out on a sunlit hillside, sloping softly into another one a little smaller. Beyond, they could see the rusted top of the old barn where the extra hay was stored.

The hill was sprinkled with small pink weeds. "Then you ain't saved?" he asked suddenly, stopping.

The girl smiled. It was the first time she had smiled at him at all. "In my economy," she said, "I'm saved and you are damned but I told you I didn't believe in God."

Nothing seemed to destroy the boy's look of admiration. He gazed at her now as if the fantastic animal at the zoo had put its paw through the bars and given him a loving poke. She thought he looked as if he wanted to kiss her again and she walked on before he had the chance.

"Ain't there somewheres we can sit down sometime?" he murmured, his voice softening toward the end of the sentence.

"In that barn," she said.

They made for it rapidly as if it might slide away like a train. It was a large two-story barn, cool and dark inside. The boy pointed up the ladder that led into the loft and said, "It's too bad we can't go up there."

"Why can't we?" she asked.

"Yer leg," he said reverently.

The girl gave him a contemptuous look and putting both hands on the ladder, she climbed it while he stood below, apparently awestruck. She pulled herself expertly through the opening and then looked down at him and said, "Well, come on if you're coming," and he began to climb the ladder, awkwardly bringing the suitcase with him.

"We won't need the Bible," she observed.

"You never can tell," he said, panting. After he had got into the loft, he was a few seconds catching his breath. She had sat down in a pile of straw. A wide sheath of sunlight, filled with dust particles, slanted over her. She lay back against a bale, her face turned away, looking out the front opening of the barn where hay was thrown from a wagon into the loft. The two pink-speckled hillsides lay back against a dark ridge of woods. The sky was cloudless and cold blue. The boy dropped down by her side and put one arm under her and the other over her and began methodically kissing her face, making little noises like a fish. He did not remove his hat but it was pushed far enough back not to interfere. When her glasses got in his way, he took them off of her and slipped them into his pocket.

The girl at first did not return any of the kisses but presently she began to and after she had put several on his cheek, she reached his lips and remained there, kissing him again and again as if she were trying to draw all the breath out of him. His breath was clear and sweet like a child's and the kisses were sticky like a child's. He mumbled about loving her and about knowing when he first seen her that he loved her, but the mumbling was like the sleepy fretting of a child being put to sleep by his mother. Her mind, throughout this, never stopped or lost itself for a second to her feelings. "You ain't said you loved me none," he whispered finally, pulling back from her. "You got to say that."

She looked away from him off into the hollow sky and then down at a black ridge and then down farther into what appeared to be two green swelling lakes. She didn't realize he had taken her glasses but this landscape could not seem exceptional to her for she seldom paid any close attention to her surroundings.

"You got to say it," he repeated. "You got to say you love me."

She was always careful how she committed herself. "In a sense," she began, "if you use the word loosely, you might say that. But it's not a word I use. I don't have illusions. I'm one of those people who see through to nothing."

The boy was frowning. "You got to say it. I said it and you got to say it," he said.

The girl looked at him almost tenderly. "You poor baby," she murmured. "It's just as well you don't understand," and she pulled him by the neck, face-down, against her. "We are all damned," she said, "but some of us have taken off our blindfolds and see that there's nothing to see. It's a kind of salvation."

The boy's astonished eyes looked blankly through the ends of her hair. "Okay," he almost whined, "but do you love me or don'tcher?"

"Yes," she said and added, "in a sense. But I must tell you something. There mustn't be anything dishonest between us." She lifted his head and looked him in the eye. "I am thirty years old," she said. "I have a number of degrees."

The boy's look was irritated but dogged. "I don't care," he said. "I don't care a thing about what all you done. I just want to know if you love me or don'tcher?" and he caught her to him and wildly planted her face with kisses until she said, "Yes, yes."

"Okay then," he said, letting her go. "Prove it."

She smiled, looking dreamily out on the shifty landscape. She had seduced him without even making up her mind to try. "How?" she asked, feeling that he should be delayed a little.

He leaned over and put his lips to her ear. "Show me where your wooden leg joins on," he whispered.

The girl uttered a sharp little cry and her face instantly drained of color. The obscenity of the suggestion was not what shocked her. As a child she had sometimes been subject to feelings of shame but education had removed the last traces of that as a good surgeon scrapes for cancer; she would no more have felt it over what he was asking than she would have believed in his Bible. But she was as sensitive about the artificial leg as a peacock about his tail. No one ever touched it but her. She took care of it as someone else would his soul, in private and almost with her own eyes turned away. "No," she said.

"I known it," he muttered, sitting up. "You're just playing me for a sucker."

"On no no!" she cried. "It joins on at the knee. Only at the knee. Why do you want to see it?"

The boy gave her a long penetrating look. "Because," he said, "it's what makes you different. You ain't like anybody else."

She sat staring at him. There was nothing about her face or her round freezing-blue eyes to indicate that this had moved her; but she felt as if her heart had stopped and left her mind to pump her blood. She decided that for the first time in her life she was face to face with real innocence. This boy, with an instinct that came from beyond wisdom, had touched the truth about her. When after a minute, she said in a hoarse high voice, "All right," it was like surrendering to him completely. It was like losing her own life and finding it again, miraculously, in his.

Very gently, he began to roll the slack leg up. The artificial limb, in a white sock and brown flat shoe, was bound in a heavy material like canvas and ended in an ugly jointure where it was attached to the stump. The boy's face and his voice were entirely reverent as he uncovered it and said, "Now show me how to take it off and on."

She took it off for him and put it back on again and then he took it off himself, handling it as tenderly as if it were a real one. "See!" he said with a delighted child's face. "Now I can do it myself!"

"Put it back on," she said. She was thinking that she would run away with him and that every night he would take the leg off and every morning put it back on again. "Put it back on," she said.

"Not yet," he murmured, setting it on its foot out of her reach. "Leave it off for awhile. You got me instead."

She gave a little cry of alarm but he pushed her down and began to kiss her again. Without the leg she felt entirely dependent on him. Her brain seemed to have stopped thinking altogether and to be about some other function that it was not very good at. Different expressions raced back and forth over her face. Every now and then the boy, his eyes like two steel spikes, would glance behind him where the leg stood. Finally she pushed him off and said, "Put it back on me now."

"Wait," he said. He leaned the other way and pulled the valise toward him and opened it. It had a pale blue spotted lining and there were only two Bibles in it. He took one of these out and opened the cover of it. It was hollow and contained a pocket flask of whiskey, a pack of cards, and a small blue box with printing on it. He laid these out in front of her one at a time in an evenly-spaced row, like one presenting offerings at the shrine of a goddess. He put the blue box in her hand. THIS PRODUCT TO BE USED ONLY FOR THE PREVENTION OF DISEASE, she read, and dropped it. The boy was unscrewing the top of the flask. He stopped and pointed, with a smile, to the deck of cards. It was not an ordinary deck but one with an obscene picture on the back of each card. "Take a swig," he said, offering her the bottle first. He held it in front of her, but like one mesmerized, she did not move.

Her voice when she spoke had an almost pleading sound. "Aren't you," she murmured, "aren't you just good country people?"

The boy cocked his head. He looked as if he were just beginning to understand that she might be trying to insult him. "Yeah," he said, curling his lip slightly, "but it ain't held me back none. I'm as good as you any day in the week."

"Give me my leg," she said.

He pushed it farther away with his foot. "Come on now, let's begin to have us a good time," he said coaxingly. "We ain't got to know one another good yet."

"Give me my leg!" she screamed and tried to lunge for it but he pushed her down easily.

"What's the matter with you all of a sudden?" he asked, frowning as he screwed the top on the flask and put it quickly back inside the Bible. "You just a while ago said you didn't believe in nothing. I thought you was some girl!"

Her face was almost purple. "You're a Christian!" she hissed. "You're a fine Christian! You're just like them all — say one thing and do another. You're a perfect Christian, you're..."

The boy's mouth was set angrily. "I hope you don't think," he said in a lofty indignant tone, "that I believe in that crap! I may sell Bibles but I know which end is up and I wasn't born yesterday and I know where I'm going!"

"Give me my leg!" she screeched. He jumped up so quickly that she barely saw him sweep the cards and the blue box back into the Bible and throw the Bible into the valise. She saw him grab the leg and then she saw it for an instant slanted forlornly across the inside of the suitcase with a Bible at either side of its opposite ends. He slammed the lid shut and snatched up the valise and swung it down the hole and then stepped through himself. When all of him had passed but his head, he turned and regarded her with a look that no longer had any admiration in it. "I've gotten a lot of interesting things," he said. "One time I got a woman's glass eye this way. And you needn't to think you'll catch me because Pointer ain't really my name. I use a different name at every house I call at and don't stay nowhere long. And I'll tell you another thing, Hulga," he said, using the name as if he didn't think much of it, "you ain't so smart. I been believing in nothing ever since I was born!" and then the toast-colored hat disappeared down the hole and the girl was left, sitting on the straw in the dusty sunlight. When she turned her churning face toward the opening, she saw his blue figure struggling successfully over the green speckled lake.

Mrs. Hopewell and Mrs. Freeman, who were in the back pasture, digging up onions, saw him emerge a little later from the woods and head across the meadow toward the highway. "Why, that looks like that nice dull young man that tried to sell me a Bible yesterday," Mrs. Hopewell said, squinting. "He must have been selling them to the Negroes back in there. He was so simple," she said, "but I guess the world would be better off if we were all that simple."

Mrs. Freeman's gaze drove forward and just touched him before he disappeared under the hill. Then she returned her attention to the evil-smelling onion shoot she was lifting from the ground. "Some can't be that simple," she said. "I know I never could."

(The text is selected from *A Good Man Is Hard to Find* (1955).)

Questions for discussion:

1. How does Joy-Hulga regard herself? Is she as worldly and free of illusions as she imagines herself to be? Cite examples to support your views.
2. How appropriate are the names of each of characters?
3. Do Mrs. Hopewell's characters in any way help to explain her daughter's character?
4. Is there anything ironic about the title? Make comment on the irony in the story and the ways in which it is conveyed.

Toni Morrison (1931 —)

The 1993 Nobel Laureate in literature, Toni Morrison is a novelist of great importance in her own right and has been the central figure in putting fiction (by and about African American women) at the forefront of the late-twentieth-century literary canon. Whereas the legacy of slavery had effaced a usable traditional, and critical stereotypes at times restricted such writer's range, Morrison's fiction serves as a model for reconstructing a culturally empowering past. She joins the great American tradition of self-invention: her own example and her editorial work have figured importantly in the careers of other writers, such as Toni Cade Bambara (included in this volume) and Gayl Jones.

Morrison was born in Lorain, Ohio, where much of her fiction is set (a departure from earlier African American narratives typically located in the rural South or urban

North). Having earned a B. A. From Howard with a major in English and minor in Classics, and an M. A. from Cornell University (with a thesis on suicide in the novels of Virginia Woolf and William Faulkner), Morrison began a teaching career in 1955 that reached from Texas Southern University back to Howard, where her students included the future activist Stokeley Carmichael and the future critic Houston A. Baker Jr. At this time she married Harold Morrison, a Jamaican architect, with whom she had two children before ending their marriage in 1964. Already writing, she took a job with the publishing firm of Random House and eventually settled in New York City, where she worked until 1983. During these same years she held visiting teaching appointments at institutions including Yale University and Bard College.

As a first novel, *The Bluest Eye* (1970) is uncommonly mature for its confident use of a variety of narrative voices. Throughout her career Morrison will be dedicated to constructing a practical cultural identity of both a race and a gender whose self-images have been obscured or denied by dominating forces, and in *The Bluest Eye* she already shows that narrative strategy is an important element in such construction. It is a girl's need to be loved that generates the novel's action, action that involves displaced and alienated affections (and eventually incestuous rape); it is the family's inability to produce a style of existence in which love can be born and thrive that leads to such a devastating fate for Morrison's protagonist. Love is also denied in *Sula* (1974), in which relationships extend in two directions: between contemporaries (Sula and her friend Nel) and with previous generations.

With *Song of Solomon* (1977) Morrison seeks more positive redemption of her characters. Turning away from his parents', loveless marriage, Milkman Dead makes a physical and mental journey to his ancestral roots. Here he discovers a more useful legacy in communal tales about Grandmother and Great-Grandfather, each long dead but infusing the local culture with emotionally sustaining lore. It is this lore that Milkman uses to learn how the spiritual guidance offered by his aunt Pilate eclipses the material concerns of his parents' world.

Allegory becomes an important strategy in *Tar Baby* (1981), drawing on the strong folk culture of Haiti where two contrasting persons form a troubled relationship based on their own distinct searches for and rejections of a heritage. Yet it is in a rebuilding of history, rather than allegory or myth, that Morrison achieves her great strength as a novelist in *Beloved* (1987), the winner of her first major award, the Pulitzer Prize. Set in the middle 1870s, when race relations in America were at their most crucial juncture (slavery having ended and the course of the South's Reconstruction not yet fully determined), this novel shows a mother (Sethe) being haunted and eventually destroyed by the ghost of a daughter (Beloved) whom she had killed eighteen years earlier rather that let her be taken by a vicious slavemaster. This novel is central to Morrison's canon because it involves so many important themes and techniques, from love and guilt to history's role in clarifying the past's influence on the present, all told in a style of magical realism that transforms (without denying) more mundane facts.

With *Jazz* (1992) Morrison reinforces her strategy of narrative voice, here modeled on the progression of a jazz solo to demonstrate how improvisation with detail can change the nature of what is expressed. Present and past weave together in her characters' lives as the narrative seeks to understand the jealousies of love and the sometimes macabre manifestations of hatred.

Presently serving as the prestigious Golheen Professor of the Humanities at Princeton University, Morrison has moved easily into the role of spokesperson for literary issues. Together with her Nobel lecture, her essays collected as *Playing in the Dark: Whiteness and the Literary Imagination* (1992) challenge stereotypes in white critical thinking about black literature. Her short story *Recitatif*, written for the 1983 anthology edited by Amiri and Amina Baraka, *Confirmation*, directly addresses the issues of individual and family, past and present, and race and its effacements that motivate the larger sense of her work. A *recitatif* is a vocal performance in which a narrative is not stated but sung. In her work Toni Morrison's voice sings proudly of a past that in the artistic nature of its reconstruction puts all Americans in touch with a more positively usable heritage.

(The text is selected from *The Norton Anthology of American Literature* (Shorter Fifth Edition))

Major Works:

Novels:

- *The Bluest Eye*, 1970 《最蓝的眼睛》
- *Sula*, 1973 《秀拉》
- *Song of Solomon*, 1977 《所罗门之歌》
- *Tar Baby*, 1981 《柏油娃》
- *Retitatif*, 1983 《宣叙》
- *Beloved*, 1987 《宠儿》(普利策奖)
- *Jazz*, 1992 《爵士乐》
- *Paradise*, 1998 《天堂》
- *Love*, 2003 《爱》
- *A Mercy*, 2008 《慈善》

Other Works:

Dreaming Emmett, 1986 《做梦的埃梅特》
Playing in the Dark: *Whiteness and the Literary Imagination*, 1992 《在黑暗中游戏：白人性与文学想象》
Race-ing Justice, *En-gendering Power*: *Essays on Anita Hill*, *Clarence Thomas*, *and the Constructing of Social Reality*, 1992 《种族公正，权利的产生：评述安妮塔·希尔、克拉伦斯·托马斯及建构社会现实的他者们》
Unspeakable Things Unspoken: *The Afro-American Presence in American Literature*, 1989 《不可言说之不被言说：美国文学中的非裔美国人》
The Big Box, 1999 《大盒子》

Recitatif[1]

My mother danced all night and Roberta's was sick. That's why we were taken to St. Bonny's. People want to put their arms around you when you tell them you were

[1] *Recitatif* is Toni Morrison's only published short story.

in a shelter, but it really wasn't bad. No big long room with one hundred beds like Bellevue[1]. There were four to a room, and when Roberta and me came, there was a shortage of state kids, so we were the only ones assigned to 406 and could go from bed to bed if we wanted to. And we wanted to, too. We changed beds every night and for the whole four months we were there we never picked one out as our own permanent bed.

It didn't start out that way. The minute I walked in and the Big Bozo introduced us, I got sick to my stomach. It was one thing to be taken out of your own bed early in the morning — it was something else to be stuck in a strange place with a girl from a whole other race. And Mary, that's my mother, she was right. Every now and then she would stop dancing long enough to tell me something important and one of the things she said was that they never washed their hair and they smelled funny. Roberta sure did. Smell funny, I mean. So when the Big Bozo (nobody ever called her Mrs. Itkin, just like nobody every said St. Bonaventure) — when she said, "Twyla, this is Roberta. Roberta, this is Twyla. Make each other welcome." I said, "My mother won't like you putting me in here."

"Good," said Bozo. "Maybe then she'll come and take you home."

How's that for mean? If Roberta had laughed I would have killed her, but she didn't. She just walked over to the window and stood with her back to us.

"Turn around," said the Bozo. "Don't be rude. Now Twyla. Roberta. When you hear a loud buzzer, that's the call for dinner. Come down to the first floor. Any fights and no movie." And then, just to make sure we knew what we would be missing, "The Wizard of Oz[2]."

Roberta must have thought I meant that my mother would be mad about my being put in the shelter. Not about rooming with her, because as soon as Bozo left she came over to me and said, "Is your mother sick too?"

---

[1] Bellevue Hospital in New York City is known for its psychiatric ward. St. Bonaventure's offers the services of a youth shelter and school.

[2] The famous children's book published in 1900 by American writer L. Frank Baum (1856 — 1919); it was made into a film in 1939.

"No," I said. "She just likes to dance all night."

"Oh," she nodded her head and I liked the way she understood things so fast. So for the moment it didn't matter that we looked like salt and pepper standing there and that's what the other kids called us sometimes. We were eight years old and got F's all the time. Me because I couldn't remember what I read or what the teacher said. And Roberta because she couldn't read at all and didn't even listen to the teacher. She wasn't good at anything except jacks, at which she was a killer: pow scoop pow scoop pow scoop.

We didn't like each other all that much at first, but nobody else wanted to play with us because we weren't real orphans with beautiful dead parents in the sky. We were dumped. Even the New York City Puerto Ricans and the upstate Indians ignored us. All kinds of kids were in there, black ones, white ones, even two Koreans. The food was good, though. At least I thought so. Roberta hated it and left whole pieces of things on her plate: Spam, Salisbury steak — even jello with fruit cocktail in it, and she didn't care if I ate what she wouldn't. Mary's idea of supper was popcorn and a can of Yoo-Hoo❶. Hot mashed potatoes and two weenies was like Thanksgiving for me.

It really wasn't bad, St. Bonny's. The big girls on the second floor pushed us around now and then. But that was all. They wore lipstick and eyebrow pencil and wobbled their knees while they watched TV. Fifteen, sixteen, even, some of them were. They were put-out girls, scared runaways most of them. Poor little girls who fought their uncles off but looked tough to us, and mean. God did they look mean. The staff tried to keep them separate from the younger children, but sometimes they caught us watching them in the orchard where they played radios and danced with each other. They'd light out after us and pull our hair or twist our arms. We were scared of them, Roberta and me, but neither of us wanted the other one to know it. So we got a good list of dirty names we could shout back when we ran from them through the orchard. I used to dream a lot and almost always the orchard was there.

---

❶ A chocolate soft drink.

Two acres, four maybe, of these little apple trees. Hundreds of them. Empty and crooked like beggar women when I first came to St. Bonny's but fat with flowers when I left. I don't know why I dreamt about that orchard so much. Nothing really happened there. Nothing all that important, I mean. Just the big girls dancing and playing the radio. Roberta and me watching. Maggie fell down there once. The kitchen woman with legs like parentheses. And the big girls laughed at her. We should have helped her up, I know, but we were scared of those girls with lipstick and eyebrow pencil. Maggie couldn't talk. The kids said she had her tongue cut out, but I think she was just born that way: mute. She was old and sandy-colored and she worked in the kitchen. I don't know if she was nice or not. I just remember her legs like parentheses and how she rocked when she walked. She worked from early in the morning till two o'clock, and if she was late, if she had too much cleaning and didn't get out till two-fifteen or so, she'd cut through the orchard so she wouldn't miss her bus and have to wait another hour. She wore this really stupid little hat — a kid's hat with ear flaps — and she wasn't much taller than we were. A really awful little hat. Even for a mute, it was dumb — dressing like a kid and never saying anything at all.

But what about if somebody tries to kill her? "I used to wonder about that." Or what if she wants to cry? Can she cry?

"Sure," Roberta said. "But just tears. No sounds come out."

"She can't scream?"

"Nope. Nothing."

"Can she hear?"

"I guess."

"Let's call her," I said. And we did.

"Dummy! Dummy!" She never turned her head.

"Bow legs! Bow legs!" Nothing. She just rocked on, the chin straps of her baby-boy hat swaying from side to side. I think we were wrong. I think she could hear and didn't let on. And it shames me even now to think there was somebody in there after all who heard us call her those names and couldn't tell on us.

We got along all right, Roberta and me. Changed beds every night, got F's in civics and communication skills and gym. The Bozo was disappointed in us, she said. Out of 130 of us state cases, 90 were under twelve. Almost all were real orphans with beautiful dead parents in the sky. We were the only ones dumped and the only ones with F's in three classes including gym. So we got along — what with her leaving whole pieces of things on her plate and being nice about not asking questions.

I think it was the day before Maggie fell down that we found out our mothers were coming to visit us on the same Sunday. We had been at the shelter twenty-eight days (Roberta twenty-eight and a half) and this was their first visit with us. Our mothers would come at ten o'clock in time for chapel, then lunch with us in the teachers' lounge. I thought if my dancing mother met her sick mother it might be good for her. And Roberta thought her sick mother would get a big bang out of a dancing one. We got excited about it and curled each other's hair. After breakfast we sat on the bed watching the road from the window. Roberta's socks were still wet. She washed them the night before and put them on the radiator to dry. They hadn't, but she put them on anyway because their tops were so pretty — scalloped in pink. Each of us had a purple construction-paper basket that we had made in craft class. Mine had a yellow crayon rabbit on it. Roberta's had eggs with wiggly lines of color. Inside were cellophane grass and just the jelly beans because I'd eaten the two marshmallow eggs they gave us. The Big Bozo came herself to get us. Smiling she told us we looked very nice and to come downstairs. We were so surprised by the smile we'd never seen before, neither of us moved.

"Don't you want to see your mommies?"

I stood up first and spilled the jelly beans all over the floor. Bozo's smile disappeared while we scrambled to get the candy up off the floor and put it back in the grass.

She escorted us downstairs to the first floor, where the other girls were lining up to file into the chapel. A bunch of grown-ups stood to one side. Viewers mostly. The old biddies who wanted servants and the fags who wanted company looking for children they might want to adopt. Once in a while a grandmother. Almost never anybody young or anybody whose face wouldn't scare you in the night. Because if any of the real orphans had young relatives they wouldn't be real orphans. I saw Mary right away. She had on those green slacks I hated and hated even more now because didn't she know we were going to chapel? And that fur jacket with the pocket linings so ripped she had to pull to get her hands out of them. But her face was pretty — like always, and she smiled and waved like she was the little girl looking for her mother — not me.

I walked slowly, trying not to drop the jelly beans and hoping the paper handle would hold. I had to use my last Chiclet because by the time I finished cutting everything out, all the Elmer's was gone. I am left-handed and the scissors never worked for me. It didn't matter, though; I might just as well have chewed the gum. Mary dropped to her knees and grabbed me, mashing the basket, the jelly beans, and the grass into her ratty fur jacket.

"Twyla, baby. Twyla, baby!"

I could have killed her. Already I heard the big girls in the orchard the next time saying, "Twyla, baby!" But I couldn't stay mad at Mary while she was smiling and hugging me and smelling of Lady Esther dusting powder. I wanted to stay buried in her fur all day.

To tell the truth I forgot about Roberta. Mary and I got in line for the traipse into chapel and I was feeling proud because she looked so beautiful even in those ugly green slacks that made her behind stick out. A pretty mother on earth is better than a beautiful dead one in the sky even if she did leave you all alone to go dancing.

I felt a tap on my shoulder, turned, and saw Roberta smiling. I smiled back, but not too much lest somebody think this visit was the biggest thing that ever happened in my life. Then Roberta said, "Mother, I want you to meet my roommate, Twyla. And that's Twyla's mother."

I looked up it seemed for miles. She was big. Bigger than any man and on her chest was the biggest cross I'd ever seen. I swear it was six inches long each way. And in the crook of her arm was the biggest Bible ever made.

Mary, simple-minded as ever, grinned and tried to yank her hand out of the pocket with the raggedy lining — to shake hands, I guess. Roberta's mother looked down at me and then looked down at Mary too. She didn't say anything, just grabbed Roberta with her Bible-free hand and stepped tout of line, walking quickly to the rear of it. Mary was still grinning because she's not too swift when it comes to what's really going on. Then this light bulb goes off in her head and she says "That bitch!" really loud and us almost in the chapel now. Organ music whining; the Bonny Angels singing sweetly. Everybody in the world turned around to look. And Mary would have kept it up — kept calling names if I hadn't squeezed her hand as hard as I could. That helped a little, but she still twitched and crossed and uncrossed her legs all through service. Even groaned a couple of times. Why did I think she would come there and act right? Slacks. No hat like the grandmothers and viewers, and groaning all the while. When we stood for hymns she kept her mouth shut. Wouldn't even look at the words on the page. She actually reached in her purse for a mirror to check her lipstick. All I could think of was that she really needed to be killed. The sermon lasted a year, and I knew the real orphans were looking smug again.

We were supposed to have lunch in the teachers' lounge, but Mary didn't bring anything, so we picked fur and cellophane grass off the mashed jelly beans and ate them. I could have killed her. I sneaked a look at Roberta. Her mother had brought chicken legs and ham sandwiches and oranges and a whole box of chocolate-covered grahams. Roberta drank milk from a thermos while her mother read the Bible to her.

Things are not right. The wrong food is always with the wrong people. Maybe that's why I got into waitress work later — to match up the right people with the right food. Roberta just let those chicken legs sit there, but she did bring a stack of grahams up to me later when the visit was over. I think she was sorry that her mother would not shake my mother's hand. And I liked that and I liked the fact that she didn't say a word about Mary groaning all the way through the service and not bringing any lunch.

Roberta left in May when the apple trees were heavy and white. On her last day we went to the orchard to watch the big girls smoke and dance by the radio. It didn't matter that they said, "Twyyyyyla, baby." We sat on the ground and breathed. Lady Esther. Apple blossoms. I still go soft when I smell one or the other. Roberta was going home. The big cross and the big Bible was coming to get her and she seemed sort of glad and sort of not. I thought I would die in that room of four beds without her and I knew Bozo had plans to move some other dumped kid in there with me. Roberta promised to write every day, which was really sweet of her because she couldn't read a lick so how could she write anybody. I would have drawn pictures and sent them to her but she never gave me her address. Little by little she faded. Her wet socks with the pink scalloped tops and her big serious-looking eyes — that's all I could catch when I tried to bring her to mind.

I was working behind the counter at the Howard Johnson's on the Thruway just before the Kingston exit. Not a bad job. Kind of a long ride from Newburgh[1], but okay once I got there. Mine was the second night shift — eleven to seven. Very light until a Greyhound checked in for breakfast around six-thirty. At that hour the sun was all the way clear of the hills behind the restaurant. The place looked better at night — more like shelter — but I loved it when the sun broke in, even if it did show all the cracks in the vinyl and the speckled floor looked dirty no matter what the mop boy did.

It was August and a bus crowd was just unloading. They would stand around a long while: going to the john, and looking at gifts and junk-for-sale machines, reluctant to sit down so soon. Even to eat. I was trying to fill the coffee pots and get them all situated on the electric burners when I saw her. She was sitting in a booth smoking a cigarette with two guys smothered in head and facial hair. Her own hair was so big and wild I could hardly see her face. But the eyes. I would know them anywhere. She had on a powder-blue halter and shorts outfit and earrings the size of bracelets. Talk about lipstick and eyebrow pencil. She made the big girls look like nuns. I couldn't get off the counter until seven o'clock, but I kept watching the

---

[1] A community eighty miles north of New York City.

booth in case they got up to leave before that. My replacement was on time for a change, so I counted and stacked my receipts as fast as I could and signed off. I walked over to the booths, smiling and wondering if she would remember me. Or even if she wanted to remember me. Maybe she didn't want to be reminded of St. Bonny's or to have anybody know she was ever there. I know I never talked about it to anybody.

I put my hands in my apron pockets and leaned against the back of the booth facing them.

"Roberta? Roberta Fisk?"

She looked up. "Yeah?"

"Twyla."

She squinted for a second and then said, "Wow."

"Remember me?"

"Sure. Hey. Wow."

"It's been a while," I said, and gave a smile to the two hairy guys.

"Yeah. Wow. You work here?"

"Yeah," I said. "I live in Newburgh."

"Newburgh? No kidding?" She laughed then a private laugh that included the guys but only the guys, and they laughed with her. What could I do but laugh too and wonder why I was standing there with my knees showing out from under that uniform. Without looking I could see the blue and white triangle on my head, my hair shapeless in a net, my ankles thick in white oxfords. Nothing could have been less sheer than my stockings. There was this silence that came downright after I laughed. A silence it was her turn to fill up. With introductions, maybe, to her boyfriends or an invitation to sit down and have a Coke. Instead she lit a cigarette off the one she'd just finished and said, "We're on our way to the Coast. He's got an appointment with Hendrix." She gestured casually toward the boy next to her.

"Hendrix[1] Fantastic," I said. "Really fantastic. What's she doing now?"

---

[1] Jimi Hendrix (1942-1970), American musician and rock music superstar.

Roberta coughed on her cigarette and the two guys rolled their eyes up at the ceiling.

"Hendrix. Jimi Hendrix, asshole. He's only the biggest — Oh, wow. Forget it."

I was dismissed without anyone saying goodbye, so I thought I would do it for her.

"How's your mother?" I asked. Her grin cracked her whole face. She swallowed. "Fine," she said. "How's yours?"

"Pretty as a picture," I said and turned away. The backs of my knees were damp. Howard Johnson's really was a dump in the sunlight.

James is as comfortable as a house slipper. He liked my cooking and I liked his big loud family. They have lived in Newburgh all of their lives and talk about it the way people do who have always known a home. His grandmother is a porch swing older than his father and when they talk about streets and avenues and buildings they call them names they no longer have. They still call the A & P[1] Rico's because it stands on property once a mom and pop store owned by Mr. Rico. And they call the new community college Town Hall because it once was. My mother-in-law puts up jelly and cucumbers and buys butter wrapped in cloth from a dairy. James and his father talk about fishing and baseball and I can see them all together on the Hudson in a raggedy skiff. Half the population of Newburgh is on welfare now, but to my husband's family it was still some upstate paradise of a time long past. A time of ice houses and vegetable wagons, coal furnaces and children weeding gardens. When our son was born my mother-in-law gave me the crib blanket that had been hers.

But the town they remembered had changed. Something quick was in the air. Magnificent old houses, so ruined they had become shelter for squatters and rent risks, were bought and renovated. Smart IBM people[2] moved out of their suburbs

[1] Supermarket, part of a national chain.

[2] High-salaried employees of the International Business Machine Corporation, headquartered in the suburbs of New York City.

back into the city and put shutters up and herb gardens in their backyards. A brochure came in the mail announcing the opening of a Food Emporium. Gourmet food it said — and listed items the rich IBM crowd would want. It was located in a new mall at the edge of town and I drove out to shop there one day — just to see. It was late in June. After the tulips were gone and the Queen Elizabeth roses were open everywhere. It railed my cart along the aisle tossing in smoked oysters and Robert's sauce and things I knew would sit in my cupboard for years. Only when I found some Klondike ice cream bars did I feel less guilty about spending James's fireman's salary so foolishly. My father-in-law ate them with the same gusto little Joseph did.

Waiting in the check-out line I heard a voice say, "Twyla!"

The classical music piped over the aisles had affected me and the woman leaning toward me was dressed to kill. Diamonds on her hand, a smart white summer dress. "I'm Mrs. Benson," I said.

"Ho. Ho. The Big Bozo," she sang.

For a split second I didn't know what she was talking about. She had a bunch of asparagus and two cartons of fancy water.

"Roberta!"

"Right."

"For heaven's sake. Roberta."

"You look great," she said.

"So do you. Where are you? Here? In Newburgh?"

"Yes. Over in Annandale."

I was opening my mouth to say more when the cashier called my attention to her empty counter.

"Meet you outside." Roberta pointed her finger and went into the express line.

I placed the groceries and kept myself from glancing around to check Roberta's progress. I remembered Howard Johnson's and looking for a chance to speak only to be greeted with a stingy "wow." But she was waiting for me and her huge hair was sleek now, smooth around a small, nicely shaped head. Shoes, dress, everything lovely and summery and rich. I was dying to know what happened to her, how she got from Jimi Hendrix to Annandale, a neighborhood full of doctors and IBM executives. Easy, I thought. Everything is so easy for them. They think they own the world.

"How long," I asked her. "How long have you been here?"

"A year. I got married to a man who lives here. And you, you're married too, right? Benson, you said."

"Yeah. James Benson."

"And is he nice?"

"Oh, is he nice?"

"Well, is he?" Roberta's eyes were steady as though she really meant the question and wanted an answer.

"He's wonderful, Roberta. Wonderful."

"So you're happy."

"Very."

"That's good," she said and nodded her head. "I always hoped you'd be happy. Any kids? I know you have kids."

"One. A boy. How about you?"

"Four."

"Four?"

She laughed. "Step kids. He's a widower."

"Oh."

"Got a minute? Let's have a coffee."

I thought about the Klondikes melting and the inconvenience of going all the way to my car and putting the bags in the trunk. Served me right for buying all that stuff I didn't need. Roberta was ahead of me.

"Put them in my car. It's right here."

And then I saw the dark blue limousine.

"You married a Chinaman?"

"No," she laughed. "He's the driver."

"Oh, my. If the Big Bozo could see you now."

We both giggled. Really giggled. Suddenly, in just a pulse beat, twenty years disappeared and all of it came rushing back. The big girls (whom we called gar girls — Roberta's misheard word for the evil stone faces described in a civics class) there dancing in the orchard, the ploppy mashed potatoes, the double weenies, the Spam with pineapple. We went into the coffee shop holding onto one another and I tried to think why we were glad to see each other this time and not before. Once, twelve years ago, we passed like strangers. A black girl and a white girl meeting in a Howard Johnson's on the road and having nothing to say. One in a blue and white triangle waitress hat — the other on her way to see Hendrix. Now we were behaving like sisters separated for much too long. Those four short months were nothing in time. Maybe it was the thing itself. Just being there, together. Two little girls who knew what nobody else in the world knew — how not to ask questions. How to believe what had to be believed. There was politeness in that reluctance and generosity as well. Is your mother sick too? No, she dances all night. Oh — and an understanding nod.

We sat in a booth by the window and fell into recollection like veterans.

"Did you ever learn to read?"

"Watch." She picked up the menu. "Special of the day. Cream of corn soup. Entrées. Two dots and a wriggly line. Quiche. Chef salad, scallops..."

I was laughing and applauding when the waitress came up.

"Remember the Easter baskets?"

"And how we tried to *introduce* them?"

"Your mother with that cross like two telephone poles."

"And yours with those tight slacks."

We laughed so loudly heads turned and made the laughter harder to suppress.

"What happened to the Jimi Hendrix date?"

Roberta made a blow-out sound with her lips.

"When he died I thought about you."

"Oh, you heard about him finally?"

"Finally. Come on, I was a small-town country waitress."

"And I was a small-town country dropout. God, were we wild. I still don't know how I got out of there alive."

"But you did."

"I did. I really did. Now I'm Mrs. Kenneth Norton."

"Sounds like a mouthful."

"It is."

"Servants and all?"

Roberta held up two fingers.

"Ow! What does he do?"

"Computers and stuff. What do I know?"

"I don't remember a hell of a lot from those days, but Lord, St. Bonny's is as clear as daylight. Remember Maggie? The day she fell down and those gar girls laughed at her?"

Roberta looked up from her salad and stared at me. "Maggie didn't fall," she said.

"Yes, she did. You remember."

"No, Twyla. They knocked her down. Those girls pushed her down and tore her clothes. In the orchard."

"I don't — that's not what happened."

"Sure it is. In the orchard. Remember how scared we were?"

"Wait a minute. I don't remember any of that."

"And Bozo was fired."

"You're crazy. She was there when I left. You left before me."

"I went back. You weren't there when they fired Bozo."

"What?"

"Twice. Once for a year when I was about ten, another for two months when I was fourteen. That's when I ran away."

"You ran away from St. Bonny's?"

"I had to. What do you want? Me dancing in that orchard?"

"Are you sure about Maggie?"

"Of course I'm sure. You've blocked it, Twyla. It happened. Those girls had behavior problems, you know."

"Didn't they, though. But why can't I remember the Maggie thing?"

"Believe me. It happened. And we were there."

"Who did you room with when you went back?" I asked her as if I would know her. The Maggie thing was troubling me.

"Creeps. They tickled themselves in the night."

My ears were itching and I wanted to go home suddenly. This was all very well but she couldn't just comb her hair, wash her face and pretend everything was hunky-dory. After the Howard Johnson's snub. And no apology. Nothing.

"Were you on dope or what that time at Howard Johnson's?" I tried to make my voice sound friendlier than I felt.

"Maybe, a little. I never did drugs much. Why?"

"I don't know; you acted sort of like you didn't want to know me then."

"Oh, Twyla, you know how it was in those days: black-white. You know how everything was."

But I didn't know. I thought it was just the opposite. Busloads of blacks and whites came into Howard Johnson's together. They roamed together then: students, musicians, lovers, protesters. You got to see everything at Howard Johnson's and blacks were very friendly with whites in those days. But sitting there with nothing on my plate but two hard tomato wedges wondering about the melting Klondikes it seemed childish remembering the slight. We went to her car, and with the help of the driver, got my stuff into my station wagon.

"We'll keep in touch this time," she said.

"Sure," I said. "Sure. Give me a call."

"I will," she said, and then just as I was sliding behind the wheel, she leaned into the window. "By the way. Your mother. Did she ever stop dancing?"

I shook my head. "No. Never."

Roberta nodded.

"And yours? Did she ever get well?"

She smiled a tiny sad smile. "No. She never did. Look, call me, okay?"

"Okay," I said, but I knew I wouldn't. Roberta had messed up my past somehow with that business about Maggie. I wouldn't forget a thing like that. Would I?

Strife came to us that fall. At least that's what the paper called it. Strife. Racial strife. The word made me think of a bird — a big shrieking bird out of 1,000,000,000 B. C. flapping its wings and cawing. Its eye with no lid always bearing down on you. All day it screeched and at night it slept on the rooftops. It woke you in the morning and from the *Today* show to the eleven o'clock news it kept you an awful company. I couldn't figure it out from one day to the next. I knew I was supposed to feel something strong, but I didn't know what, and James wasn't any help. Joseph was on the list of kids to be transferred from the junior high school to another one at some far-out-of-the-way place and I thought it was a good thing until I heard it was a bad thing. I mean I didn't know. All the schools seemed dumps to me, and the fact that one was nicer looking didn't hold much weight. But the papers were full of it and then the kids began to get jumpy. In August, mind you. Schools weren't even open yet. I thought Joseph might be frightened to go over there, but he didn't seem scared so I forgot about it, until I found myself driving along Hudson Street out there by the school they were trying to integrate and saw a line of women marching. And who do you suppose was in line, big as life, holding a sign in front of her bigger than her mother's cross? MOTHERS HAVE RIGHTS TOO! it said.

I drove on, and then changed my mind. I circled the block, slowed down, and honked my horn.

Roberta looked over and when she saw me she waved. I didn't wave back, but I didn't move either. She handed her sign to another woman and came over to where I was parked.

"Hi."

"What are you doing?"

"Picketing. What's it look like?"

"What for?"

"What do you mean 'What for?' They want to take my kids and send them out of the neighborhood. They don't want to go."

"So what if they go to another school? My boy's being bussed too, and I don't mind. Why should you?"

"It's not about us, Twyla. Me and you. It's about our kids."

"What's more *us* than that?"

"Well, it is a free country."

"Not yet, but it will be."

"What the hell does that mean? I'm not doing anything to you."

"You really think that?"

"I know it."

"I wonder what made me think you were different."

"I wonder what made me think you were different."

"Look at them," I said. "Just look. Who do they think they are? Swarming all over the place like they own it. And now they think they can decide where my child goes to school. Look at them, Roberta. They're Bozos."

Roberta turned around and looked at the women. Almost all of them were standing still now, waiting. Some were even edging toward us. Roberta looked at me out of some refrigerator behind her eyes. "No, they're not. They're just mothers."

"And what am I? Swiss cheese?"

"I used to curl your hair."

"I hated your hands in my hair."

The women were moving. Our faces looked mean to them of course and they looked as though they could not wait to throw themselves in front of a police car, or better yet, into my car and drag me away by my ankles. Now they surrounded my car and gently, gently began to rock it. I swayed back and forth like a sideways yo-yo. Automatically I reached for Roberta, like the old days in the orchard when they saw us watching them and we had to get out of there, and if one of us fell the other pulled her up and if one of us was caught the other stayed to kick and scratch, and neither would leave the other behind. My arm shot out of the car window but no receiving hand was there. Roberta was looking at me sway from side to side in the car and her face was still. My purse slid from the car seat down under the dashboard. The four policemen who had been drinking Tab[1] in their car finally got the message and strolled over, forcing their way through the women. Quietly, firmly they spoke. "Okay, ladies. Back in line or off the streets."

Some of them went away willingly; others had to be urged away from the car doors and the hood. Roberta didn't move. She was looking steadily at me. I was fumbling to turn on the ignition, which wouldn't catch because the gearshift was still in drive. The seats of the car were a mess because the swaying had thrown my grocery coupons all over it and my purse was sprawled on the floor.

"Maybe I am different now, Twyla. But you're not. You're the same little state kid who kicked a poor old black lady when she was down on the ground. You kicked a black lady and you have the nerve to call me a bigot."

The coupons were everywhere and the guts of my purse were bunched under the dashboard. What was she saying? Black? Maggie wasn't black.

"She wasn't black," I said.

"Like hell she wasn't, and you kicked her. We both did. You kicked a black lady who couldn't even scream."

"Liar!"

"You're the liar! Why don't you just go on home and leave us alone, huh?"

She turned away and I skidded away from the curb.

The next morning I went into the garage and cut the side out of the carton our portable TV had come in. It wasn't nearly big enough, but after a while I had a decent sign: red spray-painted letters on a white background—AND SO DO CHILDREN****. I meant just to go down to the school and tack it up somewhere so those cows on the picket line across the street could see it, but when I got there, some ten or so others had already assembled protesting the cows across the street. Police permits and everything. I got in line and we strutted in time on our side while Roberta's group strutted on theirs. That first day we were all dignified, pretending

---

[1] A carbonated diet soft drink.

the other side didn't exist. The second day there was name calling and finger gestures. But that was about all. People changed signs from time to time, but Roberta never did and neither did I. Actually my sign didn't make sense without Roberta's. "And so do children what?" one of the women on my side asked me. Have rights, I said, as though it was obvious.

Roberta didn't acknowledge my presence in any way and I got to thinking maybe she didn't know I was there. I began to pace myself in the line, jostling people one minute and lagging behind the next, so Roberta and I could reach the end of our respective lines at the same time and there would be a moment in our turn when we would face each other. Still, I couldn't tell whether she saw me and knew my sign was for her. The next day I went early before we were scheduled to assemble. I waited until she got there before I exposed my new creation. As soon as she hoisted her MOTHERS HAVE RIGHTS TOO I began to wave my new one, which said, HOW WOULD YOU KNOW? I know she saw that one, but I had gotten addicted now. My signs got crazier each day, and the women on my side decided that I was a kook. They couldn't make heads or tails out of my brilliant screaming posters.

I brought a painted sign in queenly red with huge black letters that said, IS YOUR MOTHER WELL? Roberta took her lunch break and didn't come back for the rest of the day or any day after. Two days later I stopped going too and couldn't have been missed because nobody understood my signs anyway.

It was a nasty six weeks. Classes were suspended and Joseph didn't go to anybody's school until October. The children — everybody's children — soon got bored with that extended vacation they thought was going to be so great. They looked at TV until their eyes flattened. I spent a couple of mornings tutoring my son, as the other mothers said we should. Twice I opened a text from last year that he had never turned in. Twice he yawned in my face. Other mothers organized living room sessions so the kids would keep up. None of the kids could concentrate so they drifted back to *The Price Is Right* and *The Brady Bunch*❶. When the school finally opened

❶ Respectively, a popular television game show and situation comedy.

there were fights once or twice and some sirens roared through the streets every once in a while. There were a lot of photographers from Albany. And just when ABC was about to send up a news crew, the kids settled down like nothing in the world had happened. Joseph hung my HOW WOULD YOU KNOW? sign in his bedroom. I don't know what became of AND SO DO CHILDREN****. I think my father-in-law cleaned some fish on it. He was always puttering around in our garage. Each of his five children lived in Newburgh and he acted as though he had five extra homes.

I couldn't help looking for Roberta when Joseph graduated from high school, but I didn't see her. It didn't trouble me much what she had said to me in the car. I mean the kicking part. I know I didn't do that, I couldn't do that. But I was puzzled by her telling me Maggie was black. When I thought about it I actually couldn't be certain. She wasn't pitch-black, I knew, or I would have remembered that. What I remember was the kiddie hat, and the semicircle legs. I tried to reassure myself about the race thing for a long time until it dawned on me that the truth was already there, and Roberta knew it. I didn't kick her; I didn't join in with the gar girls and kick that lady, but I sure did want to. We watched and never tried to help her and never called for help. Maggie was my dancing mother. Deaf, I thought, and dumb. Nobody inside. Nobody who would hear you if you cried in the night. Nobody who could tell you anything important that you could use. Rocking, dancing, swaying as she walked. And when the gar girls pushed her down, and started roughhousing, I knew she wouldn't scream, couldn't — just like me — and I was glad about that.

We decided not to have a tree, because Christmas would be at my mother-in-law's house, so why have a tree at both places? Joseph was at SUNY New Paltz❶ and we had to economize, we said. But at the last minute, I changed my mind. Nothing could be that bad. So I rushed around town looking for a tree, something small but wide. By the time I found a place, it was snowing and very late. I dawdled like it was the most important purchase in the world and the tree man was fed

❶ A campus in the State University of New York system.

up with me. Finally I chose one and had it tied onto the trunk of the car. I drove away slowly because the sand trucks were not out yet and the streets could be murder at the beginning of a snowfall. Downtown the streets were wide and rather empty except for a cluster of people coming out of the Newburgh Hotel. The one hotel in town that wasn't built out of cardboard and Plexiglas. A party, probably. The men huddled in the snow were dressed in tails and the women had on furs. Shiny things glittered from underneath their coats. It made me tired to look at them. Tired, tired, tired. On the next corner was a small diner with loops and loops of paper bells in the window. I stopped the car and went in. Just for a cup of coffee and twenty minutes of peace before I went home and tried to finish everything before Christmas Eve.

"Twyla?"

There she was. In a silvery evening gown and dark fur coat. A man and another woman were with her, the man fumbling for change to put in the cigarette machine. The woman was humming and tapping on the counter with her fingernails. They all looked a little bit drunk.

"Well. It's you."

"How are you?"

I shrugged. "Pretty good. Frazzled. Christmas and all."

"Regular?" called the woman from the counter.

"Fine," Roberta called back and then, "Wait for me in the car."

She slipped into the booth beside me. "I have to tell you something, Twyla. I made up my mind if I ever saw you again, I'd tell you."

"I'd just as soon not hear anything, Roberta. It doesn't matter now, anyway."

"No," she said. "Not about that."

"Don't be long," said the woman. She carried two regulars to go and the man peeled his cigarette pack as they left.

"It's about St. Bonny's and Maggie."

"Oh, please."

"Listen to me. I really did think she was black. I didn't make that up. I really thought so. But now I can't be sure. I just remember her as old, so old. And because she couldn't talk — well, you know, I thought she was crazy. She'd been brought up in an institution like my mother was and like I thought I would be too. And you were right. We didn't kick her. It was the gar girls. Only them. But, well, I wanted to. I really wanted them to hurt her. I said we did it, too. You and me, but that's not true. And I don't want you to carry that around. It was just that I wanted to do it so bad that day — wanting to is doing it."

Her eyes were watery from the drinks she'd had, I guess. I know it's that way with me. One glass of wine and I start bawling over the littlest thing.

"We were kids, Roberta."

"Yeah. Yeah. I know, just kids."

"Eight."

"Eight."

"And lonely."

"Scared, too."

She wiped her cheeks with the heel of her hand and smiled. "Well that's all I wanted to say."

I nodded and couldn't think of any way to fill the silence that went from the diner past the paper bells on out into the snow. It was heavy now. I thought I'd better wait for the sand trucks before starting home.

"Thanks, Roberta."

"Sure."

"Did I tell you? My mother, she never did stop dancing."

"Yes. You told me. And mine, she never got well." Roberta lifted her hands from the tabletop and covered her face with her palms. When she took them away she really was crying. "Oh shit, Twyla. Shit, Shit, Shit. What the hell happened to Maggie?"

(The text is selected from *http: //www. nbu. bg/webs/Amb/American*)

Questions for discussion:

1. At what point in the short story "Recitatif", does the reader first begin to make assump-

tion about the race and classes of the two main characters?

2. Is this basically a pessimistic story? (Or do identity, and friendship, show themselves as transcendent somehow, undamaged, in their essence by change?) What details in the story help you to decide on your answer?
3. Why does the story continually return to the references to the orchard and to Maggie? What is significant in these continual references?

Joyce Carol Oates (1938—)

Joyce Carol Oates was born in Lockport, New York, on June 16, 1938. She grew up on her parents' farm, outside the town, and went to the same one-room schoolhouse her mother had attended. This rural area of upstate New York, straddling Niagara and Erie Counties, had been hit hard by the Great Depression. The few industries the area enjoyed suffered from frequent closures and layoffs. Farm families worked desperately hard to sustain meager subsistence. But young Joyce enjoyed the natural environment of farm country, and displayed a precocious interest in books and writing. Although her parents had little education, they encouraged her ambitions. When, at age 14, her grandmother gave her first typewriter, she began consciously preparing herself, "writing novel after novel" throughout high school and college.

When she transferred to the high school in Lockport, she quickly distinguished herself. An excellent student, she contributed to her high school newspaper and won a scholarship to attend Syracuse University, where she majored in English. When she was only 19, she won the "college short story" contest sponsored by *Mademoiselle*. Joyce Carol Oates was valedictorian of her graduating class. After receiving her B. A. degree, she earned her Master's degree in a single year at the University of Wisconsin. While studying in Wisconsin she met Raymond Smith. The two were married after a three-month courtship.

In 1962, the couple settled in Detroit, Michigan. Joyce taught at the University of Detroit and had a front-row seat for the social turmoil engulfing America's cities in the 1960s. These violent realities informed much of her early fiction. Her first novel, *With Shuddering Fall*, was published when she was 28. Her novel *them* received the National Book Award.

In 1968, Joyce took a job at the University of Windsor, and the couple moved across the Detroit River to Windsor, in the Canadian province of Ontario. In the ten years that followed, Joyce Carol Oates published new books at the extraordinary rate of two or three per year, while teaching full-time. Many of her novels sold well; her short stories and critical essays solidified her reputation. Despite some critical grumbling about her phenomenal productivity, Oates had become one of the most respected and honored writers in the United States though only in her thirties.

While still in Canada, Oates and her husband started a small press and began to publish a literary magazine, *The Ontario Review*. They continued these activities after 1978, when they moved to Princeton, New Jersey. Since 1978, Joyce Carol Oates has taught in the creative writing program at Princeton University, where she has mentored numerous young writers, including Jonathan Safran Foer. Her literary work continued unabated.

In the early 1980s, Oates surprised critics and readers with a series of novels, beginning with *Bellefluer*, in which she reinvented the conventions of Gothic fiction, using them to re-imagine whole stretches of American history. Just as suddenly, she returned, at the end of the decade, to her familiar realistic ground with a series of ambitious family chronicles, including *You Must Remember This*, and *Because It Is Bitter, and Because It Is My Heart*. The novels *Solstice* and *Marya: A Life* also date from this period, and use the materials of her family and childhood to create moving studies of the female experience. In addition to her literary fiction, she has written a series of experimental suspense novels under the pseudonym Rosamond Smith.

Joyce Carol Oates has written 56 novels, over 30 collections of short stories, eight volumes of poetry, plays, innumerable essays and book reviews, as well as longer nonfiction works on literary subjects ranging from the poetry of Emily Dickinson and the fiction of Dostoyevsky and James Joyce, to studies of the gothic and horror genres, and on such non-literary subjects as the painter George Bellows and the boxer Mike Tyson. In 1996, Oates received the PEN/Malamud Award for "a lifetime of literary achievement."

Her husband, Raymond Smith, died in 2008, shortly before the publication of her 32nd collection of short stories, *Dear Husband*. The following year, Oates married Professor Charles Gross, of the Psychology Department and Neuroscience Institute at Princeton. In the months following Raymond Smith's death, and before she met Dr. Gross, she suffered from severe depression and suicidal thoughts. She described this experience vividly in the memoir, *A Widow's Tale*, published in 2011. Today, Joyce Carol Oates continues to live and write in Princeton, New Jersey, where she is Distinguished Professor of Humanities at Princeton University.

(The text is selected from *http://www.achievement.org*)

Major Works:

Novels:

- *With Shuddering Fall*, 1964 《颤栗地落下》
- *A Garden of Earthly Delights*, 1967 《人间乐园》
- *Expensive People*, 1968 《阔佬》
- *them*, 1969 《他们》

- *Wonderland*, 1971 《奇境》
- *Do With Me What You Will*, 1973 《我任你摆布》
- *The Assassins*, 1975 《刺客们》
- *Childwold*, 1976 《乔尔伍德》
- *Son of the Morning*, 1978 《晨之子》
- *Unholy Loves*, 1979 《不神圣的爱情》
- *Bellefleur*, 1980 《贝莱福勒》
- *Angel of Light*, 1981 《光明天使》
- *A Bloodsmoor Romance*, 1982 《布鲁德斯摩传奇》
- *Mysteries of Winterthurn*, 1984 《温特瑟恩的秘密》
- *Solstice*, 1985 《极致》
- *Marya: A Life*, 1986 《玛雅的一生》
- *You Must Remember This*, 1987 《你必须记住这个》
- *American Appetites*, 1989 《美国人的胃口》
- *Because It Is Bitter, and Because It Is My Heart*, 1990《因为它味苦，因为它是我的心》
- *I Lock Door Upon Myself*, 1990 《自我封闭》
- *Black Water*, 1992 《漆黑的水》
- *Foxfire: Confessions of a Girl Gang*, 1993 《狐火：一个少女帮的自白》
- *What I Lived For*, 1994 《我为何而活》
- *Zombie*（1995） 《僵尸》
- *We Were the Mulvaneys*, 1996 《我们是马尔瓦尼一家》
- *Man Crazy*, 1997《花痴》
- *My Heart Laid Bare*, 1998 《袒露我的心怀》
- *Broke Heart Blues*, 1999 《冲破忧伤心曲》
- *Blonde*, 2000 《浮生如梦》
- *Middle Age: A Romance*, 2001 《中年：浪漫之旅》
- *I'll Take You There*, 2002 《我带你去那儿》
- *The Falls*, 2004 《大瀑布》
- *Missing Mom*, 2005 《妈妈走了》

- *The Gravedigger's Daughter*, 2007 《掘墓人的女儿》
- *My Sister*, *My Love*, 2008 《我的妹妹我的爱：史盖乐·蓝派克秘史》
- *Little Bird of Heaven*, 2009 《天堂的小鸟》
- *A Fair Maiden*, 2010 《淑女》（编者译）
- *Mudwoman*, 2012 《泥妇人》
- *Daddy Love*, 2013 《父爱》（编者译）
- *The Accursed*, 2013 《受诅咒者》
- *Carthage*, 2014 《迦太基》（编者译）

Short story collections:

- *By the North Gate*, 1963 《北门边》
- *Upon the Sweeping Flood And Other Stories*, 1966《在泛滥的洪水上》
- *The Wheel of Love and Other Stories*, 1970 《爱之轮》
- *Marriages and Infidelities*, 1972 《婚姻与不贞》
- *Where are you going*, *Where have you been?: Stories of Young America*, 1974 《你从哪里来？又要去哪里？》（又译《何去何从》）

Where Are You Going, Where Have You Been?[1]

For Bob Dylan[2]

Her name was Connie. She was fifteen and she had a quick, nervous giggling habit of craning her neck to glance into mirrors or checking other people's faces to make sure her own was all right. Her mother, who noticed everything and knew everything and who hadn't much reason any longer to look at her own face, always scolded Connie about it. "Stop gawking at yourself. Who are you? You think you're so pretty?" she would say. Connie would raise her eyebrows at these familiar old complaints and look right through her mother, into a shadowy vision of herself as she

---

[1] The story was first published in *Epoch*, Fall 1966. It's included in *Prize Stories*: *O' Henry Award Winners* (1968), and *The Best American Short Stories* (1967).

[2] Bob Dylan (1941 —), American musician, singer-songwriter, artist and writer, who has been an influential figure in popular music and culture for more than 5 decades.

was right at that moment: she knew she was pretty and that was everything. Her mother had been pretty once too, if you could believe those old snapshots in the album, but now her looks were gone and that was why she was always after Connie.

"Why don't you keep your room clean like your sister? How've you got your hair fixed — what the hell stinks? Hair spray? You don't see your sister using that junk."

Her sister June was twenty-four and still lived at home. She was a secretary in the high school Connie attended, and if that wasn't bad enough — with her in the same building — she was so plain and chunky and steady that Connie had to hear her praised all the time by her mother and her mother's sisters. June did this, June did that, she saved money and helped clean the house and cooked and Connie couldn't do a thing, her mind was all filled with trashy daydreams. Their father was away at work most of the time and when he came home he wanted supper and he read the newspaper at supper and after supper he went to bed. He didn't bother talking much to them, but around his bent head Connie's mother kept picking at her until Connie wished her mother was dead and she herself was dead and it was all over. "She makes me want to throw up sometimes," she complained to her friends. She had a high, breathless, amused voice that made everything she said sound a little forced, whether it was sincere or not.

There was one good thing: June went places with girl friends of hers, girls who were just as plain and steady as she, and so when Connie wanted to do that her mother had no objections. The father of Connie's best girl friend drove the girls the three miles to town and left them at a shopping plaza so they could walk through the stores or go to a movie, and when he came to pick them up again at eleven he never bothered to ask what they had done.

They must have been familiar sights, walking around the shopping plaza in their shorts and flat ballerina slippers that always scuffed the sidewalk, with charm bracelets[1] jingling on their thin wrists; they would lean together to whisper and laugh secretly if someone passed who amused or interested them. Connie had long dark blond

---

[1] A charm bracelet is an item of jewellery worn around the wrist. It carries personal "charms": decorative pendants or trinkets which signify important things in the wearer's life.

hair that drew anyone's eye to it, and she wore part of it pulled up on her head and puffed out and the rest of it she let fall down her back. She wore a pull-over jersey blouse that looked one way when she was at home and another way when she was away from home. Everything about her had two sides to it, one for home and one for anywhere that was not home: her walk, which could be childlike and bobbing, or languid enough to make anyone think she was hearing music in her head; her mouth, which was pale and smirking most of the time, but bright and pink on these evenings out; her laugh, which was cynical and drawling at home — "Ha, ha, very funny," — but high-pitched and nervous anywhere else, like the jingling of the charms on her bracelet.

Sometimes they did go shopping or to a movie, but sometimes they went across the highway, ducking fast across the busy road, to a drive-in restaurant where older kids hung out. The restaurant was shaped like a big bottle, though squatter than a real bottle, and on its cap was a revolving figure of a grinning boy holding a hamburger aloft. One night in midsummer they ran across, breathless with daring, and right away someone leaned out a car window and invited them over, but it was just a boy from high school they didn't like. It made them feel good to be able to ignore him. They went up through the maze of parked and cruising cars to the bright-lit, fly-infested restaurant, their faces pleased and expectant as if they were entering a sacred building that loomed up out of the night to give them what haven and blessing they yearned for. They sat at the counter and crossed their legs at the ankles, their thin shoulders rigid with excitement, and listened to the music that made everything so good: the music was always in the background, like music at a church service; it was something to depend upon.

A boy named Eddie came in to talk with them. He sat backwards on his stool, turning himself jerkily around in semicircles and then stopping and turning back again, and after a while he asked Connie if she would like something to eat. She said she would and so she tapped her friend's arm on her way out — her friend pulled her face up into a brave, droll look — and Connie said she would meet her at eleven, across the way. "I just hate to leave her like that," Connie said earnestly, but the boy said that she wouldn't be alone for long. So they went out to his car, and on the way Connie couldn't help but let her eyes wander over the windshields and faces all around her, her face gleaming with a joy that had nothing to do with Eddie or even this place; it might have been the music. She drew her shoulders up and sucked in her breath with the pure pleasure of being alive, and just at that moment she happened to glance at a face just a few feet from hers. It was a boy with shaggy black hair, in a convertible[1] jalopy painted gold. He stared at her and then his lips widened into a grin. Connie slit her eyes at him and turned away, but she couldn't help glancing back and there he was, still watching her. He wagged a finger and laughed and said, "Gonna get you, baby," and Connie turned away again without Eddie noticing anything.

She spent three hours with him, at the restaurant where they ate hamburgers and drank Cokes in wax cups that were always sweating, and then down an alley a mile or so away, and when he left her off at five to eleven only the movie house was still open at the plaza. Her girl friend was there, talking with a boy. When Connie came up, the two girls smiled at each other and Connie said, "How was the movie?" and the girl said, "You should know." They rode off with the girl's father, sleepy and pleased, and Connie couldn't help but look back at the darkened shopping plaza with its big empty parking lot and its signs that were faded and ghostly now, and over at the drive-in restaurant where cars were still circling tirelessly. She couldn't hear the music at this distance.

Next morning June asked her how the movie was and Connie said, "So-So."

She and that girl and occasionally another girl went out several times a week, and the rest of the time Connie spent around the house — it was summer vacation — getting in her mother's way and thinking, dreaming about the boys she met. But all the boys fell back and dissolved into a single face that was not even a face but an idea, a feeling, mixed up with the urgent insistent pounding of the music and the humid night air of July. Connie's mother kept dragging her back to the daylight by

---

[1] A car with a soft roof that you can fold back or remove.

finding things for her to do or saying suddenly, "What's this about the Pettinger girl?"

And Connie would say nervously, "Oh, her. That dope." She always drew thick clear lines between herself and such girls, and her mother was simple and kind enough to believe it. Her mother was so simple, Connie thought, that it was maybe cruel to fool her so much. Her mother went scuffling around the house in old bedroom slippers and complained over the telephone to one sister about the other, then the other called up and the two of them complained about the third one. If June's name was mentioned her mother's tone was approving, and if Connie's name was mentioned it was disapproving. This did not really mean she disliked Connie, and actually Connie thought that her mother preferred her to June just because she was prettier, but the two of them kept up a pretense of exasperation, a sense that they were tugging and struggling over something of little value to either of them. Sometimes, over coffee, they were almost friends, but something would come up — some vexation that was like a fly buzzing suddenly around their heads — and their faces went hard with contempt.

One Sunday Connie got up at eleven — none of them bothered with church — and washed her hair so that it could dry all day long in the sun. Her parents and sister were going to a barbecue at an aunt's house and Connie said no, she wasn't interested, rolling her eyes to let her mother know just what she thought of it. "Stay home alone then," her mother said sharply. Connie sat out back in a lawn chair and watched them drive away, her father quiet and bald, hunched around so that he could back the car out, her mother with a look that was still angry and not at all softened through the windshield, and in the back seat poor old June, all dressed up as if she didn't know what a barbecue was, with all the running yelling kids and the flies. Connie sat with her eyes closed in the sun, dreaming and dazed with the warmth about her as if this were a kind of love, the caresses of love, and her mind slipped over onto thoughts of the boy she had been with the night before and how nice he had been, how sweet it always was, not the way someone like June would suppose but sweet, gentle, the way it was in movies and promised in songs; and when she opened her eyes she hardly knew where she was, the back yard ran off into weeds and a fence-like line of trees and behind it the sky was perfectly blue and still. The asbestos ranch house that was now three years old startled her — it looked small. She shook her head as if to get awake.

It was too hot. She went inside the house and turned on the radio to drown out the quiet. She sat on the edge of her bed, barefoot, and listened for an hour and a half to a program called "XYZ Sunday Jamboree❶", record after record of hard, fast, shrieking songs she sang along with, interspersed by exclamations from "Bobby King": "An'look here, you girls at Napoleon's — Son and Charley want you to pay real close attention to this song coming up!"

And Connie paid close attention herself, bathed in a glow of slow-pulsed joy that seemed to rise mysteriously out of the music itself and lay languidly about the airless little room, breathed in and breathed out with each gentle rise and fall of her chest.

After a while she heard a car coming up the drive. She sat up at once, startled, because it couldn't be her father so soon. The gravel kept crunching all the way in from the road — the driveway was long — and Connie ran to the window. It was a car she didn't know. It was an open jalopy, painted a bright gold that caught the sunlight opaquely. Her heart began to pound and her fingers snatched at her hair, checking it, and she whispered, "Christ. Christ," wondering how bad she looked. The car came to a stop at the side door and the horn sounded four short taps, as if this were a signal Connie knew.

She went into the kitchen and approached the door slowly, then hung out the screen door, her bare toes curling down off the step. There were two boys in the car and now she recognized the driver: he had shaggy, shabby black hair that looked crazy as a wig and he was grinning at her.

"I ain't late, am I?" he said.

"Who the hell do you think you are?" Connie said.

---

❶ A big noisy party or event.

"Toldja[1] I'd be out, didn't I?"

"I don't even know who you are."

She spoke sullenly, careful to show no interest or pleasure, and he spoke in a fast, bright monotone. Connie looked past him to the other boy, taking her time. He had fair brown hair, with a lock that fell onto his forehead. His sideburns[2] gave him a fierce, embarrassed look, but so far he hadn't even bothered to glance at her. Both boys wore sunglasses. The driver's glasses were metallic and mirrored everything in miniature.

"You wanta come for a ride?" he said.

Connie smirked and let her hair fall loose over one shoulder.

"Don'tcha like my car? New paint job," he said. "Hey."

"What?"

"You're cute."

She pretended to fidget, chasing flies away from the door.

"Don'tcha believe me, or what?" he said.

"Look, I don't even know who you are," Connie said in disgust.

"Hey, Ellie's got a radio, see. Mine broke down." He lifted his friend's arm and showed her the little transistor radio the boy was holding, and now Connie began to hear the music. It was the same program that was playing inside the house.

"Bobby King?" she said.

"I listen to him all the time. I think he's great."

"He's kind of great," Connie said reluctantly.

"Listen, that guy's *great*. He knows where the action is."

Connie blushed a little, because the glasses made it impossible for her to see just what this boy was looking at. She couldn't decide if she liked him or if he was just a jerk, and so she dawdled in the doorway and wouldn't come down or go back inside. She said, "What's all that stuff painted on your car?"

"Can'tcha read it?" He opened the door very carefully, as if he were afraid it

---

1. "Told you".
2. Hair grown down the sides of a man's face in front of his ears.

might fall off. He slid out just as carefully, planting his feet firmly on the ground, the tiny metallic world in his glasses slowing down like gelatine hardening, and in the midst of it Connie's bright green blouse. "This here is my name," to begin with, he said. ARNOLD FRIEND was written in tarlike black letters on the side, with a drawing of a round, grinning face that reminded Connie of a pumpkin, except it wore sunglasses. "I wanta introduce myself, I'm Arnold Friend and that's my real name and I'm gonna be your friend, honey, and inside the car's Ellie Oscar, he's kinda shy." Ellie brought his transistor radio up to his shoulder and balanced it there. "Now, these numbers are a secret code, honey," Arnold Friend explained. He read off the numbers 33, 19, 17 and raised his eyebrows at her to see what she thought of that, but she didn't think much of it. The left rear fender had been smashed and around it was written, on the gleaming gold background: DONE BY CRAZY WOMAN DRIVER. Connie had to laugh at that. Arnold Friend was pleased at her laughter and looked up at her. "Around the other side's a lot more — you wanta come and see them?"

"No."

"Why not?"

"Why should I?"

"Don'tcha wanta see what's on the car? Don'tcha wanta go for a ride?"

"I don't know."

"Why not?"

"I got things to do."

"Like what?"

"Things."

He laughed as if she had said something funny. He slapped his thighs. He was standing in a strange way, leaning back against the car as if he were balancing himself. He wasn't tall, only an inch or so taller than she would be if she came down to him. Connie liked the way he was dressed, which was the way all of them dressed: tight faded jeans stuffed into black, scuffed boots, a belt that pulled his waist in and showed how lean he was, and a white pull-over shirt that was a little soiled and showed the hard small muscles of his arms and shoulders. He looked as if he probably did hard work, lifting and carrying things. Even his neck looked muscular. And his face was a familiar face, somehow: the jaw and chin and cheeks slightly darkened because he hadn't shaved for a day or two, and the nose long and hawk-like, sniffing as if she were a treat he was going to gobble up and it was all a joke.

"Connie, you ain't telling the truth. This is your day set aside for a ride with me and you know it," he said, still laughing. The way he straightened and recovered from his fit of laughing showed that it had been all fake.

"How do you know what my name is?" she said suspiciously.

"It's Connie."

"Maybe and maybe not."

"I know my Connie," he said, wagging his finger. Now she remembered him even better, back at the restaurant, and her cheeks warmed at the thought of how she had sucked in her breath just at the moment she passed him — how she must have looked to him. And he had remembered her. "Ellie and I come out here especially for you," he said. "Ellie can sit in back. How about it?"

"Where?"

"Where what?"

"Where're we going?"

He looked at her. He took off the sunglasses and she saw how pale the skin around his eyes was, like holes that were not in shadow but instead in light. His eyes were like chips of broken glass that catch the light in an amiable way. He smiled. It was as if the idea of going for a ride somewhere, to someplace, was a new idea to him.

"Just for a ride, Connie sweetheart."

"I never said my name was Connie," she said.

"But I know what it is. I know your name and all about you, lots of things," Arnold Friend said. He had not moved yet but stood still leaning back against the side of his jalopy. "I took a special interest in you, such a pretty girl, and found out all about you — like I know your parents and sister are gone somewheres and I know where and how long they're going to be gone, and I know who you were with last night, and your best girl friend's name is Betty. Right?"

He spoke in a simple lilting voice, exactly as if he were reciting the words to a song. His smile assured her that everything was fine. In the car Ellie turned up the volume on his radio and did not bother to look around at them.

"Ellie can sit in the back seat," Arnold Friend said. He indicated his friend with a casual jerk of his chin, as if Ellie did not count and she should not bother with him.

"How'd you find out all that stuff?" Connie said.

"Listen: Betty Schultz and Tony Fitch and Jimmy Pettinger and Nancy Pettinger," he said in a chant. "Raymond Stanley and Bob Hutter — "

"Do you know all those kids?"

"I know everybody."

"Look, you're kidding. You're not from around here."

"Sure."

"But — how come we never saw you before?"

"Sure you saw me before," he said. He looked down at his boots, as if he were a little offended. "You just don't remember."

"I guess I'd remember you," Connie said.

"Yeah?" He looked up at this, beaming. He was pleased. He began to mark time with the music from Ellie's radio, tapping his fists lightly together. Connie looked away from his smile to the car, which was painted so bright it almost hurt her eyes to look at it. She looked at that name, ARNOLD FRIEND. And up at the front fender was an expression that was familiar — MAN THE FLYING SAUCERS. It was an expression kids had used the year before but didn't use this year. She looked at it for a while as if the words meant something to her that she did not yet know.

"What're you thinking about? Huh?" Arnold Friend demanded. "Not worried about your hair blowing around in the car, are you?"

"No."

"Think I maybe can't drive good?"

"How do I know?"

"You're a hard girl to handle. How come?" he said. "Don't you know I'm your friend? Didn't you see me put my sign in the air when you walked by?"

"What sign?"

"My sign." And he drew an X in the air, leaning out toward her. They were maybe ten feet apart. After his hand fell back to his side the X was still in the air, almost visible. Connie let the screen door close and stood perfectly still inside it, listening to the music from her radio and the boy's blend together. She stared at Arnold Friend. He stood there so stiffly relaxed, pretending to be relaxed, with one hand idly on the door handle as if he were keeping himself up that way and had no intention of ever moving again. She recognized most things about him, the tight jeans that showed his thighs and buttocks and the greasy leather boots and the tight shirt, and even that slippery friendly smile of his, that sleepy dreamy smile that all the boys used to get across ideas they didn't want to put into words. She recognized all this and also the singsong way he talked, slightly mocking, kidding, but serious and a little melancholy, and she recognized the way he tapped one fist against the other in homage to the perpetual music behind him. But all these things did not come together.

She said suddenly, "Hey, how old are you?"

His smiled faded. She could see then that he wasn't a kid, he was much older — thirty, maybe more. At this knowledge her heart began to pound faster.

"That's a crazy thing to ask. Can'tcha see I'm your own age?"

"Like hell you are."

"Or maybe a couple years older. I'm eighteen."

"Eighteen?" she said doubtfully.

He grinned to reassure her and lines appeared at the corners of his mouth. His teeth were big and white. He grinned so broadly his eyes became slits and she saw how thick the lashes were, thick and black as if painted with a black tarlike material. Then, abruptly, he seemed to become embarrassed and looked over his shoulder at Ellie. "*Him*, he's crazy," he said. "Ain't he a riot? He's a nut, a real character." Ellie was still listening to the music. His sunglasses told nothing about what he was thinking. He wore a bright orange shirt unbuttoned halfway to show his chest, which was a pale, bluish chest and not muscular like Arnold Friend's. His shirt collar was turned up all around and the very tips of the collar pointed out past his chin as if they were protecting him. He was pressing the transistor radio up against his ear and sat there in a kind of daze, right in the sun.

"He's kinda strange," Connie said.

"Hey, she says you're kinda strange! Kinda strange!" Arnold Friend cried. He pounded on the car to get Ellie's attention. Ellie turned for the first time and Connie saw with shock that he wasn't a kid either — he had a fair, hairless face, cheeks reddened slightly as if the veins grew too close to the surface of his skin, the face of a forty-year-old baby. Connie felt a wave of dizziness rise in her at this sight and she stared at him as if waiting for something to change the shock of the moment, make it all right again. Ellie's lips kept shaping words, mumbling along with the words blasting in his ear.

"Maybe you two better go away," Connie said faintly.

"What? How come?" Arnold Friend cried. "We come out here to take you for a ride. It's Sunday." He had the voice of the man on the radio now. It was the same voice, Connie thought. "Don'tcha know it's Sunday all day? And honey, no matter who you were with last night, today you're with Arnold Friend and don't you forget it! Maybe you better step out here," he said, and this last was in a different voice. It was a little flatter, as if the heat was finally getting to him.

"No. I got things to do."

"Hey."

"You two better leave."

"We ain't leaving until you come with us."

"Like hell I am —"

"Connie, don't fool around with me. I mean — I mean, don't fool *around*," he said, shaking his head. He laughed incredulously. He placed his sunglasses on top of his head, carefully, as if he were indeed wearing a wig, and brought the stems down behind his ears. Connie stared at him, another wave of dizziness and fear rising in her so that for a moment he wasn't even in focus but was just a blur standing there against his gold car, and she had the idea that he had driven up the driveway all right but had come from nowhere before that and belonged nowhere and that everything about him and even about the music that was so familiar to her was only half real.

"If my father comes and sees you —"

"He ain't coming. He's at a barbecue."

"How do you know that?"

"Aunt Tillie's. Right now they're uh — they're drinking. Sitting around," he said vaguely, squinting as if he were staring all the way to town and over to Aunt Tillie's back yard. Then the vision seemed to get clear and he nodded energetically. "Yeah. Sitting around. There's your sister in a blue dress, huh? And high heels, the poor sad bitch — nothing like you, sweetheart! And your mother's helping some fat woman with the corn, they're cleaning the corn — husking the corn —"

"What fat woman?" Connie cried.

"How do I know what fat woman, I don't know every goddamn fat woman in the world!" Arnold Friend laughed.

"Oh, that's Mrs. Hornsby.... Who invited her?" Connie said. She felt a little lightheaded. Her breath was coming quickly.

"She's too fat. I don't like them fat. I like them the way you are, honey," he said, smiling sleepily at her. They stared at each other for a while through the screen door. He said softly, "Now, what you're going to do is this: you're going to come out that door. You're going to sit up front with me and Ellie's going to sit in the back, the hell with Ellie, right? This isn't Ellie's date. You're my date. I'm your lover, honey."

"What? You're crazy —"

"Yes, I'm your lover. You don't know what that is but you will," he said. "I know that too. I know all about you. But look: it's real nice and you couldn't ask for nobody better than me, or more polite. I always keep my word. I'll tell you how it is, I'm always nice at first, the first time. I'll hold you so tight you won't think you have to try to get away or pretend anything because you'll know you can't. And I'll come inside you where it's all secret and you'll give in to me and you'll love me."

"Shut up! You're crazy!" Connie said. She backed away from the door. She put her hands up against her ears as if she'd heard something terrible, something not meant for her. "People don't talk like that, you're crazy," she muttered. Her heart was almost too big now for her chest and its pumping made sweat break out all over her. She looked out to see Arnold Friend pause and then take a step toward the porch, lurching❶. He almost fell. But, like a clever drunken man, he managed to catch his balance. He wobbled in his high boots and grabbed hold of one of the porch posts.

"Honey?" he said. "You still listening?"

"Get the hell out of here!"

"Be nice, honey. Listen."

"I'm going to call the police —"

He wobbled again and out of the side of his mouth came a fast spat curse, an aside not meant for her to hear. But even this "Christ!" sounded forced. Then he began to smile again. She watched this smile come, awkward as if he were smiling from inside a mask. His whole face was a mask, she thought wildly, tanned down to his throat but then running out as if he had plastered make-up on his face but had forgotten about his throat.

"Honey —? Listen, here's how it is. I always tell the truth and I promise you this: I ain't coming in that house after you."

"You better not! I'm going to call the police if you — if you don't —"

"Honey," he said, talking right through her voice, "honey, I'm not coming in there but you are coming out here. You know why?"

She was panting. The kitchen looked like a place she had never seen before, some room she had run inside but that wasn't good enough, wasn't going to help her.

---

❶ To walk or move suddenly in an uncontrolled or unsteady way.

The kitchen window had never had a curtain, after three years, and there were dishes in the sink for her to do — probably — and if you ran your hand across the table you'd probably feel something sticky there.

"You listening, honey? Hey?" "— going to call the police —"

"Soon as you touch the phone I don't need to keep my promise and can come inside. You won't want that."

She rushed forward and tried to lock the door. Her fingers were shaking. "But why lock it," Arnold Friend said gently, talking right into her face. "It's just a screen door. It's just nothing." One of his boots was at a strange angle, as if his foot wasn't in it. It pointed out to the left, bent at the ankle. "I mean, anybody can break through a screen door and glass and wood and iron or anything else if he needs to, anybody at all, and specially Arnold Friend. If the place got lit up with a fire, honey, you'd come runnin' out into my arms, right into my arms an' safe at home — like you knew I was your lover and'd stopped fooling around. I don't mind a nice shy girl but I don't like no fooling around." Part of those words were spoken with a slight rhythmic lilt, and Connie somehow recognized them — the echo of a song from last year, about a girl rushing into her boy friend's arms and coming home again —

Connie stood barefoot on the linoleum floor, staring at him. "What do you want?" she whispered.

"I want you," he said.

"What?"

"Seen you that night and thought, that's the one, yes sir. I never needed to look anymore."

"But my father's coming back. He's coming to get me. I had to wash my hair first —" "She spoke in a dry, rapid voice, hardly raising it for him to hear."

"No, your daddy is not coming and yes, you had to wash your hair and you washed it for me. It's nice and shining and all for me. I thank you sweetheart," he said with a mock bow, but again he almost lost his balance. He had to bend and adjust his boots. Evidently his feet did not go all the way down; the boots must have been stuffed with something so that he would seem taller. Connie stared out at him and behind him at Ellie in the car, who seemed to be looking off toward Connie's right, into nothing. This Ellie said, pulling the words out of the air one after another as if he were just discovering them, "You want me to pull out the phone?"

"Shut your mouth and keep it shut," Arnold Friend said, his face red from bending over or maybe from embarrassment because Connie had seen his boots. "This ain't none of your business."

"What — what are you doing? What do you want?" Connie said. "If I call the police they'll get you, they'll arrest you — "

"Promise was not to come in unless you touch that phone, and I'll keep that promise," he said. He resumed his erect position and tried to force his shoulders back. He sounded like a hero in a movie, declaring something important. But he spoke too loudly and it was as if he were speaking to someone behind Connie. "I ain't made plans for coming in that house where I don't belong but just for you to come out to me, the way you should. Don't you know who I am?"

"You're crazy," she whispered. She backed away from the door but did not want to go into another part of the house, as if this would give him permission to come through the door. "What do you... you're crazy, you..."

"Huh? What're you saying, honey?"

Her eyes darted everywhere in the kitchen. She could not remember what it was, this room.

"This is how it is, honey: you come out and we'll drive away, have a nice ride. But if you don't come out we're gonna wait till your people come home and then they're all going to get it."

"You want that telephone pulled out?" Ellie said. He held the radio away from his ear and grimaced, as if without the radio the air was too much for him.

"I toldja shut up, Ellie," Arnold Friend said, "you're deaf, get a hearing aid, right? Fix yourself up. This little girl's no trouble and's gonna be nice to me, so Ellie keep to yourself, this ain't your date right? Don't hem in on me, don't hog, don't crush, don't bird dog, don't trail me," he said in a rapid, meaningless voice, as if he were running through all the expressions he'd learned but was no longer sure which of them was in style, then rushing on to new ones, making them up with his eyes closed. "Don't crawl under my fence, don't squeeze in my chipmonk hole, don't sniff my glue, suck my popsicle, keep your own greasy fingers on yourself!"[1] He shaded his eyes and peered in at Connie, who was backed against the kitchen table. "Don't mind him, honey, he's just a creep. He's a dope. Right? I'm the boy for you, and like I said, you come out here nice like a lady and give me your hand, and nobody else gets hurt, I mean, your nice old bald-headed daddy and your mummy and your sister in her high heels. Because listen: why bring them in this?"

"Leave me alone," Connie whispered.

"Hey, you know that old woman down the road, the one with the chickens and stuff — you know her?"

"She's dead!"

"Dead? What? You know her?" Arnold Friend said.

"She's dead —"

"Don't you like her?"

"She's dead — she's — she isn't here any more —"

"But don't you like her, I mean, you got something against her? Some grudge or something?" Then his voice dipped as if he were conscious of a rudeness. He touched the sunglasses perched up on top of his head as if to make sure they were still there. "Now, you be a good girl."

"What are you going to do?"

"Just two things, or maybe three," Arnold Friend said. "But I promise it won't last long and you'll like me the way you get to like people you're close to. You will. It's all over for you here, so come on out. You don't want your people in any trouble, do you?"

She turned and bumped against a chair or something, hurting her leg, but she

---

[1] "Don't crawl under my fence, don't squeeze in my chipmonk hole, don't sniff my glue, suck my popsicle, keep your own greasy fingers on yourself!" All these slangs mean the same: Mind your own business!

ran into the back room and picked up the telephone. Something roared in her ear, a tiny roaring, and she was so sick with fear that she could do nothing but listen to it — the telephone was clammy and very heavy and her fingers groped down to the dial but were too weak to touch it. She began to scream into the phone, into the roaring. She cried out, she cried for her mother, she felt her breath start jerking back and forth in her lungs as if it were something Arnold Friend was stabbing her with again and again with no tenderness. A noisy sorrowful wailing rose all about her and she was locked inside it the way she was locked inside this house.

After a while she could hear again. She was sitting on the floor with her wet back against the wall.

Arnold Friend was saying from the door, "That's a good girl. Put the phone back."

She kicked the phone away from her.

"No, honey. Pick it up. Put it back right."

She picked it up and put it back. The dial tone stopped.

"That's a good girl. Now, you come outside."

She was hollow with what had been fear but what was now just an emptiness. All that screaming had blasted it out of her. She sat, one leg cramped under her, and deep inside her brain was something like a pinpoint of light that kept going and would not let her relax. She thought, I'm not going to see my mother again. She thought, I'm not going to sleep in my bed again. Her bright green blouse was all wet.

Arnold Friend said, in a gentle-loud voice that was like a stage voice, "The place where you came from ain't there any more, and where you had in mind to go is cancelled out. This place you are now — inside your daddy's house — is nothing but a cardboard box I can knock down any time. You know that and always did know it. You hear me?"

She thought, I have got to think. I have got to know what to do.

"We'll go out to a nice field, out in the country here where it smells so nice and it's sunny," Arnold Friend said. "I'll have my arms tight around you so you won't need to try to get away and I'll show you what love is like, what it does. The hell with this house! It looks solid all right," he said. He ran a fingernail down the screen and the noise did not make Connie shiver, as it would have the day before. "Now, put your hand on your heart, honey. Feel that? That feels solid too but we know better. Be nice to me, be sweet like you can because what else is there for a girl like you but to be sweet and pretty and give in? — and get away before her people come back?"

She felt her pounding heart. Her hand seemed to enclose it. She thought for the first time in her life that it was nothing that was hers, that belonged to her, but just a pounding, living thing inside this body that wasn't really hers either.

"You don't want them to get hurt," Arnold Friend went on. "Now, get up, honey. Get up all by yourself."

She stood.

"Now, turn this way. That's right. Come over here to me. — Ellie, put that away, didn't I tell you? You dope. You miserable creepy dope," Arnold Friend said. His words were not angry but only part of an incantation. The incantation was kindly. "Now come out through the kitchen to me, honey, and let's see a smile, try it, you're a brave, sweet little girl and now they're eating corn and hot dogs cooked to bursting over an outdoor fire, and they don't know one thing about you and never did and honey, you're better than them because not a one of them would have done this for you."

Connie felt the linoleum under her feet; it was cool. She brushed her hair back out of her eyes. Arnold Friend let go of the post tentatively and opened his arms for her, his elbows pointing in toward each other and his wrists limp, to show that this was an embarrassed embrace and a little mocking, he didn't want to make her self-conscious.

She put out her hand against the screen. She watched herself push the door slowly open as if she were back safe somewhere in the other doorway, watching this body and this head of long hair moving out into the sunlight where Arnold Friend waited.

"My sweet little blue-eyed girl," he said in a half-sung sigh that had nothing to do with her brown eyes but was taken up just the same by the vast sunlit reaches of the land behind him and on all sides of him — so much land that Connie had never seen before and did not recognize except to know that she was going to it.

(The text is selected from *http://wenku.baidu.com*)

Questions for discussion:

1. What roles do various members of Connie's family play in her life? Discuss the theme of the house as a metaphor of Connie's identity.
2. How do you interpret Arnold? Why does he dress and conduct himself in that way?
3. Where does Arnold take Connie, and what happens to her?
4. What are the characteristics of a typical American adolescent of the 1960s according to the depiction of Connie in the story?

Maxine Hong Kingston (1940 —)

Maxine Hong Kingston was born in Stockton, California, to parents who had emigrated from China. Before they emigrated, Kingston's father was a schoolteacher and a poet; her mother was a rural doctor in a profession consisting almost entirely of men. In American they took on quite different identities: her father, at times unemployed, worked in a gambling house and a laundry; her mother raised six children, of whom Kingston was the eldest.

Kingston graduated from the University of California at Berkeley, studying there in the turbulent middle sixties. Her debut as a writer was auspicious: in 1976, an unknown, she published her first and most widely read book, *The Women Warrior*, and was catapulted to literary fame. Subtitled "Memoirs of a Girlhood among Ghosts," it draws on autobiographical fact and combines it with legends, especially Asian ones, to make a distinct imaginative creation. Reviews of the book, almost universally laudatory, emphasized its poetic and lyric beauty. *The Women Warrio*r is about the cultural conflicts Americans of Chinese descent must confront. Still, what remains in the mind is its quality of vivid particularity, as for example at the beginning of *Shaman*, the book's third section:

> Once in a long while, four times so far for me, my mother brings out the metal tube that holds her medical diploma. On the tube are gold circles crossed with seven red lines each — "joy" ideographs in abstract. There are also little flowers that look like gears for a gold machine··· When I open it, the smell of China flies out, a thousand-year-old bat flying heavy-headed out of the Chinese caverns where bats are as white as dust, a smell that comes from long ago, far back in brain.

Although *The Women Warrior* received the National Book Critics' Circle award for general nonfiction, there is nothing "general" in the sensuous density of its reference.

The importance of storytelling to Kingston's enterprise in *The Women Warrior* and its successor, *China Men* (1980), cannot be overemphasized. The Chinese phrase for storytelling is "talking story," and in *No Name Women* (anthologized here), the first section from *Warrior*, the narrator's mother "talks" her a story — which she is instructed to keep silent about — of the suicide in China of her father's sister. This woman, the narrator's aunt, became pregnant out of wedlock (she may have been raped); and in response to this violation of a taboo, the village treats her with a vengeful hostility that leads to her own and her infant's death. The narrator (Kingston in no disguise) is fascinated and appalled by this family secret; how can she, as a writer, presume to publish it to the world? In an interview with Bill Moyers on public television, Kingston said that her attempt was to push the account toward "form" by giving it a "redemptive" meaning, making it a "beautiful" story rather than a sordid one. As is the case typically with her practice as a writer, her effort is to mediate between present and past: "I think that my stories have a constant breaking in and out of the present and past. So the reader might be walking along very well in the present, but the past breaks through and changes and enlightens the present and vice versa."

Kingston had originally conceived of *The Women Warrior* and *China Men* as one long book, but decided to preserve an overall division by gender: *Warrior* is about her female antecedents; while *China Men*, which won the 1980 National Book Award for nonfiction, deals with her relation to her father and complements that relation by providing epiclike biographies of earlier male forebears, especially those Chinese who came to America and worked on building the railroads. In a final section, she writes about her brother who served in the U. S. Navy during the Vietnam War. Interestingly enough, as she said in the interview with Moyers, her father annotated both of these memoir-meditations, thus carrying further the conversation between the generations.

Tripmaster Monkey (1989), presented more deliberately as a novel, is an exercise as excessive as the young fifth-generation American hero, Wittman Ah Sing, who is portrayed there. Subtitled "His Fake Book," the novel is an extended, picaresque account of Wittman's adventures as an aspiring playwright who imagines himself to be an incarnation of the legendary Monkey King — a trickster hero said to have brought the Buddha's teaching to China. Combining magic, realism, and black humor, *Tripmaster Monkey* is about a young male's search for a community in America. Although Kingston's myth-laden narratives have been called "exotic", she dislikes the word, since she has dedicated her art to exploring what it means to be a human being in American society. In fact, she thinks of her books as more American than Chinese, sees Wittmen Carlos William's *In the American Grain* as a true prose predecessor, and probably would not be unhappy to think of the hero of *Tripmaster Monkey* as a later, different version of Huck Finn or Augie March. As critic Jennie Wang explains in even larger dimensions, Kingston's Wittmen Ah Sing is "the maker/magician created in the wake of James Joyce's 'bygmester', conceived in the mind's fancy of a metafictionist," who joins in his multiculturalism both American and postmodern ambitions.

(The text is that of *The Woman Warrior* (1976))

Major Works:

- *Woman Warrior: Memoires of a Grilhood among Ghosts*, 1976 《女勇士:

一个女孩在群鬼间的生活忆往》

- *China Men*, 1980 《金山勇士》(又译《中国佬》)
- *Tripmaster Monkey*: *His Fake Book*, 1989 《孙行者: 他的即兴曲》
- *The Fifth Book of Peace*, 2003 《第五和平之书》

No Name Woman[1]

"You must not tell anyone," my mother said, "what I am about to tell you. In China your father had a sister who killed herself. She jumped into the family well. We say that your father has all brothers because it is as if she had never been born.

"In 1924 just a few days after our village celebrated seventeen hurry-up weddings — to make sure that every young man who went 'out on the road' would responsibly come home — your father and his brothers and your grandfather and his brothers and your aunt's new husband sailed for America, the Gold Mountain. It was your grandfather's last trip. Those lucky enough to get contracts waved goodbye from the decks. They fed and guarded the stowaways and helped them off in Cuba, New York, Bali, Hawaii. 'We'll meet in California next year,' they said. All of them sent money home.

"I remember looking at your aunt one day when she and I were dressing; 1 had not noticed before that she had such a protruding melon of a stomach. But I did not think, 'she's pregnant,' until she began to look like other pregnant women, her shirt pulling and the white tops of her black pants showing. She could not have been pregnant, you see, because her husband had been gone for years. No one said anything. We did not discuss it. In early summer she was ready to have the child, long after the time when it could have been possible.

"The village had also been counting. On the night the baby was to be born the villagers raided our house. Some were crying. Like a great saw, teeth strung with lights, files of people walked zigzag across our land, tearing the rice. Their lanterns doubled in the disturbed black water, which drained away through the broken

---

[1] *No Name Woman* is selected from the first part of *Woman Warrior*.

bunds[1]. As the villagers closed in, we could see that some of them, probably men and women we knew well, wore white masks. The people with long hair hung it over their faces. Women with short hair made it stand up on end. Some had tied white bands around their foreheads, arms, and legs.

"At first they threw mud and rocks at the house. Then they threw eggs and began slaughtering our stock. We could hear the animals scream their deaths — the roosters, the pigs, a last great roar from the ox. Familiar wild heads flared in our night windows; the villagers encircled us. Some of the faces stopped to peer at us, their eyes rushing like searchlights. The hands flattened against the panes, framed heads, and left red prints.

"The villagers broke in the front and the back doors at the same time, even though we had not locked the doors against them. Their knives dripped with the blood of our animals. They smeared blood on the doors and walls. One woman swung a chicken, whose throat she had slit, splattering blood in red arcs about her. We stood together in the middle of our house, in the family hall with the pictures and tables of the ancestors around us, and looked straight ahead.

"At that time the house had only two wings. When the men came back, we would build two more to enclose our courtyard and a third one to begin a second courtyard. The villagers pushed through both wings, even your grandparents' rooms, to find your aunt's, which was also mine until the men returned. From this room a new wing for one of the younger families would grow. They ripped up her clothes and shoes and broke her combs, grinding them underfoot. They tore her work from the loom. They scattered the cooking fire and rolled the new weaving in it. We could hear them in the kitchen breaking our bowls and banging the pots. They overturned the great waist-high earthenware jugs; duck eggs, pickled fruits, vegetables burst out and mixed in acrid torrents. The old woman from the next field swept a broom through the air and loosed the spirits-of-the broom over our heads. 'Pig.' 'Ghost.' 'Pig,' they sobbed and scolded while they ruined our house.

---

[1] Embankments built to control the flow of water, here probably irrigation water.

"When they left, they took sugar and oranges to bless themselves. They cut pieces from the dead animals. Some of them took bowls that were not broken and clothes that were not torn. Afterward we swept up the rice and sewed it back up into sacks. But the smells from the spilled preserves lasted. Your aunt gave birth in the pigsty that night. The next morning when I went for the water, I found her and the baby plugging up the family well.

"Don't let your father know that I told you. He denies her. Now that you have started to menstruate, what happened to her could happen to you. Don't humiliate us. You wouldn't like to be forgotten as if you had never been born. The villagers are watchful."

Whenever she had to warn us about life, my mother told stories that ran like this one, a story to grow up on. She tested our strength to establish realities. Those in the emigrant generations who could not reassert brute survival died young and far from home. Those of us in the first American generations have had to figure out how the invisible world the emigrants built around our childhoods fits in solid America.

The emigrants confused the gods by diverting their curses, misleading them with crooked streets and false names. They must try to confuse their offspring as well, who, I suppose, threaten them in similar ways — always trying to get things straight, always trying to name the unspeakable. The Chinese I know hide their names; sojourners take new names when their lives change and guard their real names with silence.

Chinese-Americans, when you try to understand what things in you are Chinese, how do you separate what is peculiar to childhood, to poverty, insanities, one family, your mother who marked your growing with stories, from what is Chinese? What is Chinese tradition and what is the movies?

If I want to learn what clothes my aunt wore, whether flashy or ordinary, I would have to begin, "Remember Father's drowned-in-the-well sister?" I cannot ask that. My mother has told me once and for all the useful parts. She will add nothing unless powered by Necessity, a riverbank that guides her life. She plants vegetable gardens rather than lawns; she carries the odd-shaped tomatoes home from the fields and eats food left for the gods.

Whenever we did frivolous things, we used up energy; we flew high kites. We children came up off the ground over the melting cones our parents brought home from work and the American movie on New Year's Day — *Oh, You Beautiful Doll* with Betty Grable one year, and *She Wore a Yellow Ribbon* with John Wayne another year. After the one carnival ride each, we paid in guilt; our tired father counted his change on the dark walk home.

Adultery is extravagance. Could people who hatch their own chicks and eat the embryos and the heads for delicacies and boil the feet in vinegar for party food, leaving only the gravel, eating even the gizzard lining — could such people engender a prodigal aunt? To be a woman, to have a daughter in starvation time was a waste enough. My aunt could not have been the lone romantic who gave up everything for sex. Women in the old China did not choose. Some man had commanded her to lie with him and be his secret evil. I wonder whether he masked himself when he joined the raid on her family.

Perhaps she had encountered him in the fields or on the mountain where the daughters-in-law collected fuel. Or perhaps he first noticed her in the marketplace. He was not a stranger because the village housed no strangers. She had to have dealings with him other than sex. Perhaps he worked an adjoining field, or he sold her the cloth for the dress she sewed and wore. His demand must have surprised, then terrified her. She obeyed him; she always did as she was told.

When the family found a young man in the next village to be her husband, she had stood tractably beside the best rooster, his proxy[1], and promised before they met that she would be his forever. She was lucky that he was her age and she would be the first wife, an advantage secure now. The night she first saw him, he had sex with her. Then he left for America. She had almost forgotten what he looked like. When she tried to envision him, she only saw the black and white face in the group photograph the men had had taken before leaving.

---

[1] Someone or something that has the power to substitute or act for another.

The other man was not, after all, much different from her husband. They both gave orders: she followed. "If you tell your family, I'll beat you. I'll kill you. Be here again next week." No one talked sex, ever. And she might have separated the rapes from the rest of living if only she did not have to buy her oil from him or gather wood in the same forest. I want her fear to have lasted just as long as rape lasted so that the fear could have been contained. No drawn-out fear. But women at sex hazarded birth and hence lifetimes. The fear did not stop but permeated everywhere. She told the man, "I think I'm pregnant!" He organized the raid against her.

On nights when my mother and father talked about their life back home, sometimes they mentioned an "outcast table" whose business they still seemed to be settling, their voices tight. In a commensal tradition❶, where food is precious, the powerful older people made wrongdoers eat alone. Instead of letting them start separate new lives like the Japanese, who could become samurais and geishas❷, the Chinese family, faces averted but eyes glowering sideways, hung on to the offenders and fed them leftovers. My aunt must have lived in the same house as my parents and eaten at an outcast table. My mother spoke about the raid as if she had seen it, when she and my aunt, a daughter-in-law to a different household, should not have been living together at all. Daughters-in-law lived with their husbands' parents, not their own; a synonym for marriage in Chinese is "taking a daughter-in-law!" Her husband's parents could have sold her, mortgaged her, stoned her. But they had sent her back to her own mother and father, a mysterious act hinting at disgraces not told me. Perhaps they had thrown her out to deflect the avengers.

She was the only daughter; her four brothers went with her father, husband, and uncles "out on the road" and for some years became western men. When the goods were divided among the family, three of the brothers took land, and the youngest, my father, chose an education. After my grandparents gave their daughter away to her husband's family, they had dispensed all the adventure and all the property. They expected her alone to keep the traditional ways, which her

---

❶ A tradition in which people eat together at the same table.

❷ In Japanese society women trained to entertain men. Samurai: the Japanese warrior elite.

brothers, now among the barbarians, could fumble without detection. The heavy, deep-rooted women were to maintain the past against the flood, safe for returning. But the rare urge west had fixed upon our family, and so my aunt crossed boundaries not delineated in space.

The work of preservation demands that the feelings playing about in one's guts not be turned into action. Just watch their passing like cherry blossoms. But perhaps my aunt, my forerunner, caught in a slow life, let dreams grow and fade and after some months or years went toward what persisted. Fear at the enormities of the forbidden kept her desires delicate, wire and bone. She looked at a man because she liked the way the hair was tucked behind his ears, or she liked the question-mark line of a long torso curving at the shoulder and straight at the hip. For warm eyes or a soft voice or a slow walk — that's all — a few hairs, a line, a brightness, a sound, a pace, she gave up family. She offered us up for a charm that vanished with tiredness, a pigtail that didn't toss when the wind died. Why, the wrong lighting could erase the dearest thing about him.

It could very well have been, however, that my aunt did not take subtle enjoyment of her friend, but, a wild woman, kept rollicking company. Imagining her free with sex doesn't fit, though. I don't know any women like that, or men either. Unless I see her life branching into mine, she gives me no ancestral help.

To sustain her being in love, she often worked at herself in the mirror, guessing at the colors and shapes that would interest him, changing them frequently in order to hit on the right combination. She wanted him to look back.

On a farm near the sea, a woman who tended her appearance reaped a reputation for eccentricity. All the married women blunt-cut their hair in flaps about their ears or pulled it back in tight buns. No nonsense. Neither style blew easily into heart-catching tangles. And at their weddings they displayed themselves in their long hair for the last time. "It brushed the backs of my knees," my mother tells me. "It was braided, and even so, it brushed the backs of my knees!"

At the mirror my aunt combed individuality into her bob. A bun could have been contrived to escape into black streamers blowing in the wind or in quiet wisps about her face, but only the older women in our picture album wear buns. She brushed her hair back from her forehead, tucking the flaps behind her ears. She looped a piece of thread, knotted into a circle between her index fingers and thumbs, and ran the double strand across her forehead. When she closed her fingers as if she were making a pair of shadow geese bite, the string twisted together catching the little hairs. Then she pulled the thread away from her skin, ripping the hairs out neatly, her eyes watering from the needles of pain. Opening her fingers, she cleaned the thread, then rolled it along her hairline and the tops of her eyebrows. My mother did the same to me and my sisters and herself. I used to believe that the expression "caught by the short hairs" meant a captive held with a depilatory string. It especially hurt at the temples, but my mother said we were lucky we didn't have to have our feet bound when we were seven. Sisters used to sit on their beds and cry together, she said, as their mothers or their slaves removed the bandages for a few minutes each night and let the blood gush back into their veins. I hope that the man my aunt loved appreciated a smooth brow, that he wasn't just a tits-and-ass man.

Once my aunt found a freckle on her chin, at a spot that the almanac said predestined her for unhappiness. She dug it out with a hot needle and washed the wound with peroxide.

More attention to her looks than these pullings of hairs and pickings at spots would have caused gossip among the villagers. They owned work clothes and good clothes, and they wore good clothes for feasting the new seasons. But since a woman combing her hair hexes beginnings, my aunt rarely found an occasion to look her best. Women looked like great sea snails — the corded wood, babies, and laundry they carried were the whorls on their backs. The Chinese did not admire a bent back; goddesses and warriors stood straight. Still there must have been a marvelous freeing of beauty when a worker laid down her burden and stretched and arched.

Such commonplace loveliness, however, was not enough for my aunt. She dreamed of a lover for the fifteen days of New Year's, the time for families to exchange visits, money, and food. She plied her secret comb. And sure enough she cursed the year, the family, the village, and herself.

Even as her hair lured her imminent lover, many other men looked at her. Uncles, cousins, nephews, brothers would have looked, too, had they been home between journeys. Perhaps they had already been restraining their curiosity, and they left, fearful that their glances, like a field of nesting birds, might be startled and caught. Poverty hurt, and that was their first reason for leaving. But another, final reason for leaving the crowded house was the never-said.

She may have been unusually beloved, the precious only daughter, spoiled and mirror gazing because of the affection the family lavished on her. When her husband left, they welcomed the chance to take her back from the in-laws; she could live like the little daughter for just a while longer. There are stories that my grandfather was different from other people, "crazy ever since the little Jap bayoneted him in the head." He used to put his naked penis on the dinner table, laughing. And one day he brought home a baby girl, wrapped up inside his brown western-style greatcoat[1]. He had traded one of his sons, probably my father, the youngest, for her. My grandmother made him trade back. When he finally got a daughter of his own, he doted on her. They must have all loved her, except perhaps my father, the only brother who never went back to China, having once been traded for a girl.

Brothers and sisters, newly men and women, had to efface their sexual color and present plain miens. Disturbing hair and eyes, a smile like no other, threatened the ideal of five generations living under one roof. To focus blurs, people shouted face to face and yelled from room to room. The immigrants I know have loud voices, unmodulated to American tones even after years away from the village where they called their friendships out across the fields. I have not been able to stop my mother's screams in public libraries or over telephones. Walking erect (knees straight, toes pointed forward, not pigeon-toed, which is Chinese-feminine) and speaking in an inaudible voice, I have tried to turn myself American-feminine. Chinese communication was loud, public. Only sick people had to whisper. But at the dinner table, where the family members came nearest one another, no one could

---

[1] A heavy overcoat.

talk, not the outcasts nor any eaters. Every word that falls from the mouth is a coin lost. Silently they gave and accepted food with both hands. A preoccupied child who took his bowl with one hand got a sideways glare. A complete moment of total attention is due everyone alike. Children and lovers have no singularity here, but my aunt used a secret voice, a separate attentiveness.

She kept the man's name to herself throughout her labor and dying; she did not accuse him that he be punished with her. To save her inseminator's name she gave silent birth.

He may have been somebody in her own household, but intercourse with a man outside the family would have been no less abhorrent. All the village were kinsmen, and the titles shouted in loud country voices never let kinship be forgotten. Any man within visiting distance would have been neutralized as a lover — "brother," "younger brother," "older brother" — one hundred and fifteen relationship titles. Parents researched birth charts probably not so much to assure good fortune as to circumvent incest in a population that has but one hundred surnames. Everybody has eight million relatives. How useless then sexual mannerisms, how dangerous.

As if it came from an atavism[1] deeper than fear, I used to add "brother" silently to boys' names. It hexed the boys, who would or would not ask me to dance, and made them less scary and as familiar and deserving of benevolence as girls.

But, of course, I hexed myself also — no dates. I should have stood up, both arms waving, and shouted out across libraries, "Hey, you! Love me back." I had no idea, though, how to make attraction selective, how to control its direction and magnitude. If I made myself American-pretty so that the five or six Chinese boys in the class fell in love with me, everyone else — the Caucasian, Negro, and Japanese boys — would too. Sisterliness, dignified and honorable, made much more sense.

Attraction eludes control so stubbornly that whole societies designed to organize relationships among people cannot keep order, not even when they bind people to

---

[1] A trait with origins farther back than the preceding generation — a throwback.

one another from childhood and raise them together. Among the very poor and the wealthy, brothers married their adopted sisters, like doves. Our family allowed some romance, paying adult brides' prices and providing dowries so that their sons and daughters could marry strangers. Marriage promises to turn strangers into friendly relatives — a nation of siblings.

In the village structure, spirits shimmered among the live creatures, balanced and held in equilibrium by time and land. But one human being flaring up into violence could open up a black hole, a maelstrom[1] that pulled in the sky. The frightened villagers, who depended on one another to maintain the real, went to my aunt to show her a personal, physical representation of the break she had made in the "roundness." Misallying couples snapped off the future, which was to be embodied in true offspring. The villagers punished her for acting as if she could have a private life, secret and apart from them.

If my aunt had betrayed the family at a time of large grain yields and peace, when many boys were born, and wings were being built on many houses, perhaps she might have escaped such severe punishment. But the men — hungry, greedy, tired of planting in dry soil — had been forced to leave the village in order to send food-money home. There were ghost plagues, bandit plagues, wars with the Japanese, floods. My Chinese brother and sister had died of an unknown sickness. Adultery, perhaps only a mistake during good times, became a crime when the village needed food.

The round moon cakes and round doorways, the round tables of graduated sizes that fit one roundness inside an other, round windows and rice bowls — these talismans had lost their power to warn this family of the law: a family must be whole, faithfully keeping the descent line by having sons to feed the old and the dead, who in turn look after the family. The villagers came to show my aunt and her lover-in-hiding a broken house. The villagers were speeding up the circling of events because she was too shortsighted to see that her infidelity had already harmed the village, that

---

[1] A powerful, violent whirlpool.

waves of consequences would return unpredictably, sometimes in disguise, as now, to hurt her. This roundness had to be made coin-sized so that she would see its circumference: punish her at the birth of her baby. Awaken her to the inexorable. People who refused fatalism because they could invent small resources insisted on culpability. Deny accidents and wrest fault from the stars.

After the villagers left, their lanterns now scattering in various directions toward home, the family broke their silence and cursed her. "Aiaa, we're going to die. Death is coming. Death is coming. Look what you've done. You've killed us. Ghost! Dead ghost! Ghost! You've never been born." She ran out into the fields, far enough from the house so that she could no longer hear their voices, and pressed herself against the earth, her own land no more. When she felt the birth coming, she thought that she had been hurt. Her body seized together. "They've hurt me too much," she thought. "This is gall, and it will kill me." With forehead and knees against the earth, her body convulsed and then relaxed. She turned on her back, lay on the ground. The black well of sky and stars went out and out and out forever; her body and her complexity seemed to disappear. She was one of the stars, a bright dot in blackness, without home, without a companion, in eternal cold and silence. An agoraphobia[1] rose in her, speeding higher and higher, bigger and bigger; she would not be able to contain it; there would no end to fear.

Flayed, unprotected against space, she felt pain return, focusing her body. This pain chilled her — a cold, steady kind of surface pain. Inside, spasmodically, the other pain, the pain of the child, heated her. For hours she lay on the ground, alternately body and space. Sometimes a vision of normal comfort obliterated reality: she saw the family in the evening gambling at the dinner table, the young people massaging their elders' backs. She saw them congratulating one another, high joy on the mornings the rice shoots came up. When these pictures burst, the stars drew yet further apart. Black space opened.

She got to her feet to fight better and remembered that old-fashioned women gave

---

[1] An abnormal fear of open space.

birth in their pigsties to fool the jealous, pain-dealing gods, who do not snatch piglets. Before the next spasms could stop her, she ran to the pigsty, each step a rushing out into emptiness. She climbed over the fence and knelt in the dirt. It was good to have a fence enclosing her, a tribal person alone.

Laboring, this woman who had carried her child as a foreign growth that sickened her every day, expelled it at last. She reached down to touch the hot, wet, moving mass, surely smaller than anything human, and could feel that it was human after all — fingers, toes, nails, nose. She pulled it up on to her belly, and it lay curled there, butt in the air, feet precisely tucked one under the other. She opened her loose shirt and buttoned the child inside. After resting, it squirmed and thrashed and she pushed it up to her breast. It turned its head this way and that until it found her nipple. There, it made little snuffling noises. She clenched her teeth at its preciousness, lovely as a young calf, a piglet, a little dog.

She may have gone to the pigsty as a last act of responsibility: she would protect this child as she had protected its father. It would look after her soul, leaving supplies on her grave. But how would this tiny child without family find her grave when there would be no marker for her anywhere, neither in the earth nor the family hall? No one would give her a family hall name. She had taken the child with her into the wastes. At its birth the two of them had felt the same raw pain of separation, a wound that only the family pressing tight could close. A child with no descent line would not soften her life but only trail after her, ghostlike, begging her to give it purpose. At dawn the villagers on their way to the fields would stand around the fence and look.

Full of milk, the little ghost slept. When it awoke, she hardened her breasts against the milk that crying loosens. Toward morning she picked up the baby and walked to the well.

Carrying the baby to the well shows loving. Otherwise abandon it. Turn its face into the mud. Mothers who love their children take them along. It was probably a girl; there is some hope of forgiveness for boys.

"Don't tell anyone you had an aunt. Your father does not want to hear her name. She has never been born." I have believed that sex was unspeakable and words so strong and fathers so frail that "aunt" would do my father mysterious harm. I have thought that my family, having settled among immigrants who had also been their neighbors in the ancestral land, needed to clean their name, and a wrong word would incite the kinspeople even here. But there is more to this silence: they want me to participate in her punishment. And I have.

In the twenty years since I heard this story I have not asked for details nor said my aunt's name; I do not know it. People who can comfort the dead can also chase after them to hurt them further — a reverse ancestor worship. The real punishment was not the raid swiftly inflicted by the villagers, but the family's deliberately forgetting her. Her betrayal so maddened them, they saw to it that she would suffer forever, even after death. Always hungry, always needing, she would have to beg food from other ghosts, snatch and steal it from those whose living descendants give them gifts. She would have to fight the ghosts massed at crossroads for the buns a few thoughtful citizens leave to decoy her away from village and home so that the ancestral spirits could feast unharassed. At peace, they could act like gods, not ghosts, their descent lines providing them with paper suits and dresses, spirit money, paper houses, paper automobiles, chicken, meat, and rice[1] into eternity — essences delivered up in smoke and flames, steam and incense rising from each rice bowl. In an attempt to make the Chinese care for people outside the family, Chairman Mao encourages us now to give our paper replicas to the spirits of outstanding soldiers and workers, no matter whose ancestors they may be. My aunt remains forever hungry. Goods are not distributed evenly among the dead.

My aunt haunts me — her ghost drawn to me because now, after fifty years of neglect, I alone devote pages of paper to her, though not origamied into houses and clothes. I do not think she always means me well. I am telling on her, and she was a spite suicide, drowning herself in the drinking water. The Chinese are always very frightened of the drowned one, whose weeping ghost, wet hair hanging and skin

---

[1] Traditionally, offerings left at the graves of ancestors.

bloated, waits silently by the water to pull down a substitute.

(The text is selected from *http://wenku.baidu.com*)

Questions for discussion:

1. What purpose does Kinston have in telling her aunt's story "No Name Woman"?
2. "You must not tell anyone," my mother said, "what I am about to tell you." That's the beginning sentence of the story. Why does the mother tell her the story of the missing aunt?
3. What is your understanding about the social position of Chinese women in the past? Is your understanding the same as Kinston's?

Alice Walker (1944 —)

Of the two daughters (at odds over family heirlooms) in the story *Everyday Use*, Alice Walker resembles each one. Like the burned Maggie, she spent a childhood even more limited than her family's rural poverty dictated, for as a little girl she was shot in the eye with a BB gun; the disfigurement plagued her until it was corrected during her college years. Like Dee, she was able to attend college — first Spelman College and then prestigious Sarah Lawrence College on a scholarship — and acquire urban sophistications from the North. Many of Walker's characters become adept in the mew cultural language of Black Art and black power to which the author herself contributed as a young writer — and all of them are subjected to the same dismay Dee's mother feels at having to rule against this daughter's wishes. Like the mother, therefore, Alice Walker is given to seeing both sides of a situation; and when it comes to making a choice between her characters' opposing positions, she tends to be self-critical of her own personality first and extremely sparing in her judgment of others.

From her birthplace in Eatonton, Georgia, Alice Walker gained a thorough understanding of the rural South, an understanding she employs when evaluating the importance of Flannery O'Connor, an older white writer who lived in nearby Milledgeville. As her essay *Beyond the Peacock* shows, Walker's own eminence as a writer invites readers to see the region and its heritage in a different perspective, as visitors' habits of romanticizing how the bricks of the O'Connor home were handmade on the site by slaves as contrasted to the author's pained awareness of how the slaves surely suffered in the process. That O'Connor's work survives and even profits by such critical reexamination speaks again for Alice Walker's sense of balance. As a child of sharecroppers educated at an excellent, sophisticated northern college, Walker is able to weigh human and artistic concerns in a way that lets Flannery O'Connor be read for the complex writer she is.

After college Alice Walker returned to the South, first to work against segregation in the civil rights movement and then to begin her teaching career at Jackson State College in Mississippi. Her first novel, T*he Third Life of Grange Copeland* (1970), follows its protagonist through three generations of domestic experience. In *Meridian* (1976) Walker changes her narrative approach to encompass fragmentary recollections of the 1960s among characters trying to make sense of their recent past. This novel reflects many of the topics treated in the author's short story collection, *In Love & Trouble* (1973), in which a range of African American women almost always have unhappy relationships with men. Walker's third novel, *The Color Purple* (1982), makes her strongest narrative statement, formulated as it is from what she calls a "womanist" (as opposed to strictly feminist) perspective. This approach draws on the black folk expression "womanish", which in a mother-to-daughter context signifies a call to adult, mature, responsible (and courageous) behavior. Such behavior is beneficial to both women and men, and is necessary, Walker argues, for the survival of all African Americans by keeping creativity alive. Both the plot and the stylistic nature of *The Color Purple* show how this happens, as the young black woman Celie draws on her sister's letters (written from Africa) for her own letters that she writes to God. Though Celie's life by any other terms could be considered disastrous (including rape, incest, and the killing of her babies by her father and both physical and psychological abuse by her husband), her ability to express herself successfully gives her status as an individual in the world. To everything that will listen, Celie says "I am here."

Alice Walker's work has continued with other novels, short stories, collections of poetry, and several important volumes of essays. In *The Same River Twice* (1996) she wrote how the filming of *The Color Purple* both challenged and changed her life. As a sociocultural critic, she has examined the atrocity of female genital mutilation in parts of Africa, reporting her conclusions in her novel *Possessing the Secret of Joy*, and as a literary critic has spoken for a richer and more complete understanding of Zora Neale Hurston, whose employment of folk materials in narrative anticipates Walker's own. Throughout her career she speaks for the need for strength from African American women, and her writing is ever conscious of providing workable models for such strength Beijing achieved.

(The text is selected from *In Love & Trouble* (1973))

Major Works:

Poetry:

- *Once*, 1968 《曾经》
- *Revolutionary Petunias & Other Poems*, 1973 《革命的牵牛花和其他诗歌》
- *Good Night, Willie Lee, I'll See You in the Morning*, 1979 《晚安，威利·李，早晨见》
- *Horses Make a Landscape Look More Beautiful*, 1985 《马儿使风景更美丽》
- *Her Blue Body Everything We Know: Earthling Poems*, 1991 《她蓝色的躯体我们知道一切：世人的诗》

- *Absolute Trust in the Goodness of the Earth*, 2003 《绝对信任大地的良善》
- *A Poem Traveled Down My Arm*: *Poems And Drawings*, 2003 《诗歌沿着我的手臂而行：诗与画》
- *Hard Times Require Furious Dancing*: *New Poems*, 2010 《艰难时世需要狂野的舞蹈：新诗》

Novels:

- *The Third Life of Grange Copeland*, 1970 《格兰奇·科普兰的第三次生命》
- *Meridian*, 1976 《梅里迪安》
- *The Color Purple*, 1982 《紫色》
- *The Temple of My Familiar*, 1989 《灵物的圣殿》
- *Possessing the Secret of Joy*, 1992 《拥有快乐的秘密》
- *By the Light of My Father's Smile*, 1998 《父亲的微笑之光》
- *Now Is The Time to Open Your Heart*, 2005 《现在是你敞开心扉之际》

Everyday Use

For your grandmama

I will wait for her in the yard that Maggie and I made so clean and wavy yesterday afternoon. A yard like this is more comfortable than most people know. It is not just a yard. It is like an extended living room. When the hard clay is swept clean as a floor and the fine sand around the edges lined with tiny, irregular grooves, anyone can come and sit and look up into the elm tree and wait for the breezes that never come inside the house.

Maggie will be nervous until after her sister goes: she will stand hopelessly in corners, homely and ashamed of the burn scars down her arms and legs, eying her sister with a mixture of envy and awe. She thinks her sister has held life always in the palm of one hand, that "no" is a word the world never learned to say to her.

You've no doubt seen those TV shows where the child who has "made it" is confronted, as a surprise, by her own mother and father, tottering in weakly from backstage[1]. (A pleasant surprise, of course: What would they do if parent and child came on the show only to curse out and insult each other?) On TV mother and child embrace and smile into each other's face. Sometimes the mother and father weep; the child wraps them in her arms and leans across the table to tell how she would not have made it without their help. I have seen these programs.

Sometimes I dream a dream in which Dee and I are suddenly brought together on a TV program of this sort. Out of a dark and soft-seated limousine I am ushered into a bright room filled with many people. There I meet a smiling, gray, sporty man like Johnny Carson who shakes my hand and tells me what a fine girl I have. Then we are on the stage, and Dee is embracing me with tear s in her eyes. She pins on my dress a large orchid, even though she has told me once that she thinks orchides are tacky flowers.

In real life I am a large, big-boned woman with rough, man-working hands. In the winter I wear flannel nightgowns to bed and overalls during the day. I can kill and clean a hog as mercilessly as a man. My fat keeps me hot in zero weather. I can work outside all day, breaking ice to get water for washing; I can eat pork liver cooked over the open fire minutes after it comes steaming from the hog. One winter I knocked a bull calf straight in the brain between the eyes with a sledge hammer and had the meat hung up to chill before nightfall. But of course all this does not show on television. I am the way my daughter would want me to be: a hundred pounds lighter, my skin like an uncooked barley pancake. My hair glistens in the hot bright lights. Johnny Carson[2] has much to do to keep up with my quick and witty tongue.

But that is a mistake. I know even before I wake up. Who ever knew a Johnson with a quick tongue? Who can even imagine me looking a strange white man in the eye? It seems to me I have talked to them always with one foot raised in flight, with

---

[1] A reference to the popular TV program entitled *This Is Your Life*, in which celebrities were taken to a studio and surprised by a gathering of their friends, relatives, and associates.

[2] A famous U. S. comedian and television presenter, who hosted the popular program "Tonight Show" from 1962 to 1992.

my head turned in whichever way is farthest from them. Dee, though. She would always look anyone in the eye. Hesitation was no part of her nature.

"How do I look, Mama?" Maggie says, showing just enough of her thin body enveloped in pink skirt and red blouse for me to know she's there, almost hidden by the door.

"Come out into the yard," I say.

Have you ever seen a lame animal, perhaps a dog run over by some careless person rich enough to own a car, sidle up to someone who is ignorant enough to be kind of him? That is the way my Maggie walks. She has been like this, chin on chest, eyes on ground, feet in shuffle, ever since the fire that burned the other house to the ground.

Dee is lighter than Maggie, with nicer hair and a fuller figure. She's a woman now, though sometimes I forget. How long ago was it that the other house burned? Ten, twelve years? Sometimes I can still hear the flames and feel Maggie's arms sticking to me, her hair smoking and her dress falling off her in little black papery flakes. Her eyes seemed stretched open, blazed open by the flames reflected in them. And Dee. I see her standing off under the sweet gum tree she used to dig gum out of, a look of concentration on her face as she watched the last dingy gray board of the house fall in toward the red-hot brick chimney. Why don't you do a dance around the ashes? I'd wanted to ask her. She had hated the house that much.

I used to think she hated Maggie, too. But that was before we raised the money, the church and me, to send her to Augusta[1] to school. She used to read to us without pity, forcing words, lies, other folks' habits, whole lives upon us two, sitting trapped and ignorant underneath her voice. She washed us in a river of make-believe, burned us with a lot of knowledge we didn't necessarily need to know. Pressed us to her with the serious ways she read, to shove us away at just the moment, like dimwits, we seemed about to understand.

Dee wanted nice things. A yellow organdy dress to wear to her graduation from

---

[1] A city in Georgia, U. S., where Paine College is located.

high school; black pumps to match a green suit she'd made from an old suit somebody gave me. She was determined to stare down any disaster in her efforts. Her eyelids would not flicker for minutes at a time. Often I fought off the temptation to shake her. At sixteen she had a style of her own and knew what style was.

I never had an education myself. After second grade the school was closed down. Don't ask me why. In 1927 colored asked fewer questions than they do now. Sometimes Maggie reads to me. She stumbles along good-naturedly but can't see well. She knows she is not bright. Like good looks and money, quickness passed her by. She will marry John Thomas (who has mossy teeth in an earnest face) and then I'll be free to sit here and I guess just sing church songs to myself. Although I never was a good singer. Never could carry a tune. I was always better at a man's job. I used to love to milk till I was hooked in the side in '49. Cows are soothing and slow and don't bother you, unless you try to milk them the wrong way.

I have deliberately turned my back on the house. It is three rooms, just like the one that burned, except the roof is tin; they don't make shingle roofs any more. There are no real windows, just some holes cut in the sides, like the portholes in a ship, but not round and not square, with rawhide holding the shutters up on the outside. This house is in a pasture, too, like the other one. No doubt when Dee sees it she will want to tear it down. She wrote me once that no matter where we "choose" to live, she will manage to come see us. But she will never bring her friends. Maggie and I thought about this and Maggie asked me, "Mama, when did Dee ever *have* any friends?"

She had a few. Furtive❶ boys in pink shirts hanging about on washday after school. Nervous girls who never laughed. Impressed with her, they worshiped the well-turned phrase, the cute shape, the scalding humor that erupted like bubbles in lye. She read to them.

When she was courting Jimmy T, she didn't have much time to pay to us but turned all her faultfinding power on him. He flew to marry a cheap city girl from a

---

❶ Behaving in a way that he wants to keep something secret and do not want to be noticed.

family of ignorant, flashy people. She hardly had time to recompose herself.

When she comes I will meet — but there they are!

Maggie attempts to make a dash for the house, in her shuffling way, but I stay her with my hand. "Come back here," I say. And she stops and tries to dig a well in the sand with her toe.

It is hard to see them clearly through the strong sun. But even the first glimpse of leg out of the car tells me it is Dee. Her feet were always neat-looking, as it God himself had shaped them with a certain style. From the other side of the car comes a short, stocky man. Hair is all over his head a foot long and hanging from his chin like a kinky mule tail. I hear Maggie suck in her breath. "Uhnnnh" is what it sounds like. Like when you see the wriggling end of a snake just in front of your toot on the road. "Uhnnnh."

Dee next. A dress down to the ground, in this hot weather. A dress so loud it hurts my eyes. There are yellows and oranges enough to throw back the light of the sun. I feel my whole face warming from the heat waves it throws out. Earrings gold, too, and hanging down to her shoulders. Bracelets dangling and making noises when she moves her arm up to shake the folds of the dress out of her armpits. The dress is loose and flows, and as she walks closer, I like it. I hear Maggie go "Uhnnnh" again. It is her sister's hair. It stands straight up like the wool on a sheep. It is black as night and around the edges are two long pigtails that rope about like small lizards disappearing behind her ears.

"Wa-su-zo-Tean-o![1]" she says, coming on in that gliding way the dress makes her move. The short stocky fellow with the hair to his navel is all grinning and he follows up with "Asalamalakim[2], my mother and sister!" He moves to hug Maggie but she falls back, right up against the back of my chair. I feel her trembling there and when I look up I see the perspiration falling off her chin.

"Don't get up," says Dee. Since I am stout, it takes something of a push. You can see me trying to move a second or two before I make it. She turns, showing

---

[1] Muslim greeting.

[2] African dialect greeting.

white heels through her sandals, and goes back to the car. Out she peeks next with a Polaroid. She stoops down quickly and lines up picture after picture of me sitting there in front of the house with Maggie cowering behind me. She never takes a shot without making sure the house is included. When a cow comes nibbling around the edge of the yard, she snaps it and me and Maggie and the house. Then she puts the Polaroid in the back seat of the car and comes up and kisses me on the forehead.

Meanwhile Asalamalakim is going through motions with Maggie's hand. Maggie's hand is as limp as a fish, and probably as cold, despite the sweat, and she keeps trying to pull it back. It looks like Asalamalakim wants to shake hands but wants to do it fancy. Or maybe he don't know how people shake hands. Anyhow, he soon gives up on Maggie.

"Well," I say. "Dee."

"No, Mama," she says. "Not 'Dee', Wangero Leewanika Kemanjo!"

"What happened to 'Dee'?" I wanted to know.

"She's dead," Wangero said. "I couldn't bear it any longer, being named after the people who oppress me."

"You know as well as me you was named after your aunt Dicle," I said. Dicie is my sister. She named Dee. We called her "Big Dee" after Dee was born.

"But who was *she* named after?" asked Wangero.

"I guess after Grandma Dee," I said.

"And who was she named after?" asked Wangero.

"Her mother," I said, and saw Wangero was getting tired. "That's about as far back as I can trace it," I said. Though, in fact, I probably could have carried it back beyond the Civil War through the branches.

"Well," said Asalamalakim, "there you are."

"Uhnnnh," I heard Maggie say.

"There I was not," I said, "before 'Dicie' cropped up in our family, so why should I try to trace it that far back?"

He just stood there grinning, looking down on me like somebody inspecting a

Model A[1] car. Every once in a while he and Wangero sent eye signals over my head.

"How do you pronounce this name?" I asked.

"You don't have to call me by it if you don't want to," said Wangero.

"Why shouldn't I?" I asked. "If that's what you want us to call you, we'll call you."

"I know it might sound awkward at first," said Wangero.

"I'll get used to it," I said. "Ream it out again."

Well, soon we got the name out of the way. Asalamalakim had a name twice as long and three times as hard. After I tripped over it two or three times he told me to just call him Hakim-a-barber. I wanted to ask him was he a barber, but I didn't really think he was, so I didn't ask.

"You must belong to those beet-cattle peoples down the road," I said. They said "Asalamalakim" when they met you too, but they didn't shake hands. Always too busy feeding the cattle, fixing the fences, putting up salt-lick shelters[2], throwing down hay. When the white folks poisoned some of the herd, the men stayed up all night with rifles in their hands. I walked a mile and a half just to see the sight.

Hakim-a-barber said, "I accept some of their doctrines, but farming and raising cattle is not my style." (They didn't tell me, and I didn't ask, whether Wangero — Dee — had really gone and married him.)

We sat down to eat and right away he said he didn't eat collards, and pork was unclean. Wangero, though, went on through the chitlins[3] and corn bread, the greens and everything else. She talked a blue streak over the sweet potatoes. Everything delighted her. Even the fact that we still used the benches her daddy made for the table when we couldn't afford to buy chairs.

"Oh, Mama!" she cried. Then turned to Hakim-a-barber. "I never knew

---

[1] A very old automobile designed by Henry Ford.

[2] A shelter where cows are given salt to protect them from the heat.

[3] Hog intestines or guts.

how lovely these benches are. You can feel the rump prints," she said, running her hands underneath her and along the bench. Then she gave a sigh, and her hand closed over Grandma Dee's butter dish. "That's it!" she said. "I knew there was something I wanted to ask you if I could have." She jumped up from the table and went over in the corner where the churn stood, the milk in it clabber by now[1]. She looked at the churn and looked at it.

"This churn top is what I need," she said. "Didn't Uncle Buddy whittle it out of a tree you all used to have?"

"Yes," I said.

"Uh huh," she said happily. "And I want the dasher, too."

"Uncle Buddy whittle that, too?" asked the barber.

Dee (Wangero) looked up at me.

"Aunt Dee's first husband whittled the dash," said Maggie so low you almost couldn't hear her. "His name was Henry, but they called him Stash."

"Maggie's brain is like an elephants," Wanglero said, laughing. "I can use the churn top as a center piece for the alcove table," she said, sliding a plate over the churn, "and I'll think of something artistic to do with the dasher[2]."

When she finished wrapping the dasher, the handle stuck out. I took it for a moment in my hands. You didn't even have to look close to see where hands pushing the dasher up and down to make butter had left a kind of sink in the wood. In fact, there were a lot of small sinks; you could see where thumbs and fingers had sunk into the wood. It was beautiful light-yellow wood, from a tree that grew in the yard where Big Dee and Stash had lived.

After dinner Dee (Wangero) went to the trunk at the foot of my bed and started rifling through it. Maggie hung back in the kitchen over the dishpan. Out came Wangero with two quilts. They had been pieced by Grandma Dee, and then Big Dee and me had hung them on the quilt frames on the front porch and quilted them. One was in the Lone Star pattern. The other was Walk Around the Mountain. In both of

---

[1] Curdled milk.

[2] The churn and dasher are used for making butter out of milk.

them were scraps of dresses Grandma Dee had worn fifty and more years ago. Bits and pieces of Grandpa Jarrell's Paisley shirts. And one teeny faded blue piece, about the size of a penny matchbox, that was from Great Grandpa Ezra's uniform that he wore in the Civil War.

"Mama," Wangero said sweet as a bird. "Can I have these old quilts?"

I heard something fall in the kitchen, and a minute later the kitchen door slammed.

"Why don't you take one or two of the others?" I asked. "These old things was just done by me and Big Dee from some tops your grandma pieced before she died."

"No," said Wangero. "I don't want those. They are stitched around the borders by machine."

"That'll make them last better," I said.

"That's not the point," said Wanglero. "These are all pieces of dresses Grandma used to wear. She did all this stitching by hand. Imagine!" She held the quilts securely in her arms, stroking them.

"Some of the pieces, like those lavender ones, come from old clothes her mother handed down to her," I said, moving up to touch the quilts. Dee (Wangero) moved back just enough so that I couldn't reach the quilts. They already belonged to her.

"Imagine!" she breathed again, clutching them closely to her bosom.

"The truth is," I said, "I promised to give them quilts to Maggie, for when she marries John Thomas."

She gasped like a bee had stung her.

"Maggie can't appreciate these quilts!" she said. "She'd probably be backward enough to put them to everyday use."

"I reckon she would," I said. "God knows I been savage'em for long enough with nobody using 'em. I hope she will!" I didn't want to bring up how I had offered Dee (Wangero) a quilt when she went away to college. Then she had told me they were old-fashioned, out of style.

"But they're *priceless*!" she was saying now, furiously; for she has a temper.

"Maggie would put them on the bed and in five years they'd be in rags. Less than that!"

"She can always make some more," I said. "Maggie knows how to quilt."

Dee (Wangero) looked at me with hatred. "You just will not understand. The point is *these* quilts, these quilts!"

"Well," I said, stumped. "What would *you* do with them?"

"Hang them," she said. As it that was the only thing you *could* do with quilts.

Maggie by now was standing in the door. I could almost hear the sound her feet made as they scraped over each other.

"She can have them, Mama," she said like somebody used to never winning anything, or having anything reserved for her. "I can 'member Grandma Dee without the quilts."

I looked at her hard. She had filled her bottom lip with checkerberry snuff, and it gave her face a kind of dopey, hangdog look. It was Grandma Dee and Big Dee who taught her how to quilt herself. She stood there with her scarred hands hidden in the folds of her skirt. She looked at her sister with something like fear, but she wasn't mad at her. This was Maggie's portion. This was the way she knew God to work.

When I looked at her like that something hit me in the top of my head and ran down to the soles of my feet. Just like when I'm in church and the spirit of God touches me and I get happy and shout. I did something I never had done before: hugged Maggie to me, then dragged her on into the room, snatched the quilts out of Miss Wangero's hands and dumped them into Maggie's lap. Maggie just sat there on my bed with her mouth open.

"Take one or two of the others," I said to Dee.

But she turned without a word and went out to Hakim-a-barber.

"You just don't understand," she said, as Maggie and I came out to the car.

"What don't I understand?" I wanted to know.

"Your heritage," she said. And then she turned to Maggie, kissed her, and said, "You ought to try to make something of yourself, too, Maggie. It's really a new day for us. But from the way you and Mama still live you'd never know it."

She put on some sunglasses that hid everything above the tip of her nose and her chin.

Maggie smiled, maybe at the sunglasses. But a real mile, not scared. After we watched the car dust settle, I asked Maggie to bring me a dip of snuff. And then the two of us sat there just enjoying, until it was time to go in the house and go to bed.

(The text is selected from *http://wenku.baidu.com*)

Questions for discussion:

1. What are the differences in characte between the two sisters, Dee and Maggie?
2. Why has Dee changed her name? Why does she want the churn and dasher and the hand-made quilts?
3. What do you think the quilts stand for? Why does the mother give the quilts to Maggie instead of Dee?
4. What's your understanding of the title "Everyday Use"?

Amy Tan (1952 —)

Amy Tan was born in Oakland, California. Her family lived in several communities in Northern California before settling in Santa Clara. Both of her parents were Chinese immigrants. Her father, John Tan, was an electrical engineer and Baptist minister who came to America to escape the turmoil of the Chinese Civil War.

The harrowing early life of her mother, Daisy, inspired Amy Tan's novel *The Kitchen God's Wife*. In China, Daisy had divorced an abusive husband but lost custody of her three daughters. She was forced to leave them behind when she escaped on the last boat to leave Shanghai before the Communist takeover in 1949. Her marriage to John Tan produced three children, Amy and her two brothers.

Tragedy struck the Tan family when Amy's father and oldest brother both died of brain tumors within a year of each other. Mrs. Tan moved her surviving children to Switzerland, where Amy finished high school, but by this time mother and daughter were in constant conflict.

Mother and daughter did not speak for six months after Amy Tan left the Baptist college her mother had selected for her to follow her boyfriend to San Jose City College. Tan further defied her mother by abandoning the pre-med course her mother had urged to pursue the study of English and linguistics. She received her bachelor's and master's degrees in these fields at San Jose State University. In 1974, she and her boyfriend, Louis DeMattei, were married. They were later to settle in San Francisco.

DeMattei, an attorney, took up the practice of tax law, while Tan studied for a doctorate in linguistics, first at the University of California at Santa Cruz, later at Berkeley. By this time, she had developed an interest in the problems of the developmentally disabled. She left the doctoral program in 1976 and took a job as a language development consultant to the Alameda County Association for Retarded Citizens, and later directed a training project for developmentally disabled children.

With a partner, she started a business writing firm, providing speeches for the salesmen and executives of large corporations. After a dispute with her partner, who believed she should give up writing to concentrate on the management side of the business, she became a full-time freelance writer. Among her business works, written under non-Chinese-sounding pseudonyms, were a 26-chapter booklet called "Telecommunications and You," produced for IBM.

Amy Tan prospered as a business writer. After a few years in business for herself, she had saved enough money to buy a house for her mother. She and her husband lived well on their double income, but the harder Tan worked at her business, the more dissatisfied she became. The work had become a compulsive habit, and she sought relief in creative efforts. She studied jazz piano, hoping to channel the musical training forced on her by her parents in childhood into a more personal expression. She also began to write fiction.

Her first story, "Endgame," won her admission to the Squaw Valley writer's workshop taught by novelist Oakley Hall. The story appeared in *FM* literary magazine, and was reprinted in *Seventeen*. A literary agent, Sandra Dijkstra, was

- Lindo Jong — Waverly Jong
- Ying-ying St. Clair — Lena St. Clair

Feathers From a Thousand LI Away

The old woman remembered a swan she had bought many years ago in Shanghai for a foolish sum. This bird, boasted the market vendor, was once a duck that stretched its neck in hopes of becoming a goose, and now look! — it is too beautiful to eat.

Then the woman and the swan sailed across an ocean many thousands of li wide, stretching their necks toward America. On her journey she cooed to the swan: "In America I will have a daughter just like me. But over there nobody will say her worth is measured by the loudness of her husband's belch. Over there nobody will look down on her, because I will make her speak only perfect American English. And over there she will always be too full to swallow any sorrow! She will know my meaning, because I will give her this swan — a creature that became more than what was hoped for."

But when she arrived in the new country, the immigration officials pulled her swan away from her, leaving the woman fluttering her arms and with only one swan feather for a memory. And then she had to fill out so many forms she forgot why she had come and what she had left behind.

Now the woman was old. And she had a daughter who grew up speaking only English and swallowing more Coca-Cola than sorrow. For a long time now the woman had wanted to give her daughter the single swan feather and tell her, "This feather may look worthless, but it comes from afar and carries with it all my good intentions." And she waited, year after year, for the day she could tell her daughter this in perfect American English.

Jing-Mei Woo

My father has asked me to be the fourth corner at the Joy Luck Club. I am to replace my mother, whose seat at the mah jong table has been empty since she died two months ago. My father thinks she was killed by her own thoughts.

"She had a new idea inside her head," said my father. "But before it could come out of her mouth, the thought grew too big and burst. It must have been a very bad idea."

The doctor said she died of a cerebral aneurysm. And her friends at the Joy Luck Club said she died just like a rabbit: quickly and with unfinished business left behind. My mother was supposed to host the next meeting of the Joy Luck Club.

The week before she died, she called me, full of pride, full of life: "Auntie Lin cooked red bean soup for Joy Luck. I'm going to cook black sesame-seed soup."

"Don't show off," I said.

"It's not showoff." She said the two soups were almost the same, *chabudwo*. Or maybe she said *butong*, not the same thing at all. It was one of those Chinese expressions that means the better half of mixed intentions. I can never remember things I didn't understand in the first place.

My mother started the San Francisco version of the Joy Luck Club in 1949, two years before I was born. This was the year my mother and father left China with one stiff leather trunk filled only with fancy silk dresses. There was no time to pack anything else, my mother had explained to my father after they boarded the boat. Still his hands swam frantically between the slippery silks, looking for his cotton shirts and wool pants.

When they arrived in San Francisco, my father made her hide those shiny clothes. She wore the same brown-checked Chinese dress until the Refugee Welcome Society gave her two hand-me-down dresses, all too large in sizes for American women. The society was composed of a group of white-haired American missionary ladies from the First Chinese Baptist Church. And because of their gifts, my parents could not refuse their invitation to join the church. Nor could they ignore the old ladies' practical advice to improve their English through Bible study class on Wednesday nights and, later, through choir practice on Saturday mornings. This was how my parents met the Hsus, the Jongs, and the St. Clairs. My mother could sense that the women of these families also had unspeakable tragedies they had left behind in China and hopes they couldn't begin to express in their fragile English. Or at least, my mother recognized the numbness in these women's faces. And she saw how quickly their eyes moved when she told them her idea for the Joy Luck Club.

Joy Luck was an idea my mother remembered from the days of her first marriage in Kweilin, before the Japanese came. That's why I think of Joy Luck as her Kweilin story. It was the story she would always tell me when she was bored, when there was nothing to do, when every bowl had been washed and the Formica[1] table had been wiped down twice, when my father sat reading the newspaper and smoking one Pall Mall cigarette after another, a warning not to disturb him. This is when my mother would take out a box of old ski sweaters sent to us by unseen relatives from Vancouver. She would snip the bottom of a sweater and pull out a kinky thread of yarn, anchoring it to a piece of cardboard. And as she began to roll with one sweeping rhythm, she would start her story. Over the years, she told me the same story, except for the ending, which grew darker, casting long shadows into her life, and eventually into mine.

"I dreamed about Kweilin before I ever saw it," my mother began, speaking Chinese. "I dreamed of jagged peaks lining a curving river, with magic moss greening the banks. At the tops of these peaks were white mists. And if you could float down this river and eat the moss for food, you would be strong enough to climb the peak. If you slipped, you would only fall into a bed of soft moss and laugh. And once you reached the top, you would be able to see everything and feel such happiness it would be enough to never have worries in your life ever again.

"In China, everybody dreamed about Kweilin. And when I arrived, I realized how shabby my dreams were, how poor my thoughts. When I saw the hills, I laughed and shuddered at the same time. The peaks looked like giant fried fish heads trying to jump out of a vat of oil. Behind each hill, I could see shadows of another fish, and then another and another. And then the clouds would move just a little and the hills would suddenly become monstrous elephants marching slowly toward me! Can you see this? And at the root of the hill were secret caves. Inside grew hanging

---

[1] A hard plastic that can resist heat, used for covering work surfaces, etc.

rock gardens in the shapes and colors of cabbage, winter melons, turnips, and onions. These were things so strange and beautiful you can't ever imagine them.

"But I didn't come to Kweilin to see how beautiful it was. The man who was my husband brought me and our two babies to Kweilin because he thought we would be safe. He was an officer with the Kuomintang, and after he put us down in a small room in a two-story house, he went off to the northwest, to Chungking.

"We knew the Japanese were winning, even when the newspapers said they were not. Every day, every hour, thousands of people poured into the city, crowding the sidewalks, looking for places to live. They came from the East, West, North, and South. They were rich and poor, Shanghainese, Cantonese, northerners, and not just Chinese, but foreigners and missionaries[1] of every religion. And there was, of course, the Kuomintang and their army officers who thought they were top level to everyone else."

"We were a city of leftovers mixed together. If it hadn't been for the Japanese, there would have been plenty of reason for fighting to break out among these different people. Can you see it? Shanghai people with north-water peasants, bankers with barbers, rickshaw pullers with Burma refugees. Everybody looked down on someone else. It didn't matter that everybody shared the same sidewalk to spit on and suffered the same fast-moving diarrhea. We all had the same stink, but everybody complained someone else smelled the worst. Me? Oh, I hated the American air force officers who said habba-habba sounds to make my face turn red. But the worst were the northern peasants who emptied their noses into their hands and pushed people around and gave everybody their dirty diseases.

"So you can see how quickly Kweilin lost its beauty for me. I no longer climbed the peaks to say, How lovely are these hills! I only wondered which hills the Japanese had reached. I sat in the dark corners of my house with a baby under each arm, waiting with nervous feet. When the sirens cried out to warn us of bombers, my neighbors and I jumped to our feet and scurried to the deep caves to hide like wild

---

[1] A person who is sent to a foreign country to teach people about Christianity.

animals. But you can't stay in the dark for so long. Something inside of you starts to fade and you become like a starving person, crazy-hungry for light. Outside I could hear the bombing. Boom! Boom! And then the sound of raining rocks. And inside I was no longer hungry for the cabbage or the turnips of the hanging rock garden. I could only see the dripping bowels of an ancient hill that might collapse on top of me. Can you imagine how it is, to want to be neither inside nor outside, to want to be nowhere and disappear?

"So when the bombing sounds grew farther away, we would come back out like newborn kittens scratching our way back to the city. And always, I would be amazed to find the hills against the burning sky had not been torn apart.

"I thought up Joy Luck on a summer night that was so hot even the moths fainted to the ground, their wings were so heavy with the damp heat. Every place was so crowded there was no room for fresh air. Unbearable smells from the sewers rose up to my second-story window and the stink had nowhere else to go but into my nose. At all hours of the night and day, I heard screaming sounds. I didn't know if it was a peasant slitting the throat of a runaway pig or an officer beating a half-dead peasant for lying in his way on the sidewalk. I didn't go to the window to find out. What use would it have been? And that's when I thought I needed something to do to help me move.

"My idea was to have a gathering of four women, one for each corner of my mah jong table. I knew which women I wanted to ask. They were all young like me, with wishful faces. One was an army officer's wife, like myself. Another was a girl with very fine manners from a rich family in Shanghai. She had escaped with only a little money. And there was a girl from Nanking who had the blackest hair I have ever seen. She came from a low-class family, but she was pretty and pleasant and had married well, to an old man who died and left her with a better life.

"Each week one of us would host a party to raise money and to raise our spirits. The hostess had to serve special *dyansyin* foods to bring good fortune of all kinds —

dumplings shaped like silver money ingots[1], long rice noodles for long life, boiled peanuts for conceiving sons, and of course, many good-luck oranges for a plentiful, sweet life.

"What fine food we treated ourselves to with our meager allowances! We didn't notice that the dumplings were stuffed mostly with stringy squash and that the oranges were spotted with wormy holes. We ate sparingly, not as if we didn't have enough, but to protest how we could not eat another bite, we had already bloated ourselves from earlier in the day. We knew we had luxuries few people could afford. We were the lucky ones.

"After filling our stomachs, we would then fill a bowl with money and put it where everyone could see. Then we would sit down at the mah jong table. My table was from my family and was of a very fragrant red wood, not what you call rosewood, but *hong mu*, which is so fine there's no English word for it. The table had a very thick pad, so that when the mah jong *pai* were spilled onto the table the only sound was of ivory tiles washing against one another.

"Once we started to play, nobody could speak, except to say '*Pung*!' or '*Chr*!' when taking a tile. We had to play with seriousness and think of nothing else but adding to our happiness through winning. But after sixteen rounds, we would again feast, this time to celebrate our good fortune. And then we would talk into the night until the morning, saying stories about good times in the past and good times yet to come.

"Oh, what good stories! Stories spilling out all over the place! We almost laughed to death. A rooster that ran into the house screeching on top of dinner bowls, the same bowls that held him quietly in pieces the next day! And one about a girl who wrote love letters for two friends who loved the same man. And a silly foreign lady who fainted on a toilet when firecrackers went off next to her.

"People thought we were wrong to serve banquets every week while many people in the city were starving, eating rats and, later, the garbage that the poorest rats

---

[1] Pieces of solid metal, especially gold or silver, usually shaped like a brick.

used to feed on. Others thought we were possessed by demons — to celebrate when even within our own families we had lost generations, had lost homes and fortunes, and were separated, husband from wife, brother from sister, daughter from mother. Hnnnh! How could we laugh, people asked.

"It's not that we had no heart or eyes for pain. We were all afraid. We all had our miseries. But to despair was to wish back for something already lost. Or to prolong what was already unbearable. How much can you wish for a favorite warm coat that hangs in the closet of a house that burned down with your mother and father inside of it? How long can you see in your mind arms and legs hanging from telephone wires and starving dogs running down the streets with half-chewed hands dangling from their jaws? What was worse, we asked among ourselves, to sit and wait for our own deaths with proper somber faces? Or to choose our own happiness?

"So we decided to hold parties and pretend each week had become the new year. Each week we could forget past wrongs done to us. We weren't allowed to think a bad thought. We feasted, we laughed, we played games, lost and won, we told the best stories. And each week, we could hope to be lucky. That hope was our only joy. And that's how we came to call our little parties Joy Luck."

My mother used to end the story on a happy note, bragging about her skill at the game. "I won many times and was so lucky the others teased that I had learned the trick of a clever thief," she said. "I won tens of thousands of *yuan*. But I wasn't rich. No. By then paper money had become worthless. Even toilet paper was worth more. And that made us laugh harder, to think a thousand-*yuan* note wasn't even good enough to rub on our bottoms."

I never thought my mother's Kweilin story was anything but a Chinese fairy tale. The endings always changed. Sometimes she said she used that worthless thousand-*yuan* note to buy a half-cup of rice. She turned that rice into a pot of porridge. She traded that gruel for two feet from a pig. Those two feet became six eggs, those eggs six chickens. The story always grew and grew.

And then one evening, after I had begged her to buy me a transistor radio, after she refused and I had sulked in silence for an hour, she said, "Why do you think you are missing something you never had?" And then she told me a completely different ending to the story.

"An army officer came to my house early one morning," she said, "and told me to go quickly to my husband in Chungking. And I knew he was telling me to run away from Kweilin. I knew what happened to officers and their families when the Japanese arrived. How could I go? There were no trains leaving Kweilin. My friend from Nanking, she was so good to me. She bribed a man to steal a wheelbarrow used to haul coal. She promised to warn our other friends."

I packed my things and my two babies into this wheelbarrow and began pushing to Chungking four days before the Japanese marched into Kweilin. On the road I heard news of the slaughter from people running past me. It was terrible. Up to the last day, the Kuomintang insisted that Kweilin was safe, protected by the Chinese army. But later that day, the streets of Kweilin were strewn with newspapers reporting great Kuomintang victories, and on top of these papers, like fresh fish from a butcher, lay rows of people — men, women, and children who had never lost hope, but had lost their lives instead. When I heard this news, I walked faster and faster, asking myself at each step, Were they foolish? Were they brave?

"I pushed toward Chungking, until my wheel broke. I abandoned my beautiful mah jong table of *hong mu*. By then I didn't have enough feeling left in my body to cry. I tied scarves into slings and put a baby on each side of my shoulder. I carried a bag in each hand, one with clothes, the other with food. I carried these things until deep grooves grew in my hands. And I finally dropped one bag after the other when my hands began to bleed and became too slippery to hold onto anything.

"Along the way, I saw others had done the same, gradually given up hope. It was like a pathway inlaid with treasures that grew in value along the way. Bolts of fine fabric and books. Paintings of ancestors and carpenter tools. Until one could see cages of ducklings now quiet with thirst and, later still, silver urns lying in the road, where people had been too tired to carry them for any kind of future hope. By the time I arrived in Chungking I had lost everything except for three fancy silk dresses which I wore one on top of the other."

"What do you mean by 'everything'?" I gasped at the end. I was stunned to realize the story had been true all along. "What happened to the babies?"

She didn't even pause to think. She simply said in a way that made it clear there was no more to the story: "Your father is not my first husband. You are not those babies."

When I arrive at the Hsus' house, where the Joy Luck Club is meeting tonight, the first person I see is my father. "There she is! Never on time!" he announces. And it's true. Everybody's already here, seven family friends in their sixties and seventies. They look up and laugh at me, always tardy, a child still at thirty-six.

I'm shaking, trying to hold something inside. The last time I saw them, at the funeral, I had broken down and cried big gulping sobs. They must wonder now how someone like me can take my mother's place. A friend once told me that my mother and I were alike, that we had the same wispy hand gestures, the same girlish laugh and sideways look. When I shyly told my mother this, she seemed insulted and said, "You don't even know little percent of me! How can you be me?" And she's right. How can I be my mother at Joy Luck?

"Auntie, Uncle," I say repeatedly, nodding to each person there. I have always called these old family friends Auntie and Uncle. And then I walk over and stand next to my father.

He's looking at the Jongs' pictures from their recent China trip. "Look at that," he says politely, pointing to a photo of the Jongs' tour group standing on wide slab steps. There is nothing in this picture that shows it was taken in China rather than San Francisco, or any other city for that matter. But my father doesn't seem to be looking at the picture anyway. It's as though everything were the same to him, nothing stands out. He has always been politely indifferent. But what's the Chinese word that means indifferent because you can't see any differences? That's how troubled I think he is by my mother's death.

"Will you look at that," he says, pointing to another nondescript picture.

The Hsus' house feels heavy with greasy odors. Too many Chinese meals cooked in a too small kitchen, too many once fragrant smells compressed onto a thin layer of invisible grease. I remember how my mother used to go into other people's houses and restaurants and wrinkle her nose, then whisper very loudly: "I can see and feel the stickiness with my nose."

I have not been to the Hsus' house in many years, but the living room is exactly the same as I remember it. When Auntie An-mei and Uncle George moved to the Sunset district from Chinatown twenty-five years ago, they bought new furniture. It's all there, still looking mostly new under yellowed plastic. The same turquoise couch shaped in a semicircle of nubby tweed. The colonial end tables made out of heavy maple. A lamp of fake cracked porcelain. Only the scroll-length calendar, free from the Bank of Canton, changes every year.

I remember this stuff, because when we were children, Auntie An-mei didn't let us touch any of her new furniture except through the clear plastic coverings. On Joy Luck nights, my parents brought me to the Hsus'. Since I was the guest, I had to take care of all the younger children, so many children it seemed as if there were always one baby who was crying from having bumped its head on a table leg.

"You are responsible," said my mother, which meant I was in trouble if anything was spilled, burned, lost, broken, or dirty. I was responsible, no matter who did it. She and Auntie An-mei were dressed up in funny Chinese dresses with stiff stand-up collars and blooming branches of embroidered silk sewn over their breasts. These clothes were too fancy for real Chinese people, I thought, and too strange for American parties. In those days, before my mother told me her Kweilin story, I imagined Joy Luck was a shameful Chinese custom, like the secret gathering of the Ku Klux Klan or the tom-tom dances of TV Indians preparing for war.

But tonight, there's no mystery. The Joy Luck aunties are all wearing slacks, bright print blouses, and different versions of sturdy walking shoes. We are all seated around the dining room table under a lamp that looks like a Spanish candelabra. Uncle George puts on his bifocals and starts the meeting by reading the minutes:

"Our capital account is $24825, or about $6206 a couple, $3103 per person. We sold Subaru for a loss at six and three-quarters. We bought a hundred shares of Smith International at seven. Our thanks to Lindo and Tin Jong for the goodies. The red bean soup was especially delicious. The March meeting had to be canceled until further notice. We were sorry to have to bid a fond farewell to our dear friend Suyuan and extended our sympathy to the Canning Woo family. Respectfully submitted, George Hsu, president and secretary."

That's it. I keep thinking the others will start talking about my mother, the wonderful friendship they shared, and why I am here in her spirit, to be the fourth corner and carry on the idea my mother came up with on a hot day in Kweilin.

But everybody just nods to approve the minutes. Even my father's head bobs up and down routinely. And it seems to me my mother's life has been shelved for new business.

Auntie An-mei heaves herself up from the table and moves slowly to the kitchen to prepare the food. And Auntie Lin, my mother's best friend, moves to the turquoise sofa, crosses her arms, and watches the men still seated at the table. Auntie Ying, who seems to shrink even more every time I see her, reaches into her knitting bag and pulls out the start of a tiny blue sweater.

The Joy Luck uncles begin to talk about stocks they are interested in buying. Uncle Jack, who is Auntie Ying's younger brother, is very keen on a company that mines gold in Canada.

"It's a great hedge on inflation," he says with authority. He speaks the best English, almost accentless. I think my mother's English was the worst, but she always thought her Chinese was the best. She spoke Mandarin slightly blurred with a Shanghai dialect.

"Weren't we going to play mah jong tonight?" I whisper loudly to Auntie Ying, who's slightly deaf.

"Later," she says, "after midnight."

"Ladies, are you at this meeting or not?" says Uncle George. After everybody votes unanimously for the Canada gold stock, I go into the kitchen to ask Auntie An-mei why the Joy Luck Club started investing in stocks.

"We used to play mah jong, winner take all. But the same people were always winning, the same people always losing," she says. She is stuffing wonton, one chopstick jab of gingery meat dabbed onto a thin skin and then a single fluid turn with her hand that seals the skin into the shape of a tiny nurse's cap. "You can't have luck when someone else has skill. So long time ago, we decided to invest in the stock market. There's no skill in that. Even your mother agreed."

Auntie An-mei takes count of the tray in front of her. She's already made five rows of eight wonton each. "Forty wonton, eight people, ten each, five row more," she says aloud to herself, and then continues stuffing. "We got smart. Now we can all win and lose equally. We can have stock market luck. And we can play mah jong for fun, just for a few dollars, winner take all. Losers take home leftovers! So everyone can have some joy. Smart-hanh?"

I watch Auntie An-mei make more wonton. She has quick, expert fingers. She doesn't have to think about what she is doing. That's what my mother used to complain about, that Auntie An-mei never thought about what she was doing.

"She's not stupid," said my mother on one occasion, "but she has no spine. Last week, I had a good idea for her. I said to her, Let's go to the consulate and ask for papers for your brother. And she almost wanted to drop her things and go right then. But later she talked to someone. Who knows who? And that person told her she can get her brother in bad trouble in China. That person said FBI will put her on a list and give her trouble in the U. S. the rest of her life. That person said, You ask for a house loan and they say no loan, because your brother is a communist. I said, You already have a house! But still she was scared."

"Aunti An-mei runs this way and that," said my mother, "and she doesn't know why."

As I watch Auntie An-mei, I see a short bent woman in her seventies, with a heavy bosom and thin, shapeless legs. She has the flattened soft fingertips of an old woman. I wonder what Auntie An-mei did to inspire a lifelong stream of criticism from my mother. Then again, it seemed my mother was always displeased with all her friends, with me, and even with my father. Something was always missing. Something always needed improving. Something was not in balance. This one or that had too much of one element, not enough of another.

The elements were from my mother's own version of organic chemistry. Each person is made of five elements, she told me.

Too much fire and you had a bad temper. That was like my father, whom my mother always criticized for his cigarette habit and who always shouted back that she should keep her thoughts to herself. I think he now feels guilty that he didn't let my mother speak her mind.

Too little wood and you bent too quickly to listen to other people's ideas, unable to stand on your own. This was like my Auntie An-mei.

Too much water and you flowed in too many directions, like myself, for having started half a degree in biology, then half a degree in art, and then finishing neither when I went off to work for a small ad agency as a secretary, later becoming a copywriter.

I used to dismiss her criticisms as just more of her Chinese superstitions, beliefs that conveniently fit the circumstances. In my twenties, while taking *Introduction to Psychology*, I tried to tell her why she shouldn't criticize so much, why it didn't lead to a healthy learning environment.

"There's a school of thought," I said, "that parents shouldn't criticize children. They should encourage instead. You know, people rise to other people's expectations. And when you criticize, it just means you're expecting failure."

"That's the trouble," my mother said. "You never rise. Lazy to get up. Lazy to rise to expectations."

"Time to eat," Auntie An-mei happily announces, bringing out a steaming pot of the wonton she was just wrapping. There are piles of food on the table, served buffet style, just like at the Kweilin feasts. My father is digging into the chow mein❶, which still sits in an oversize aluminum pan surrounded by little plastic packets of soy sauce. Auntie An-mei must have bought this on Clement Street. The wonton soup smells wonderful with delicate sprigs of cilantro floating on top. I'm drawn first to a large platter of *chaswei*, sweet barbecued pork cut into coin-sized

---

❶ A Chinese-style dish of fried noodles served with small pieces of meat and vegetables.

slices, and then to a whole assortment of what I've always called finger goodies — thin-skinned pastries filled with chopped pork, beef, shrimp, and unknown stuffings that my mother used to describe as "nutritious things."

Eating is not a gracious event here. It's as though everybody had been starving. They push large forkfuls into their mouths, jab at more pieces of pork, one right after the other. They are not like the ladies of Kweilin, who I always imagined savored their food with a certain detached delicacy.

And then, almost as quickly as they started, the men get up and leave the table. As if on cue, the women peck at last morsels and then carry plates and bowls to the kitchen and dump them in the sink. The women take turns washing their hands, scrubbing them vigorously. Who started this ritual? I too put my plate in the sink and wash my hands. The women are talking about the Jongs' China trip, then they move toward a room in the back of the apartment. We pass another room, what used to be the bedroom shared by the four Hsu sons. The bunk beds with their scuffed, splintery ladders are still there. The Joy Luck uncles are already seated at the card table. Uncle George is dealing out cards, fast, as though he learned this technique in a casino. My father is passing out Pall Mall cigarettes, with one already dangling from his lips.

And then we get to the room in the back, which was once shared by the three Hsu girls. We were all childhood friends. And now they've all grown and married and I'm here to play in their room again. Except for the smell of camphor, it feels the same — as if Rose, Ruth, and Janice might soon walk in with their hair rolled up in big orange-juice cans and plop down on their identical narrow beds. The white chenille bedspreads are so worn they are almost translucent. Rose and I used to pluck the nubs out while talking about our boy problems. Everything is the same, except now a mahogany-colored mah jong table sits in the center. And next to it is a floor lamp, a long black pole with three oval spotlights attached like the broad leaves of a rubber plant.

Nobody says to me, "Sit here, this is where your mother used to sit." But I can tell even before everyone sits down. The chair closest to the door has an emptiness to it. But the feeling doesn't really have to do with the chair. It's her place on the table. Without having anyone tell me, I know her corner on the table was the East.

The East is where things begin, my mother once told me, the direction from which the sun rises, where the wind comes from.

Auntie An-mei, who is sitting on my left, spills the tiles onto the green felt tabletop and then says to me, "Now we wash tiles." We swirl them with our hands in a circular motion. They make a cool swishing sound as they bump into one another.

"Do you win like your mother?" asks Auntie Lin across from me. She is not smiling.

"I only played a little in college with some Jewish friends."

"Annh! Jewish mah jong," she says in disgusted tones. "Not the same thing." This is what my mother used to say, although she could never explain exactly why.

"Maybe I shouldn't play tonight. I'll just watch," I offer.

Auntie Lin looks exasperated, as though I were a simple child: "How can we play with just three people? Like a table with three legs, no balance. When Auntie Ying's husband died, she asked her brother to join. Your father asked you. So it's decided."

"What's the difference between Jewish and Chinese mah jong?" I once asked my mother. I couldn't tell by her answer if the games were different or just her attitude toward Chinese and Jewish people.

"Entirely different kind of playing," she said in her English explanation voice. "Jewish mah jong, they watch only for their own tile, play only with their eyes."

Then she switched to Chinese: "Chinese mah jong, you must play using your head, very tricky. You must watch what everybody else throws away and keep that in your head as well. And if nobody plays well, then the game becomes like Jewish mah jong. Why play? There's no strategy. You're just watching people make mistakes."

These kinds of explanations made me feel my mother and I spoke two different languages, which we did. I talked to her in English, she answered back in Chinese.

"So what's the difference between Chinese and Jewish mah jong?" I ask Auntie Lin.

"Aii-ya," she exclaims in a mock scolding voice. "Your mother did not teach you anything?"

Auntie Ying pats my hand. "You a smart girl. You watch us, do the same. Help us stack the tiles and make four walls."

I follow Auntie Ying, but mostly I watch Auntie Lin. She is the fastest, which means I can almost keep up with the others by watching what she does first. Auntie Ying throws the dice and I'm told that Auntie Lin has become the East wind. I've become the North wind, the last hand to play. Auntie Ying is the South and Auntie An-mei is the West. And then we start taking tiles, throwing the dice, counting back on the wall to the right number of spots where our chosen tiles lie. I rearrange my tiles, sequences of bamboo and balls, doubles of colored number tiles, odd tiles that do not fit anywhere.

"Your mother was the best, like a pro," says Auntie An-mei while slowly sorting her tiles, considering each piece carefully.

Now we begin to play, looking at our hands, casting tiles, picking up others at an easy, comfortable pace. The Joy Luck aunties begin to make small talk, not really listening to each other. They speak in their special language, half in broken English, half in their own Chinese dialect. Auntie Ying mentions she bought yarn at half price, somewhere out in the avenues. Auntie An-mei brags about a sweater she made for her daughter Ruth's new baby. "She thought it was store-bought," she says proudly.

Auntie Lin explains how mad she got at a store clerk who refused to let her return a skirt with a broken zipper. "I was *chiszle*[1]," she says, still fuming, "mad to death."

---

[1] "气死了" in Chinese, meaning "mad to death" in English.

"But Lindo, you are still with us. You didn't die," teases Auntie Ying, and then as she laughs Auntie Lin says "*Pung*!" and "*mah jong*!" and then spreads her tiles out, laughing back at Auntie Ying while counting up her points. We start washing tiles again and it grows quiet. I'm getting bored and sleepy.

"Oh, I have a story," says Auntie Ying loudly, startling everybody. Auntie Ying has always been the weird auntie, someone lost in her own world. My mother used to say, "Auntie Ying is not hard of hearing. She is hard of listening."

"Police arrested Mrs. Emerson's son last weekend," Auntie Ying says in a way that sounds as if she were proud to be the first with this big news. "Mrs. Chan told me at church. Too many TV sets found in his car."

Auntie Lin quickly says, "Aii-ya, Mrs. Emerson good lady," meaning Mrs. Emerson didn't deserve such a terrible son. But now I see this is also said for the benefit of Auntie An-mei, whose own youngest son was arrested two years ago for selling stolen car stereos. Auntie An-mei is rubbing her tile carefully before discarding it. She looks pained.

"Everybody has TVs in China now," says Auntie Lin, changing the subject. "Our family there all has TV sets — not just black-and-white, but color and remote! They have everything. So when we asked them what we should buy them, they said nothing, it was enough that we would come to visit them. But we bought them different things anyway, VCR and Sony Walkman for the kids. They said, No, don't give it to us, but I think they liked it."

Poor Auntie An-mei rubs her tiles ever harder. I remember my mother telling me about the Hsus' trip to China three years ago. Auntie An-mei had saved two thousand dollars, all to spend on her brother's family. She had shown my mother the insides of her heavy suitcases. One was crammed with See's Nuts & Chews, M & M's, candy-coated cashews, instant hot chocolate with miniature marshmallows. My mother told me the other bag contained the most ridiculous clothes, all new: bright California-style beachwear, baseball caps, cotton pants with elastic waists, bomber jackets, Stanford sweatshirts, crew socks.

My mother had told her, "Who wants those useless things? They just want money." But Auntie An-mei said her brother was so poor and they were so rich by comparison. So she ignored my mother's advice and took the heavy bags and their two thousand dollars to China. And when their China tour finally arrived in Hangzhou, the whole family from Ningbo was there to meet them. It wasn't just Auntie An-mei's little brother, but also his wife's stepbrothers and stepsisters, and a distant cousin, and that cousin's husband and that husband's uncle. They had all brought their mothers-in-law and children, and even their village friends who were not lucky enough to have overseas Chinese relatives to show off.

As my mother told it, "Auntie An-mei had cried before she left for China, thinking she would make her brother very rich and happy by communist standards. But when she got home, she cried to me that everyone had a palm out and she was the only one who left with an empty hand."

My mother confirmed her suspicions. Nobody wanted the sweatshirts, those useless clothes. The M & M's were thrown in the air, gone. And when the suitcases were emptied, the relatives asked what else the Hsus had brought.

Auntie An-mei and Uncle George were shaken down, not just for two thousand dollars' worth of TVs and refrigerators but also for a night's lodging for twenty-six people in the Overlooking the Lake Hotel, for three banquet tables at a restaurant that catered to rich foreigners, for three special gifts for each relative, and finally, for a loan of five thousand *yuan* in foreign exchange to a cousin's so-called uncle who wanted to buy a motorcycle but who later disappeared for good along with the money. When the train pulled out of Hangzhou the next day, the Hsus found themselves depleted of some nine thousand dollars' worth of goodwill. Months later, after an inspiring Christmastime service at the First Chinese Baptist Church, Auntie An-mei tried to recoup her loss by saying it truly was more blessed to give than to receive, and my mother agreed, her longtime friend had blessings for at least several lifetimes.

Listening now to Auntie Lin bragging about the virtues of her family in China, I realize that Auntie Lin is oblivious to Auntie An-mei's pain. Is Auntie Lin being mean, or is it that my mother never told anybody but me the shameful story of Auntie

An-mei's greedy family?

"So, Jing-mei, you go to school now?" says Auntie Lin.

"Her name is June. They all go by their American names," says Auntie Ying.

"That's okay," I say, and I really mean it. In fact, it's even becoming fashionable for American-born Chinese to use their Chinese names.

"I'm not in school anymore, though," I say. "That was more than ten years ago."

Auntie Lin's eyebrows arch. "Maybe I'm thinking of someone else's daughter," she says, but I know right away she's lying. I know my mother probably told her I was going back to school to finish my degree, because somewhere back, maybe just six months ago, we were again having this argument about my being a failure, a "college drop-off," about my going back to finish.

Once again I had told my mother what she wanted to hear: "You're right. I'll look into it."

I had always assumed we had an unspoken understanding about these things: that she didn't really mean I was a failure, and I really meant I would try to respect her opinions more. But listening to Auntie Lin tonight reminds me once again: My mother and I never really understood one another. We translated each other's meanings and I seemed to hear less than what was said, while my mother heard more. No doubt she told Auntie Lin I was going back to school to get a doctorate.

Auntie Lin and my mother were both best friends and arch enemies who spent a lifetime comparing their children. I was one month older than Waverly Jong, Auntie Lin's prized daughter. From the time we were babies, our mothers compared the creases in our belly buttons, how shapely our earlobes were, how fast we healed when we scraped our knees, how thick and dark our hair, how many shoes we wore out in one year, and later, how smart Waverly was at playing chess, how many trophies she had won last month, how many newspapers had printed her name, how many cities she had visited.

I know my mother resented listening to Auntie Lin talk about Waverly when she had nothing to come back with. At first my mother tried to cultivate some hidden genius in me. She did housework for an old retired piano teacher down the hall who gave me lessons and free use of a piano to practice on in exchange. When I failed to become a concert pianist, or even an accompanist for the church youth choir, she finally explained that I was late-blooming, like Einstein, who everyone thought was retarded until he discovered a bomb.

Now it is Auntie Ying who wins this hand of mah jong, so we count points and begin again.

"Did you know Lena move to Woodside?" asks Auntie Ying with obvious pride, looking down at the tiles, talking to no one in particular. She quickly erases her smile and tries for some modesty. "Of course, it's not best house in neighborhood, not million-dollar house, not yet. But it's good investment. Better than paying rent. Better than somebody putting you under their thumb to rub you out."

So now I know Auntie Ying's daughter, Lena, told her about my being evicted from my apartment on lower Russian Hill. Even though Lena and I are still friends, we have grown naturally cautious about telling each other too much. Still, what little we say to one another often comes back in another guise. It's the same old game, everybody talking in circles.

"It's getting late," I say after we finish the round. I start to stand up, but Auntie Lin pushes me back down into the chair.

"Stay, stay. We talk awhile, get to know you again," she says. "Been a long time."

I know this is a polite gesture on the Joy Luck aunties' part — a protest when actually they are just as eager to see me go as I am to leave. "No, I really must go now, thank you, thank you," I say, glad I remembered how the pretense goes.

"But you must stay! We have something important to tell you, from your mother," Auntie Ying blurts out in her too-loud voice. The others look uncomfortable, as if this were not how they intended to break some sort of bad news to me.

I sit down. Auntie An-mei leaves the room quickly and returns with a bowl of peanuts, then quietly shuts the door. Everybody is quiet, as if nobody knew where to begin.

It is Auntie Ying who finally speaks. "I think your mother die with an important thought on her mind," she says in halting English. And then she begins to speak in Chinese, calmly, softly.

"Your mother was a very strong woman, a good mother. She loved you very much, more than her own life. And that's why you can understand why a mother like this could never forget her other daughters. She knew they were alive, and before she died she wanted to find her daughters in China."

The babies in Kweilin, I think. I was not those babies. The babies in a sling on her shoulder. Her other daughters. And now I feel as if I were in Kweilin amidst the bombing and I can see these babies lying on the side of the road, their red thumbs popped out of their mouths, screaming to be reclaimed. Somebody took them away. They're safe. And now my mother's left me forever, gone back to China to get these babies. I can barely hear Auntie Ying's voice.

"She had searched for years, written letters back and forth," says Auntie Ying. "And last year she got an address. She was going to tell your father soon. Aii-ya, what a shame. A lifetime of waiting."

Auntie An-mei interrupts with an excited voice: "So your aunties and I, we wrote to this address," she says. "We say that a certain party, your mother, want to meet another certain party. And this party write back to us. They are your sisters, Jing-mei."

My sisters, I repeat to myself, saying these two words together for the first time.

Auntie An-mei is holding a sheet of paper as thin as wrapping tissue. In perfectly straight vertical rows I see Chinese characters written in blue fountain-pen ink. A word is smudged. A tear? I take the letter with shaking hands, marveling at how smart my sisters must be to be able to read and write Chinese.

The aunties are all smiling at me, as though I had been a dying person who has now miraculously recovered. Auntie Ying is handing me another envelope. Inside is a check made out to June Woo for $1,200. I can't believe it.

"My sisters are sending *me* money?" I ask.

"No, no," says Auntie Lin with her mock exasperated voice. "Every year we save our mah jong winnings for big banquet at fancy restaurant. Most times your mother win, so most is her money. We add just a little, so you can go Hong Kong, take a train to Shanghai, see your sisters. Besides, we all getting too rich, too fat." she pats her stomach for proof.

"See my sisters," I say numbly. I am awed by this prospect, trying to imagine what I would see. And I am embarrassed by the end-of-the-year-banquet lie my aunties have told to mask their generosity. I am crying now, sobbing and laughing at the same time, seeing but not understanding this loyalty to my mother.

"You must see your sisters and tell them about your mother's death," says Auntie Ying. "But most important, you must tell them about her life. The mother they did not know, they must now know."

"See my sisters, tell them about my mother," I say, nodding. "What will I say? What can I tell them about my mother? I don't know anything. She was my mother."

The aunties are looking at me as if I had become crazy right before their eyes.

"Not know your own mother?" cries Auntie An-mei with disbelief. "How can you say? Your mother is in your bones!"

"Tell them stories of your family here. How she became success," offers Auntie Lin.

"Tell them stories she told you, lessons she taught, what you know about her mind that has become your mind," says Auntie Ying. "You mother very smart lady."

I hear more choruses of "Tell them, tell them" as each Auntie frantically tries to think what should be passed on.

"Her kindness."

"Her smartness."

"Her dutiful nature to family."

"Her hopes, things that matter to her."

"The excellent dishes she cooked."

"Imagine, a daughter not knowing her own mother!"

And then it occurs to me. They are frightened. In me, they see their own daughters, just as ignorant, just as unmindful of all the truths and hopes they have brought to America. They see daughters who grow impatient when their mothers talk in Chinese, who think they are stupid when they explain things in fractured English. They see that joy and luck do not mean the same to their daughters, that to these closed American-born minds "joy luck" is not a word, it does not exist. They see daughters who will bear grandchildren born without any connecting hope passed from generation to generation.

"I will tell them everything," I say simply, and the aunties look at me with doubtful faces.

"I will remember everything about her and tell them," I say more firmly. And gradually, one by one, they smile and pat my hand. They still look troubled, as if something were out of balance. But they also look hopeful that what I say will become true. What more can they ask? What more can I promise?

They go back to eating their soft boiled peanuts, saying stories among themselves. They are young girls again, dreaming of good times in the past and good times yet to come. A brother from Ningbo who makes his sister cry with joy when he returns nine thousand dollars plus interest. A youngest son whose stereo and TV repair business is so good he sends leftovers to China. A daughter whose babies are able to swim like fish in a fancy pool in Woodside. Such good stories. The best. They are the lucky ones.

And I am sitting at my mother's place at the mah jong table, on the East, where things begin.

(The text is selected from *The Joy Luck Club* (1989))

Questions for discussion:

1. What do you think the "feather" stands for?
2. Why the gathering of women is named as "the joy-luck-club"?
3. How do you understand the relationship between Jing-Mei Woo and her mother? Can you identify with them?

Rita Dove (1952 —)

What she has called the "friction" between the beauty of a poetic form and a difficult or painful subject appeals to Rita Dove. Her own formal control and discipline create a beautiful design and a hunting music in *Parsley*, a poem based on a murderous event: in 1957 the dictator of the Dominican Republic, Rafael Trujillo, ordered twenty thousand black Haitians killed because they could not pronounce the letter "r" in the Spanish word for "parsley". What compels Dove in this poem is the way a "single, beautiful word" has the power of life and death. More astonishing is that she writes from the perspective of both the Haitians in the cane fields and General Trujillo in his place. When asked in an interview about her capacity to imagine Trujillo, Dove responded, "I frankly don't believe anyone who says they've never felt any evil, that they cannot understand that process of evil. It was important to me to try to understand that arbitrary quality of his cruelty... Making us get into his head may shock us all into seeing what the human being is capable of, because if we can go that far into his head, we are halfway there ourselves." An ability to enter into different points of view in a single poem is characteristic of Dove's disinterested imagination. Her method is to avoid commentary, to let the imagined person or object, the suggestive detail, speak for itself. Often her work suggests what Keats called "negative capability," the gift of the poet to become what he or she is not.

Born in Akron, Dove attended Miami University of Ohio and, after her graduation, studied modern European literature as a Fulbright/Hays fellow at the University of Tvbingen in Germany. When she returned from Europe she took an M. F. A. at the University of Iowa (in 1977). Later she taught creative writing at Arizona State University before joining the University of Virginia, where she is now Commonwealth Professor of English. Over the past two decades since her Fulbright year she has also frequently returned to live abroad, in Ireland, Israel, France, and especially Germany. Her travel in Europe and elsewhere suggests part of the imperative she fells as a poet: to range widely through fields of experience to cross boundaries of space as well as time. Her first book, *The Yellow House on the Corner* (1980), is notable for its intense poems about adolescence; her second book, *Museum* (1983), dramatically exterds the range of her work. "When I started *Museum*," she has said, "I was in Europe, and I had a way of looking back on America and distancing myself from my experience." As well as for several fine poems about her father (a subject that may also have needed distance), the book is remarkable for the way distance allowed Dove to move out of her immediate experience, freed her to imagine widely different lives.

As if to show that it is also possible to travel widely while staying at home, Dove's *Thomas and Beulah* (1986) is an extended sequence based on her grandparents' lives. Her continuing fascination with imagining different perspectives on the same event is evident in this sequence. Dove herself has described the origins of the book this way:

> My grandmother had told me a story that had happened to my grandfather when he was young, coming up on a riverboat to Akron, Ohio, my hometown. But that was all I had basically. And the story so fascinated me that I tried to write about it. I started off writing stories about my grandfather and soon, because I ran out of real fact, in order to keep going, I made up facts for this character, Thomas... Then this poem "Dusting" appeared, really out of nowhere. I didn't realize this was Thomas's wife saying, "I want to talk. And you can't do his side without my side..."

This is the story, in part, of a marriage and of a black couple's life in the industrial Midwest in the period from 1900 to 1960. Thomas's point of view controls the poems of the book's first section, while the second part imagines his wife's, the larger framework of the sequence links family history to social history. Thomas's journey from the rural South to the industrial city of Akron (where he finds employment in the Goodyear Zeppelin factory until the Depression puts him out of work) is part of the larger social movement of southern African Americans into northern industrial cities in the first part of this century. The individual lyrics of Dove's sequence create and sustain the story through distinct and often ordinary moments in which each life is vividly portrayed. It is part of Dove's gift that she can render the apparently unimportant moments that inform a life and set them against a background of larger historical forces, as do Robert Hayden in *Elegies for Paradise Valley* and Robert Lowell in *Notebook.*

Many of the figures in Dove's poems are displaced, on the border between different worlds: for example, Thomas and Beulah and Benjamin Banneker ("Banneker"). The experience of displacement, of what she has called living in "two different worlds, seeing things with double vision," consistently compels this poet's imagination. It takes both detachment and control to maintain (and to live with) such doubleness. This may be why Dove's rich sense of language and her love of sound are joined to a disciplined formal sense. The form of her poems often holds in place difficult or ambiguous feelings, and keeps the expression of feeling understated. While restraint is one of the strengths of Dove's poems, her work can sometimes seem austere. She is perhaps too careful not to risk excess. Such careful control recalls Elizabeth Bishop's early work, also highly controlled and even, at times, guarded. As Bishop grew to relax her restraints, to open into an extraordinary expressiveness, so Dove, now only in her early forties, has gifts to suggest a similar growth, and her most recent collections, *Grace Notes* (1989) and *Mother Love* (1995), suggest just such a relaxing of the poet's guard. The evidence so far is that with each book she asks something more from herself, and there is every reason to believe she will become one of our indispensable poets. Dove was Poet Laureate of the United States from 1993 to 1995.

(The text is selected from *The Norton Anthology of American Literature* (Shorter Fifth Edition))

Major Works:

Poetry Collections:

- *The Yellow House on the Corner*, 1980 《街角的黄房子》
- *Museum*, 1983 《博物馆》
- *Thomas and Beulah*, 1986 《托马斯和比尤拉》
- *Grace Notes*, 1989 《花音》
- *Mother Love*, 1995 《母亲的爱》
- *On the Bus with Rosa Parks*, 1999 《与罗莎·帕克斯在公车上》

Other Works:

- *The Poet's World*, 1995《诗人的世界》(散文集)
- *The Darker Face of the Earth: A Verse Play in Fourteen Scenes*, 1994《地球较暗的脸》(又译《农庄苍茫夜》, 戏剧)
- *Through the Ivory Gate*, 1992 《穿过象牙门》(小说)
- *Fifth Sunday*, 1985 《第五个星期天》(短篇小说集)

I have been a stranger in a strange land

It wasn't bliss[1]. What was bliss
but the ordinary life? She'd spend hours
in patter, moving through whole days
touching, sniffing, tasting... exquisite
housekeeping in a charmed world.
And yet there was always

more of the same, all that happiness,
the aimless Being There.
So she wandered for a while, bush to arbor[2],
lingered to look through a pond's restive mirror.
He was off cataloging the universe, probably,
pretending he could organize
what was clearly someone else's chaos.

That's when she found the tree,
the dark, crabbed branches
bearing up such speechless bounty,
she knew without being told
this was forbidden. It wasn't
a question of ownership —
who could lay claim to
such maddening perfection?

And there was no voice in her head,
no whispered intelligence lurking

---

[1] Extreme happiness.

[2] A shelter in a garden for people to sit under, made by growing climbing plants over a frame.

in the leaves — just an ache that grew
until she knew she'd already lost everything
except desire, the red heft of it
warming her outstretched palm.

Flirtation

After all, there's no need
to say anything

at first. An orange, peeled
and quartered, flares

like a tulip on a wedge wood[1] plate
Anything can happen.

Outside the sun
has rolled up her rugs

and night strewn salt
across the sky. My heart

is humming a tune
I haven't heard in years!

Quiet's cool flesh —
let's sniff and eat it.

There are ways

---

[1] A brand of English fine china tableware sets.

to make of the moment

a topiary[1]
so the pleasure's in

walking through.

Lady Freedom Among Us

Don't lower your eyes
or stare straight ahead to where
you think you ought to be going

don't mutter *oh no*
not another one
get a job fly a kite
go bury a bone

with her oldfashioned sandals
with her leaden[2] skirts
with her stained cheeks and whiskers and
heaped up trinkets
she has risen among us in blunt reproach

she has fitted her hair under a hand-me-down cap
and spruced it up with feathers and stars
slung over her shoulder she bears
the rainbowed layers of charity and murmurs
all of you even the least of you

---

[1] The art of cutting bushes into shapes such as birds or animals.
[2] Dull grey in color.

don't cross to the other side of the square
don't think another item to fit on a
tourist's agenda

consider her drenched gaze her shining brow
she who has brought mercy back into the streets
and will not retire politely to the potter's field

having assumed the thick skin of this town
its gritted exhaust its sunscorch and blear
she rests in her weathered plumage
bigboned resolute

don't think you can ever forget her
don't even try
she's not going to budge

no choice but to grant her space
crown her with sky
for she is one of the many
and she is each of us

November for Beginners

Snow would be the easy
way out — that softening
sky like a sigh of relief
at finally being allowed
to yield. No dice.
We stack twigs for burning

in glistening patches
but the rain won't give.

So we wait, breeding
mood, making music
of decline. We sit down
in the smell of the past
and rise in a light
that is already leaving.
We ache in secret,
memorizing

a gloomy line
or two of German.
When spring comes
we promise to act
the fool. Pour,
rain! Sail, wind,
with your cargo of zithers[1]!

(The poems above are selected from *http://www.poets.org*)

Teach Us to Number Our Days

In the old neighborhood, each funeral parlor
is more elaborate than the last.
The alleys smell of cops, pistols bumping their thighs,
each chamber steeled with a slim blue bullet.

Low-rent balconies stacked to the sky.

[1] A musical instrument with a lot of metal strings stretched over a flat wooden box, that you play with your fingers or a plectrum.

Rita Dove (1952 —)

A boy plays tic-tac-toe[1] on a moon
crossed by TV antennae, dreams

he has swallowed a blue bean.
It takes root in his gut, sprouts
and twines upward, the vines curling
around the sockets and locking them shut.

And this sky, knotting like a dark tie?
The patroller, disinterested, holds all the beans.
(The poem is selected from *http: //www. poemhunter. com/*)

Questions for discussion:

1. Could you summarize the main metrical and rhythmical features of the poems?
2. What is your understanding of the "Lady Freedom"?
3. What is the theme of "Teach Us Number Our Days"?

[1] Tic-tac-toe = noughts and crosses: a simple game in which two players take turns to write Os or Xs in a set of nine squires. The first player to complete a row of three Os or three Xs is the winner.

References

[1] Tan A. *The Joy Luck Club* [M]. New York: Ivy Books, 1989.

[2] Baym, N. *The Norton Anthology of American Literature* (Shorter Fifth Edition) [M]. New York: W. W. Norton & Company, 1999.

[3] Birch E L. *Black American Women's Writing: A Quilt of Many Colours* [M]. London: Harvester Wheatsheaf, 1994.

[4] Buck P S. *The Good Earth* [M]. New York: Simon & Schuster, 2004.

[5] Chafe W H. *The Paradox of Change: American Women in the Twentieth Century* [M]. New York: Oxford University Press, 1997.

[6] Drabble, M, *et al*. *The Oxford Companion to English Literature* [M]. Beijing: Foreign Language Teaching and Research Press, 2005.

[7] Mitchell M. *Gone with the Wind* [M]. London: Pan Books Ltd., 1974.

[8] 常耀信. 美国文学史 [M]. 天津: 南开大学出版社, 2002.

[9] 陈晓兰. 外国女星文学教程 [M]. 上海: 复旦大学出版社, 2011.

[10] 黄铁池. 当代美国小说研究 [M]. 上海: 学林出版社, 2000.

[11] 金莉. 20世纪美国女性小说研究 [M]. 北京: 北京大学出版社, 2010.

[12] 钱青. 美国20世纪文学选读 [M]. 北京: 外语教学与研究出版社, 2009.

[13] 萨克文·科伯维奇, 剑桥美国文学史 [M]. 孙宏主译. 北京: 中央编译出版社, 2005.

[14] 石坚, 王欣. 似是故人来: 新历史主义视角下的20世纪英美文学 [M]. 重庆: 重庆大学出版社, 2008.

[15] 陶洁. 灯下西窗: 美国文学和美国文化 [M]. 北京: 北京大学出版社, 2004.

[16] 陶洁. 20世纪美国文学选读 [M]. 北京: 北京大学出版社, 2006.

[17] 王恩铭, 等. 当代美国社会与文化 (第二版) [M]. 上海: 上海外语教育出版社, 2007.

[18] 王守仁, 刘海平. 新编美国文学史 [M]. 上海: 上海外语教育出版社, 2002.

[19] 徐颖果，马红旗．美国女性文学：从殖民地时期到20世纪［M］．天津：南开大学出版社，2010.

[20] 徐颖果．美国华裔文学选读（第二版）［M］．天津：南开大学出版社，2008.

[21] 闫小青．20世纪美国女性文学发展历程透视［M］．长春：吉林大学出版社，2012.

[22] 杨建政．女性的书写：英美女性文学研究［M］．北京：经济管理出版社，2012.

[23] 尹晓煌．美国华裔文学史［M］．徐颖果，等译．天津：南开大学出版社，2006.

[24] 朱刚．新编美国文学史［M］．上海：上海外语教育出版社，2004.

[25] 朱永涛．英美文学基础教程［M］．北京：外语教学与研究出版社，1991.

[26] *http：//baike. baidu. com.*

[27] *http：//wenku. baidu. com.*

[28] *http：//www. nbu. bg.*

[29] *http：//en. wikipedia. org.*

[30] *http：//www. encyclopedia. com.*

[31] *http：//www. amazon. com.*

[32] *http：//www. poetry. com.*

[33] *http：//www. poets. org.*

[34] *http：//www. womenwriters. net.*

[35] *http：//www. english. upenn. edu.*

[36] *http：//www. achievement. org.*

[37] *http：//www. classicreader. com.*